Fifteen Thousand Hours

Secondary schools and their effects on children

Michael Rutter

Barbara Maughan

Peter Mortimore

Janet Ouston

with Alan Smith

P·C·P
Paul Chapman
Publishing Ltd

First published in 1979 by Open Books Publishing

Reissued by Paul Chapman Publishing 1994

Copyright © 1979 and 1994, Michael Rutter, Barbara Maughan, Peter Mortimore and Janet Ouston

Paul Chapman Publishing Ltd
144 Liverpool Road
London
N1 1LA

British Library Cataloguing in Publication Data

Rutter, Michael
  Fifteen Thousand Hours: Secondary Schools
  and Their Effects on Children. – New ed
  I. Title
  373.0941

  ISBN 1–85396–281–3

Printed and bound by The Baskerville Press, Salisbury, Wiltshire.

A B C D E F G H   9 8 7 6 5 4

Contents

Preface and Acknowledgements

The research reported in this book would have been impossible without the generous help we have received at every stage from the Head Teachers and staff of the schools involved. A large number of both primary and secondary schools contributed to the earlier stages of the work, from 1970 onwards, and our thanks are due both to the teaching and the secretarial staff who helped in providing all the information from which the present study grew. More recently, our debt has been to the twelve secondary schools which have formed the focus of this part of the study. Throughout three years of field work the Heads and staff allowed us unlimited access to all aspects of school life, and gave most generously of their own time. Each stage of the research has been planned in conjunction with a working party of teachers from local schools, who have given us invaluable guidance and encouragement. The project is as much theirs as ours, and the ideas and suggestions of the teachers taking part in the research have done much to shape both the study itself and this report. Because of the demands of confidentiality none of these teachers can be named or adequately thanked here, but we hope that they will feel that all the time, energy and thought they have given to the research has been worthwhile.

Many research workers have been involved with the project during the last eight years. We are particularly indebted to Bridget Yule who first developed co-operative working relationships with the schools, and who was primarily responsible for the follow through of the children from 1970 to 1974 in the first stage of the project. Michael Rutter has directed the work from the outset; Barbara Maughan, Peter Mortimore and Janet Ouston developed the measures of the schools and were responsible for the field work and data analysis from 1975 onwards; Alan Smith has given invaluable advice and guidance on data preparation and statistical procedures and provided the brief outline of log-linear modelling in Appendix H. The research has drawn on ideas from many different branches of the social sciences, as reflected

in the different professional backgrounds of those involved. Barbara
Maughan's background was in social work and social administration,
Peter Mortimore is an experienced teacher and educational psychologist, Janet Ouston a developmental psychologist, Michael Rutter
a child psychiatrist, and Alan Smith a statistician.

The findings are based on complex and extensive data which have
required detailed statistical analyses. Some of these have been included
in the text, but those thought most likely to be of interest just to
research workers have been placed in appendices at the end of the
book. As many readers may not be familiar with all the statistical
techniques used, we have included brief descriptions of the methods of
analysis at various points through the book. These do not give
mathematical details but merely provide an outline of the methods
used, which we hope will make both the rationale of the study and the
findings accessible to teachers, parents and others interested in secondary education.

The research has been generously supported throughout by the
Inner London Education Authority. The Research and Statistics Division, the Divisional Officers, and many individual members of staff in
local offices have provided constant encouragement for the work and
have allowed us access to statistical data. The I.L.E.A. provided fun-
ding for the earlier stages of the work, and from 1975 onwards the
project has been financially supported by the Department of Education
and Science. Our thanks are also due to the Metropolitan Police, for
enabling us to use data from their Juvenile Bureaux. The 'Statistical
Package for the Social Sciences' (Nie et al., 1975) was used for all data
analyses apart from the log-linear modelling.

Finally, we would like to thank Kathy Brook, Pauline Ellerman, Joy
Maxwell and Libby Ryan who typed the several drafts of the
manuscript with great speed, accuracy and patience. Joy Maxwell also
prepared the list of references and Pauline Ellerman, as project
secretary, has helped us in innumerable ways over the last four years.

Preface for 1994 reissue

Research studies are inevitably products of their time. Since *Fifteen Thousand Hours* was first published, in 1979, there have been major reforms in many different countries, and important advances in the methods used to assess the effects of schools. New British readers of this book will find no mention here of the National Curriculum or of local management of schools. New North American readers will find no reference to the restructuring that has been taking place in recent years. Similarly, new readers from Australia or New Zealand will find no discussion of the various experiments in educational review or other interesting developments in evaluation. The book is not concerned with curricular issues, but rather with school organisation as a whole. Hence, it is likely to have relevance even when there have been major changes in the curriculum and other similar matters. We believe, therefore, that the central findings of this study are as relevant now as in the 1970s.

The principal finding of our investigation into secondary schooling was that considerable variation existed in the ability of schools to promote the progress of their pupils and that this was relatively independent of the intake characteristics of the school. Furthermore, we found that schools that had good attendance rates, reasonable pupil behaviour in school and low delinquency rates out of school usually also achieved good examination results. This general picture has not altered, as numerous reports by Her Majesty's Inspectorate (in Britain) and research studies (in many different countries), have shown. What *is* new is an acceptance – worldwide – of the potential of schools to affect pupils' performance. Whereas, in 1979, this was seen as contentious, today it is accepted as the norm.

The other major finding of our study concerned the *reasons* why some schools were more effective than others. Our original fieldwork identified a series of process variables which were associated with better outcomes in the more effective schools. These process factors have passed the test of time and many have been replicated in other studies. Whilst the detail may, in some ways, be different, the underlying processes appear similar to those being identified in the most recent empirical investigations.

The first publication of *Fifteen Thousand Hours* generated considerable controversy. Our methods have since been discussed in numerous scientific publications and, as a result, improvements in techniques of analysing and processing data have been brought about.

We welcome this opportunity to re-issue this book with a new publisher. Over the last decade and a half, we have discussed its findings with educational practitioners all over the world. We hope this edition – although reporting on schools as they were – will stimulate educationalists to strive for schools as they might be.

1

Introduction: previous studies

For almost a dozen years during a formative period of their development children spend almost as much of their waking life at school as at home. Altogether this works out at some *15,000 hours* (from the age of five until school leaving) during which schools and teachers may have an impact on the development of the children in their care. Do a child's experiences at school have any effect; does it matter *which* school he goes to; and which are the features of school that matter? These are the issues which gave rise to the study of twelve London secondary schools described in this book. The research findings provide a clear 'yes' in response to the first two questions. Schools do indeed have an important impact on children's development and it does matter which school a child attends. Moreover, the results provide strong indications of what are the particular features of school organisation and functioning which make for success.

Our finding that schooling *does* make a difference will come as no surprise to parents who often go to a good deal of trouble to get their children into schools of their choice. On the other hand, at the time the study was started there was a widespread acceptance among academics that schools made little difference. This view largely stemmed from two very influential books from the United States: James Coleman's (1966) report on *Equality of Educational Opportunity* and Christopher Jencks' (1972) *Inequality: A Reassessment of the Effect of Family and Schooling in America*. Coleman conducted a large scale survey of the achievement of some 645,000 students in 4000 elementary and secondary schools. The results were held to indicate that educational attainment was largely independent of the schooling a child received. Jencks reassessed a mass of statistical evidence from a variety of investigations, including the 'Coleman Report'. His analyses led to the rather startling conclusions that: 'equalizing the quality of high schools would reduce cognitive inequality by one per cent or less' and that 'additional school expenditures are unlikely to increase achievement, and redistributing resources will not reduce test score inequality'. At about the same time Arthur Jensen (1969) reviewed the evidence on the factors which influence IQ and scholastic attainment and drew his controversial conclusion that: 'Compensatory education has been tried and it apparently has failed'.

At the same time British writers were drawing rather similar conclusions about the limited influence of schools on the development of their pupils. The Plowden Report (1967), which drew on evidence comparable in many respects to that in the Coleman study, concluded that home influences far outweighed those of the school. David Farrington (1972) wrote an article entitled 'Delinquency begins at home', which claimed to show that Michael Power's (1967) earlier demonstration that schools varied greatly in delinquency rates was largely a reflection of the fact that schools varied greatly in the proportions of their children who had already shown troublesome behaviour at primary school.

There was a widespread pessimism about the extent that schools could have any impact on children's development and Basil Bernstein's (1970) view that 'Education cannot compensate for society' was generally accepted. However, it is important to recognise that there was immense *dis*agreement on just what *did* have an influence on children's behaviour and attainments. Jensen (1969) saw hereditary factors as predominant; Jencks (1972), on the other hand, mainly put it down to 'luck'; many people saw family influences, especially during the preschool years, as the most important factor (e.g. Coleman *et al.*, 1966; Plowden, 1967; West and Farrington, 1973); whereas sociologists were more inclined to see the roots of inequality in the economic and political structure of society itself. Thus, Bowles (1971; see also Bowles & Gintis, 1976) argued that 'educational inequalities are rooted in the basic institutions of our economy ... (its sources are to be found) in the mutual reinforcement of class subcultures and social class biases in the operation of the school system itself'.

Clearly, there is considerable disagreement about the influence of schooling on children's development. At first sight, too, there appears to be a hopelessly confusing chaos of contradictory research findings. In fact, that is not so. A careful examination of the various studies shows that when like is compared with like the results of different investigations are pretty much in agreement on the main findings. The apparent clashes in evidence arise largely because the studies have gathered different kinds of data or have used different statistical analyses to answer quite different questions. In order to appreciate just what these differences in approach mean and what the effects of posing the questions in different ways are, it is necessary to briefly review other work before describing our own research.

Large-scale surveys of attainment

It is appropriate to begin with the large-scale cross-sectional surveys which were most influential in creating the impression that education made little difference. Their basic strategy was to gather information on the attainments of very large numbers of children using standardised tests. Variations in children's achievement on these tests were then related to available measures on the children, their homes and their schools. Clearly the results are likely to be influenced by the particular measures used, by the extent to which children or schools actually vary on these measures, and by the methods of statistical analysis employed.

Measures of scholastic attainment

The first point that is immediately striking is that the original American studies used measures of attainment which bore little relationship to anything most schools would aim to teach. Thus, Coleman *et al.* (1966) placed reliance on a single measure of verbal ability. This was necessary because American school children do not take national examinations in school subjects in the way that British children do. However, subsequent research has shown that reliance on a general intellectual measure rather than attainment in subjects specifically taught at school led to an underestimate of the importance of schooling.

The International Educational Achievement (IEA) Survey used specially constructed achievement tests to study school influences on attainment across twenty-two different countries (Postlethwaite, 1975). The findings showed a more substantial school effect than that evident in the Coleman report. However, there is reason to suppose that the construction of standardised tests, which often involves the exclusion of items which show major school differences, is likely to minimise school effects (Brimer *et al.*, 1977). Certainly, recent studies in Ireland (Madaus *et al.*, 1976) and England (Brimer *et al.*, 1977) of public examination successes have shown greater school effects than those of the IEA survey. Davis (1977) showed that among comprehensive schools (i.e. those taking children of all levels of ability) in one county in England, the proportion of children obtaining 6 or more passes in GCE 'O' level ranged from 6 per cent to 32 per cent. Among grammar schools (taking roughly the 15 per cent most able children) the rates varied from 26 per cent to 78 per cent.

Moreover, the choice of school subject is also liable to influence findings. Thus, the IEA studies (Postlethwaite, 1975; Coleman, 1975), the American *Project Talent* (Shaycoft, 1967) and the British research (Brimer *et al.*, 1977) all indicated that subjects such as mathematics or science which are generally learned mainly at school show greater school differences than do those such as reading which a child may learn in part at home from his parents, or those like English Literature or Social Studies where a child's learning from television or from books at home as well as family conversation are all likely to play a part.

A further point in this connection is that the subjects chosen for the study of school influences should be appropriate to the age group being investigated. Thus, tests of reading are unlikely to show much of a secondary school influence simply because for most children reading skills are largely acquired at primary school level.

School variables

The second major point about the large-scale surveys is that they examined a very narrow range of school variables. The main focus was on resources, as reflected in items like average expenditure per pupil, number of books in the school library and teacher-pupil ratio. It is clear now from many studies in both Britain and the United States that the variations between schools or between local authorities in either financial resources or size of school class show no clear relationships to differences in scholastic attainment (see Jencks *et al.*, 1972; Averch *et al.*, 1972; Rutter and Madge, 1976; Summers and Wolfe, 1977). On the other hand, these rather concrete variables say nothing about a whole range of school features which *might* influence children's behaviour and attainments. As Jencks *et al.* (1972) themselves pointed out, they 'ignored not only attitudes and values but the internal life of schools'. They were therefore quite unable to consider whether children were influenced by differences in things such as the style or quality of teaching, the types of teacher-child interaction in the classroom, the overall social climate of the school, or its characteristics and qualities as a social organisation. Other studies, which we consider below, suggest that these were grave omissions — inevitable in the context of a massive questionnaire survey but nevertheless liable to lead to rather misleading conclusions. If the effects of schooling are to be judged in terms of the strength of associations between particular school variables and measures of attainment, it is essential that the school variables should be the right ones (meaning that they reflect those aspects of school life which do in fact have an impact). A lack of association may simply mean that an irrelevant variable was chosen.

Gains in attainment

A major problem in all cross-sectional surveys designed to examine school influences is the lack of information on what the children were like when they entered the school. As Coleman (1975) put it: 'the principal villain (in the statistical analyses) is the fact that student populations in different schools differ at the outset. ... because of this difference, it is not possible merely to judge the quality of a school by the achievements of the students leaving it. It is necessary to control in some way for the variations in student input with which the teachers and staff of the school are confronted. In some way, it is the *increment* in achievement that the school provides which should be the measure of the school's quality'. This can only be determined through longitudinal studies in which repeated measurements are made on the same group of pupils at several different points during their school career. The surveys considered so far all lacked any kind of measure of the children's attainments on entry to school, and so a variety of statistical adjustments had to be made in order to estimate the size of any possible effect. There has been considerable controversy about the best way to do this (see, for example, Mosteller and Moynihan, 1972; Coleman, 1975; Brimer *et al.*, 1977). The statistical details need not concern us here but it is necessary to recognise that different assumptions underlie different methods of statistical analysis. Perhaps the most important difficulty is raised by the (common) circumstance of children from disadvantaged homes being more likely to attend disadvantaged schools. If the whole of home influences on development are statistically eliminated *before* determining school effects, school influences will be automatically (and misleadingly) reduced by the extent of overlap between disadvantages at home and at school. There are various ways of handling this problem statistically but none provide a really satisfactory alternative to using measures of attainment on the same children both before and after school entry.

Variations between homes and between schools

Much research in the past two decades has been concerned with attempts to estimate the relative importance of homes and schools in terms of their impact on children's development. The question is very difficult to answer because, statistically speaking, the size or degree of effect of any factor is strongly dependent on the range or extent of variation on that factor or measure.

The point is perhaps best illustrated by an example. One might ask which is more important in determining how fast a car can go – the size of its engine or the skills of its driver? If we studied the issue by looking at the races won by professional drivers, all of whom used cars in the same racing class, we would probably find that the driver made the most difference – simply because the car engines varied so little in size. On the other hand, if the same comparison was made with cars whose engines ranged from, say, 650cc to four litre capacity the answer would be likely to be the other way round. The result would be dependent in part on whether the difference between the 'best' and 'worst' driver was more or less than that between the biggest and smallest engine.

The point is of some relevance when considering the relative importance of homes and schools. All studies which have compared the two have clearly shown that for almost all measures of scholastic attainment, the differences between schools accounted for far less of the variance than did features of the family or home (Rutter and Madge, 1976). The findings are important in showing the limits of what would be achieved by bringing the 'worst' schools up to the level of the 'best', but too much should not be read into them. The results do not necessarily mean that school influences are of little importance. Instead, they may be a consequence of the fact that there is a bigger difference between the 'best' and 'worst' home than that between the 'best' and 'worst' school. If schools vary in quality less than do homes (as is probably the case) then their statistical 'effect' on children's attainment will also appear less.

Inequalities in attainment or levels of attainment

The last issue with respect to the large-scale survey concerns the questions being examined. The main distinction to bear in mind is that between *inequalities* in attainment and overall *levels* of attainment. Jencks' analyses were primarily concerned with the first issue − namely, if the quality of schooling was greatly improved, what effect would this have in making children more similar to one another (i.e. reducing inequalities in attainment)? The answer was that it would make very little difference. The differences in attainment between children within any one school are much greater than any differences in average attainment between schools. Raising the quality of education does not have the effect of making every one alike. This is because children vary (as a result of both genetic endowment and home experiences) in their ability to profit from educational opportunities. Improving schools will not necessarily make any difference to individual variations.

But it may have a decisive impact in raising overall standards of attainment. The distinction is very nicely brought out by Jack Tizard's (1975) study of the height of London school children. Over the last half-century their average height has risen nine centimetres − a very considerable gain − but of course children still vary enormously in how tall they are. Improved living conditions (probably in terms of better nutrition) have led to major changes in *level*, without any reduction in *inequality*. Similarly, Skodak and Skeels (1949) showed that when children born to seriously disadvantaged mothers were adopted into good homes their average level of intelligence rose greatly, but as with any other group of children, they still differed a lot between themselves.

Conclusions from the large-scale surveys

The large-scale surveys, then, are agreed in showing that differences between schools have rather little to do with the variations between individual children in general cognitive ability. On the other hand, the effects are somewhat greater with respect to subjects such as maths and science which are largely learned at school. Adequate estimates of the size of any school effect, however, are not possible in the absence of information on what the children's behaviour and attainments were like *before* school entry. Insofar as school influences are important, the crucial factor does not appear to consist of the overall level of school resources. Other studies are needed to determine which school characteristics are most likely to foster successful development.

Studies of school variations in attendance, behaviour and delinquency

The studies considered so far all refer to one or other aspect of scholastic attainment. However, other investigations have also shown quite large differences between schools in other aspects of children's performance — in their attendance, behaviour and delinquency rates.

Michael Power and his colleagues (1967) found huge differences in delinquency rates between the twenty secondary schools serving one inner London borough, even after excluding the schools taking the 15 per cent most academic children. Annual average rates varied from 1 per cent in the school with the 'best' record to 19 per cent in the one with the 'worst'. These school differences remained remarkably stable over a six year period and did not appear to be explicable in terms of differences in the catchment area served (Power *et al.*, 1972). The differences applied both to first offenders and to recidivists.

More recently, Dennis Gath and his research team (1977) have produced broadly similar findings for children living in an outer London borough of rather different social characteristics to that studied by Power. Both primary and secondary schools differed widely in probation rates (reflecting delinquency) and in rates of referral to child psychiatric clinics. The two sets of rates showed parallel trends, schools with a high referral rate tending also to have a high delinquency rate. As in the Power study, the school variations could not be explained in terms of the areas where the children lived.

Neither of these studies had data on the children's characteristics at school entry and neither was able to determine which school features were associated with low or high delinquency rates. Studies by Donald West and David Farrington (1973) and by David Reynolds (Reynolds and Murgatroyd, 1977; Reynolds *et al.*, 1976) make up for one or other of these deficiencies but neither has data to deal with both problems. West and Farrington's work is based on a prospective study of some four hundred boys living in a working class area in inner London. The sample size was rather small for an investigation of this kind and only four secondary schools took as many as forty children each. However, Farrington (1972) was able to show that much of the school variation was explicable in terms of intake differences. The high delinquency schools took a higher proportion of boys already showing troublesome behaviour at primary school. The study strongly emphasises the importance of having longitudinal data in order to look at *changes* in behaviour according to the school attended. The findings have been interpreted as showing that schools do not influence delinquency rates (West and Farrington, 1973). However, examination of the data shows that there were some school variations. Thus, for boys with 'average' behaviour at primary school, 20 per cent became delinquent at low delinquency schools whereas 31 per cent did so at high delinquency schools.

David Reynolds, on the other hand, did not have any information on the children prior to secondary school entry, although there was evidence that the schools he studied had roughly comparable intakes. He found major variations between them in rates of academic attainment, attendance, delinquency and also unemployment four months after school leaving. These school differences remained stable over a six year period from 1966 to 1972. Preliminary findings on school practices (as observed by Reynolds) showed that enforcement of uniforms, a prefect system and a low level of corporal punishment were all significantly correlated with good attendance. The study is important, not only because of the range of 'outcomes' studied but also because it begins to provide pointers to what sort of features may be influential in schools. The suggestion is that the impact lies in characteristics of the schools in the formal and informal rules they have and in their internal organisation rather than anything directly to do with finances or buildings.

Heal (1978) found that primary schools differed significantly in the level of misbehaviour reported by their pupils (even after controlling for differences in the schools' catchment areas). Misbehaviour was higher in schools with more formal systems of punishment and in schools in which a large increase in pupil numbers had been met by the provision of temporary accommodation. Interestingly, the children's behaviour in their first year of secondary school was unrelated to the feeder primary school they had attended, suggesting that the primary school influences were not very persistent.

We may conclude that there is very good evidence that schools vary greatly in rates of attendance, psychiatric referral and delinquency, but that it is uncertain how far these variations are due to differences in the kinds of children admitted to each school. Little is known, however, on what makes some schools more 'successful' than others in these terms.

School features

It is necessary now to turn to some rather different sorts of studies which have looked at various aspects of school functioning which could have an influence on children's behaviour and attainments. Because very few of the studies provide statistical links between the school measures and the children's performance it is rarely possible to conclude with any confidence that the school variables are directly related to children's performance but the investigations provide valuable leads on what might be important.

Previous work in this area will be considered under seven broad headings: (1) amount of teaching experienced by the children; (2) the size of school; (3) organisation of teaching groups; (4) the effects on pupils of differing teacher expectations; (5) teaching styles and classroom management; (6) patterns of discipline; and (7) overall school climate.

Amount of teaching

The findings on whether nursery school attendance has any significant long-term impact on later scholastic attainment are contradictory and inconclusive, but there is evidence that missed schooling has adverse effects on measured intelligence and also that more years of schooling during adolescence has beneficial effects (see Jencks *et al.*, 1972; Rutter and Madge, 1976). These findings refer to the effects of quite large differences in the amount of schooling on scores on tests of general ability rather than attainment in school subjects. However, there is also evidence from the British National Child Development Study that children who show a poor attendance rate at secondary school have worse reading and mathematics scores at sixteen years (Fogelman, 1978). The Isle of Wight study found that among physically handicapped children those who missed a lot of school were more likely to experience serious difficulties in reading (Rutter, Tizard and Whitmore, 1970). Could it also be that schools which foster good attendance are more likely to have better levels of scholastic attainment?

Moreover, will scholastic success be greater in schools which provide more hours of active teaching or a greater academic emphasis? The findings are meagre but the suggestion is that it will be. Several studies have shown modest, but positive, associations between the time spent actively involved in particular subject work and attainments in those subjects (see Bennett, 1978). Opportunities for pupil practice and frequent teacher feedback both seem to help. Furthermore, there appear to be benefits from extra teaching in the summer holidays during the middle and later school years (Yinger *et al.*, 1977). McDill and Rigsby (1973), in a cross-sectional study, also showed that schools with a strong academic emphasis (as assessed from questionnaires completed by pupils and teachers) tended to have somewhat better attainments in mathematics. Ainsworth and Batten (1974), in a follow-up of the children first studied for the Plowden (1967) enquiry, found that academically successful schools tended to have an emphasis on examinations and on homework; they also had better qualified staff. However, the results also showed that the school environment was strongly linked with the initial ability of the pupil intake. Schools with a more able intake tended to have better amenities all round.

As already mentioned within the relatively narrow range found in local authority schools, neither average size of school class nor pupil-teacher ratio seems to be consistently associated with school behaviour or attainment (see Rutter and Madge, 1976). Indeed, what trend exists is for *larger* class size to be associated with *better* attainments – the opposite of what most people would expect. The reason for this curious finding is not known and it may be that only really small classes make an educational difference. Perhaps the differences in class size studied were not great enough to allow any modification in style of teaching. Whatever the explanation, it seems that reducing the number of very large classes would be unlikely to do much on its own to improve overall educational attainments. On the other hand, there is a suggestion from one study (Summers and Wolfe, 1977) that the effects may be different for pupils of different ability. These findings point to the possibility that it is only low ability pupils who benefit much from being in small classes. The matter needs further study.

Size of school

It seems likely that the character and atmosphere of a school will be influenced by its size, but the findings are contradictory on whether the net effect is positive or negative with respect to the children's behaviour and progress. Barker and Gump (1964) showed that pupils in large schools were less likely to be involved in after-school activities than those attending small schools. Ross *et al.* (1972) found much the same but, as most of the large schools were in urban areas, it seemed that the location of the school may be as important as its size.

Galloway (1976) examined persistent absenteeism in thirty British comprehensive secondary schools and found no significant association between the size of the school and the absence rate (there was a non-significant trend for absence rates to be higher in small schools). Reynolds and Murgatroyd (1977), in contrast, found a tendency for attendance to be worse in large schools. However, the two studies are difficult to compare in that Reynolds' large schools would have been regarded as small in Galloway's investigation. Heal (1978) found misbehaviour more common in large primary schools but the association might well have been explained by the fact that the larger schools had to use temporary accommodation in order to cope with rising rolls. Altogether, the findings are too few and too contradictory to allow any firm conclusions. Moreover, the findings mean little without data on other characteristics of the schools.

Organisation of teaching groups

While there has been great educational controversy on the effects of different balances with respect to pupil mix and on the merits and demerits of teaching children in groups of similar ability, the empirical findings on this issue are contradictory and inconclusive (see Jencks *et al.*, 1972; Kelsall and Kelsall, 1971; Mabey, 1974; Barnes and Lucas, 1974). On the whole, the American studies suggest that a high proportion of socially disadvantaged children in a school is associated with less satisfactory school attainments but the British evidence suggests that social mix only makes a difference at the extremes. Less is known on how school functioning and pupil progress are affected by the balance of intellectually less able to behaviourally disruptive pupils.

It also appears that, *on average*, children in streamed and unstreamed (tracked and untracked) schools make similar progress and gain comparable attainment (Passow *et al.*, 1967; Lunn, 1970; Jencks *et al.*, 1972). On the other hand, within *streamed* schools there is some scholastic advantage associated with being in the higher stream even after initial differences in achievement and social background have been taken into account (Acland, 1973; Lunn, 1970). The net effect on attainment which stems from which stream a child is in amounts to the equivalent of no more than five IQ points – a small difference but not a trivial one.

Streaming probably also affects children's attitudes and behaviour. In a participant-observer case study of one secondary school, Hargreaves (1967) noted the way in which pupil sub-cultures and teacher attitudes became polarised along the lines of streaming arrangements. There was a tendency for lower-stream children to be labelled as failures and to perceive themselves as such. Many became delinquent. Lacey (1970 and 1974) looked at the effects of streaming in an academically selective school. In a follow-up study of the same school after it had changed to mixed ability groupings, he found that the less able boys (actually still above average in ability because the school was selective in its intake) improved their exam performance whereas the change made no difference to the pass rate of the most able group. Much the same was shown with respect to the long-term effects of early streamed or mixed ability teaching in the Banbury Enquiry (Postlethwaite and Denton, 1978). The public examination results at age sixteen years showed only quite small differences between pupils who had been taught in streamed groups and those who had been in mixed ability classes in their early years at secondary school (all the children were streamed in the later years). However, there was some evidence of better overall performance for the less able boys in the mixed ability classes, without any lowering of the standards achieved by the more able. Few differences were found for girls.

Less information is available on the behavioural consequences of mixed ability teaching. However, the study of comprehensive schools undertaken by Ross *et al.* (1972) showed a higher proportion of pupils rated as ill-behaved in mixed ability schools (possibly because of different standards of comparison) but the same schools also seemed to have a reduced tendency to develop delinquent sub-cultures and the formation of particularly difficult classes. The data are far too few for any conclusion about the balance of advantages and disadvantages resulting from streamed or mixed ability teaching.

King (1973) examined other aspects of school organisation in terms of possible effects on pupils' participation in school activities. The findings showed no overall advantage of any one type of organisation but different patterns of association for different age groups suggested that further study of the issue would be worthwhile.

Teacher expectations

In 1968, Rosenthal and Jacobson (1968) published *Pygmalion in the Classroom*, an experimental study which claimed to show that teacher expectations had an important impact on pupil performance. Researchers told teachers that tests indicated that certain pupils (actually randomly selected) would make unusual intellectual gains during the coming years. It was said that these predictions were then fulfilled. In fact the study has serious methodological faults and the results do not truly indicate what the book claims. More importantly, several attempts by other researchers to repeat the experiment have produced largely negative findings (see review by Pilling and Pringle, 1978). It appears that teachers are not that easily taken in by spurious test findings when the test results run counter to their own observations of the children. On the other hand, several studies of naturally occurring (rather than experimentally induced) teacher expectations have shown significant (although generally fairly small) effects on pupil progress. For example, Seaver (1973) found that pupils taught by the same teachers as their older siblings had higher academic attainments than pupils taught by different teachers if their older siblings had been academically bright, but lower achievement if their siblings had been dull. Other studies (reviewed by Pilling and Pringle, 1978) have shown that teachers' expectations and attitudes have an impact on how they behave towards their pupils. However, not all teachers respond in the same way – some give more attention and praise to those for whom they have high expectations whereas others give most encouragement to the low-achievers whom they think need it more.

Almost all the studies of teacher expectations refer to individual teachers rather than to schools. Nevertheless, the findings raise the question of whether schools in which there were high expectations of the pupils would obtain higher levels of scholastic attainment than those in which low achievement was expected to be the norm.

Teaching style and classroom management

Early comparisons between so-called traditional and progressive methods of teaching showed few overall differences in effects on pupil progress (Gardner, 1966; Gooch and Pringle, 1966). Each suited some children and some teachers and not others. More recently, in an influential study which caught the public eye, Bennett (1976) looked at the associations between teaching style and changes in children's performance on standard tests of reading, mathematics and English during the final year of junior school before secondary transfer at eleven years. In general, Bennett found that children taught by teachers using a 'formal' style showed greater gains in attainment than those taught in 'informal' classrooms. The study constituted a distinct advance on its predecessors both in terms of its longitudinal design (allowing *changes* in attainment to be measured) and of its assessment of the teaching styles of individual teachers. Even so there are important difficulties in interpreting the findings. The most serious confounding factor was that some schools operated within a selective system with secondary school allocation based on the test scores obtained at the age of eleven, whereas others functioned in the context of a non-selective system with automatic progression to comprehensive schools. As it turned out, although the 'formal' group did best overall, the most favourable results were actually obtained by children taught according to 'informal' methods in a selective district. In addition there are problems in interpreting just what the formal-informal dichotomy meant in practical terms. Some teachers were very informal in their use of the classroom but nevertheless were highly structured in their planning and recording of pupils' work. A teacher of this kind was cited by Bennett as one whose class made particularly good progress. Unfortunately the statistical analyses which were undertaken did not allow a really satisfactory disentangling of effects. The study undoubtedly points to the value of further investigations of styles of teaching but the results obtained so far do not justify much in the way of firm conclusions.

The complexities are well-illustrated in Stallings' (1975) American longitudinal study of teaching practices with elementary school children in first and third grades. In this study, unlike Bennett's, the practices were assessed by classroom observations rather than by teacher reports. Two main findings stand out. First, children's attainments in reading and in maths were significantly better when the teachers used systematic instruction with much question and answer and a liberal use of praise for correct answers (less able children were most helped by praise). Second, flexible open classrooms with more exploratory materials, more choices by the child and a greater use by the teacher of open-ended questions were associated with better attendance, higher scores on a test of reasoning and a greater willingness to work independently.

Similarly, in a study of different types of pre-school programme, Miller and Dyer (1975) found that highly structured formal approaches were associated with the greatest immediate cognitive gains but also the greatest falls later when the children moved on to primary school. These investigations were all of much younger children than those in our own secondary school study, there are disagreements about the most appropriate way to analyse results of this kind, and the findings from one age group cannot be readily generalised to another. However, it is clear that no simple conclusion is possible about the effects of 'structure'. Not only is 'structure' a multi-faceted concept but also there has to be a concern with the effects of teaching practices on information transmitted, on styles of work and on approaches to learning.

This differentiation is also brought out by the White and Lippitt (1960) studies of ten and eleven year old children in small experimental groups. These showed that an authoritarian approach led to a high work out-put but some aggression to the 'teacher'. Children in democratic groups in which they were led and guided but also were involved in decision-making had nearly as high a work-output, got on best with the 'teacher' and worked slightly better than the authoritarian group when the 'teacher' was out of the room. Children in the laissez-faire group did worst on all criteria.

Of course, as this study shows, styles of teaching involve methods of group management as well as methods of teaching. Experienced teachers clearly recognise the attention to detail which is required to conduct a class skilfully (this is well illustrated in Michael Marland's 1975 book *The Craft of the Classroom: A Survival Guide*). Kounin's (1970) research has been influential in this context. He emphasised the importance of teachers keeping in touch with all that's going on in the classroom while still going on teaching (with-it-ness), of maintaining a smooth flow of activities without delays and interruptions, of keeping the *whole* class alert and interested, of being able to deal with several things at the same time, and of providing the pupils with varied and challenging tasks. In one of the few studies to test these ideas systematically, Brophy and Evertson (1976) confirm that these teaching practices were indeed associated with increased learning gains by pupils. Schools vary greatly in the amount of time spent by pupils 'getting organised', clearing up and just waiting for the teacher (Bennett, 1978) and it seems that children show greater involvement in lessons when there is little time-wasting of this kind.

Patterns of discipline

There has been surprisingly little systematic research into the effects of different patterns of discipline. However, the few studies that have been undertaken both point to its importance and emphasise that discipline and punishment should not be seen as synonymous. As already mentioned, Reynolds observed that the combination of good discipline (in terms of rule enforcement), the involvement of pupils in discipline (as shown by the use of a prefect system), and a low use of corporal punishment was most likely to be associated with good attendance. Heal (1978) found that misbehaviour was worst in schools with formal punishment systems; and Clegg and Megson (1968) noted that delinquency rates tended to be highest in schools with a great deal of corporal punishment. They also describe the improvement in one school where a new head reduced the number of rules and reduced the use of corporal punishment but also increased the monitoring and enforcement of the rules that remained and insisted on higher standards of staff behaviour. Other studies have found that firm, quiet reprimands are more effective than angry punitive responses (Kounin, 1970; O'Leary *et al.*, 1970). Experimental studies of teacher-child interaction in the classroom show that teacher approval and attention when the children are behaving appropriately encourages its continuation; also it may be better to ignore disruptive behaviour when it has an attention-seeking purpose (see Becker, 1973). It seems possible that different patterns of discipline may be needed for children of different ages but the matter has been little studied.

School climate or atmosphere

Halpin (1966) developed teacher questionnaires to assess school climates and morale and Finlayson (1973) expanded the approach to include the perceptions of pupils as well as teachers. A comparison of four schools which were similar on social indicators but which differed in delinquency rates showed that pupil perceptions differed according to the school delinquency rates (Finlayson and Loughran, 1975). Pupils in high delinquency schools perceived the teachers as more authoritarian and the schools as less committed to learning (this was so both for delinquent and non-delinquent pupils within the schools). The finding suggests the importance of the school ethos or atmosphere but, of course, it leaves entirely open the crucial question of what actions by the staff (or others) serve to establish particular types of climate.

Overview of school features

It is evident that schools differ on a variety of quite different features and there are strong suggestions that these differences may have an important influence on the children's behaviour and scholastic progress. The possibly relevant features include the amount of teaching and degree of academic emphasis, the extent and nature of ability groupings, teacher expectations, styles of teaching and classroom management, the size of the school, patterns of discipline and the characteristics of the overall school climate or atmosphere. The findings provide important leads as to what school features deserve further study but so far the research results allow few firm conclusions. This is largely because so few studies have had longitudinal data and hence it has been very difficult to sort out whether the children's behaviour and attainments resulted from what they were like before they entered secondary school, or rather whether the school practices were having an influence on them. Furthermore, many of the studies concerned classrooms rather than schools, and many focussed on pre-school or primary school age rather than secondary school children.

Other institutions

The studies discussed up to now imply that children may be influenced by the characteristics of schools as social organisations as well as by the styles and quality of pedagogy they encounter in the classroom. However, the investigations have all been concerned with schools of one type or another and it is appropriate to ask whether the characteristics of *other* types of institution have also been found to have an impact on the people in them. A variety of investigations indicate that they do. For example, Ian Sinclair (1971) found that boys' success in probation hostels was greatest in those with warm but strict wardens whose wives agreed with them on how the hostels should be run; Bartak and Rutter (1973; Rutter and Bartak, 1973) found that autistic children made most progress in structured units with systematic teaching; King et al. (1971) showed remarkable differences in child management practices between different types of institution catering for mentally handicapped children; Raynes et al. (1977) showed that staff involvement in decision making was related to the quality of care provided; Wing and Brown (1970) showed close associations between the behaviour of schizophrenic patients and the social environment provided by the hospitals in which they lived; Revans (1964) found that patients stayed longer in general hospitals with low staff morale; Millham et al. (1975) examined the associations between the characteristics of schools for delinquents and the boys' attitudes and subsequent re-conviction rates; and several studies examined associations between college environments and academic productivity there (Getzels, 1969). The institutional characteristics examined in these studies were quite varied and it is not possible to draw any close parallels between them. Moreover, most were concerned with residential care of one kind or another for individuals with problems or handicaps. In both respects they differ greatly from the day schools we studied. However, the findings are important in drawing attention to the value of considering patterns of social organisation in institutions; patterns which reflect styles of management and control, quality of relationships, participation and involvement, responsibilities and decision-making, and the overall emotional climate as well as the details of how individuals interact with one another. It is likely that these will be important in schools as well as in other kinds of institution.

Research implications

There is good evidence from other research that secondary schools vary greatly with respect to rates of examination success, attendance, misbehaviour and delinquency. There are also indications that these variations may reflect school *influences* on children's behaviour and attainments. However, it is not possible to draw inferences about possible causal effects in view of the fact that so few investigations have had information on what the children were like *before* entry to the secondary school. It was evident that a longitudinal study following children through from primary school to secondary school was necessary to examine the matter. Accordingly, that was how our project began.

The earlier work also emphasised that school influences were more likely to be shown with respect to attainments directly relevant to what is taught at school rather than in relation to general tests of intelligence. However, it was also clear that the school variations applied to children's attitudes, attendance and behaviour as well as to their scholastic accomplishments so that it would be important to examine a wide range of indicators of pupil progress. Interestingly, and perhaps surprisingly, the evidence suggested that schools may influence children's behaviour outside as well as inside school — as shown by differences between schools in delinquency rates.

A variety of studies in both Britain and the United States have clearly indicated that the main source of variations between schools in their effects on the children does not lie in factors such as buildings or resources. Rather, the crucial differences seemed to concern aspects of school life to do with its functioning as a social organisation. Observers had noted differences between schools in morale, climate and atmosphere but little was known about what staff actions or activities lay behind these intangible but important features. Accordingly, it seemed important to study schools in some detail over a prolonged period of time in which the many different facets of school life could be assessed by direct observation as well as by interviews with staff and pupils. This we sought to do.

2

Background to the study

A great deal of educational research has been devoted to questions of the curriculum and of pedagogic practice, but, as we have seen in our review of earlier work in the first chapter, relatively little is known about the broader patterns of life in schools and about the kinds of environments for learning which they present to their pupils. That was the prime focus of our study.

The comparative surveys of children in inner London and on the Isle of Wight

However, before describing our study of *schools*, it is necessary to consider the investigations of *children* which constituted the basis for the work. The study had its roots in a comparative survey of all ten year old children living in an inner London borough, and children of the same age with homes on the Isle of Wight (Rutter *et al.*, 1974; 1975a, b, & c; Berger *et al.*, 1975; Yule *et al.*, 1975). The research gave rise to two main findings. First, it was found that emotional, behavioural and reading problems were twice as common in inner London as on the Isle of Wight. The findings clearly showed the heavy burdens faced by children and teachers in this area.

Secondly, the results indicated that the problems and difficulties shown by the children were strongly linked with various types of family adversity. Family discord and disharmony, parental mental disorder, criminality in the parents, large family size and overcrowding in the home, admission of the child into care of the local authority, and low occupational status were all associated with emotional or behavioural disturbance and/or reading retardation. As with previous studies, there was ample evidence of the immense importance of family circumstances and family relationships in shaping children's development. Indeed, these family variables were so influential that they largely accounted for the much higher rate of problems in London school children compared with the Isle of Wight.

However, there was also a third finding — namely that primary schools in London differed markedly in their rates of both behaviour problems and reading difficulties. As far as could be determined, these differences between schools were not wholly due to variations in the sorts of children admitted to each of the schools. The inference was that the schools might be having an effect on the way the children functioned. But we could not be sure of this because we did not know what the children had been like when they first entered primary school.

However, the data already collected did provide information on the children's behaviour and attainments prior to *secondary* school transfer. Thus, if we followed the progress of the same children through secondary school we would be able to determine how far any changes were a consequence of what the children were like when they entered secondary school and how far the result of some kind of school influence. This we did.

The 1970 survey

The survey of London ten year olds was undertaken in 1970 when the children were nearing the end of their time at primary school, before their transfer to secondary school in September 1971. Group tests were used to assess the intellectual level and reading attainments of all children attending local authority primary schools in one inner London borough (or attending special schools situated outside the Borough, the placement having been made by the local authority). Information on the child's behaviour and family circumstances were obtained for the same group of children.

The NFER* test NV5 (Pidgeon, 1965) provided a measure of non-verbal intelligence and the NFER reading test SRA (a lengthened version of the earlier Sentence Reading Test 1 — Watts, 1955) gave an assessment of reading comprehension.

Information on parental occupation, together with the place of birth of the child and both his parents, was provided by the teacher. A large sample of parents was interviewed to provide a check on the accuracy

* National Foundation for Educational Research.

of this information. Occupations were classified according to the Registrar General's (1970) criteria.

The behavioural questionnaire completed by teachers was originally developed and tested during earlier surveys of school children in Aberdeen and the Isle of Wight (Rutter, 1967; Rutter, Tizard and Whitmore, 1970). It was then slightly modified and the layout improved for the 1970 Isle of Wight—Inner London comparative study (Rutter *et al.*, 1975a). The questionnaire was designed as a screening instrument to pick out children with possible emotional or behavioural difficulties and there is good evidence from a variety of studies that it does this well (see Rutter, 1967; Rutter, Tizard and Whitmore, 1970; Rutter *et al.*, 1975a). Different teachers tend to rate the same children in a fairly comparable fashion and the questionnaire scores generally agree with more detailed individual diagnostic psychiatric assessments. The questionnaire functions well as a screening measure of possible current difficulties and group comparisons using questionnaire scores have been shown to be valid. However, the instrument was *not* designed for, nor is it appropriate for, individual diagnosis. Further, it provides an assessment of how a child behaves in one particular setting and it is known that children often behave differently in different settings (see Rutter, Tizard and Whitmore, 1970). Moreover, it assesses *current* behaviour and not enduring personality characteristics. As a result, associations with the child's behaviour in later years are only modest (see Rutter, 1977).

The questionnaire is designed both to give an overall measure of possible emotional or behavioural difficulties and also to indicate whether the difficulties mainly involve emotional disturbance or problems of conduct.

The 1974 survey

About two-thirds of the 1970 sample went on to one of twenty non-selective schools in three educational divisions in South London — a much larger geographical area than the one with which we first started. The remainder of the children transferred either to selective schools in London or else moved out of the area to secondary schools elsewhere.

All the children were retested in 1974 when they were aged approximately fourteen years and in their third year of secondary school.

The same teacher questionnaire as at age ten years was employed to give an indication of the proportion of children showing emotional problems or behavioural difficulties at school. The educational tests were chosen to be appropriate for children in the middle of their secondary schooling but otherwise they were closely comparable to those used at ten. The NFER test NV-DH provided a measure of non-verbal intelligence and the NFER Reading Test NS6 a measure of reading comprehension. At the same time we gathered further information on ethnic background and parental occupational status, and obtained figures on the children's delinquency. All children who had been involved in the ten year old testing were followed up, including those who had moved out of London.

However, as our main interest with respect to this study was in school differences, we concentrated our analyses on the twenty non-selective schools in the local area which had taken the majority of the children in the ten year old 'cohort'.* As London secondary schools take children from a much wider geographical area than do primary schools, the 'cohort' group constituted only a proportion of their age group in the twenty schools.

Obviously, it was important both to check whether the 'cohort' children differed in any way from the rest of the children in the schools and to obtain a picture of the attainments and behaviour of the complete age group in the twenty schools. Accordingly, identical tests and questionnaires were completed at the same time for all the children who entered the schools in 1971. The population numbered 3485 in all, 1487 'cohort' children, plus 1998 others from adjacent boroughs. There were no significant differences between the 'cohort' and 'non-cohort' children on any of the measures we obtained. However, when the schools were considered individually, significant differences on one or other of the measures were found in four of the twenty schools. Clearly, these differences would need to be taken into account in planning later stages of the research.

---

* The term 'cohort' is used to describe a particular group of individuals followed over time – in this case the children in the original 1970 survey. It is not the same as an 'age group' in that all the schools included children of the same age who came from other primary schools not included in the 1970 survey. Moreover, it will be appreciated that while the 'cohort' was aged ten years at the beginning of the study they are now over eighteen and have left school.

School differences in 1974

The next step was to examine the variations between the twenty schools in terms of their rates of delinquency, emotional/behavioural problems, and reading difficulties. Very large variations were found. Thus, for boys, the school delinquency rates varied from 0 to 31 per cent; rates of behavioural deviance on the teacher questionnaire ranged from 0 to 48 per cent; and rates of severe reading difficulties from 6 to 26 per cent.

These major school variations were in keeping with the findings from previous research. However, as we pointed out in the first chapter, it was not possible to assume that all schools have similar intakes. As a result, it could be that the school variations were merely reflections of differences between the schools in the proportion of difficult or backward children they admitted from primary schools. As we had already collected data relevant to this question we were able to examine the patterns of intake to each of the twenty schools. This analysis showed that there were considerable differences between schools. Thus, for boys, some schools admitted as few as 7 per cent of children with behavioural or reading difficulties whereas others took as many as 48–50 per cent with these problems. On the other hand, the schools with a high proportion of 'difficult' children at intake were not always those with highest proportion of children with problems at follow-up.

Controlling for variations in intake

Clearly, it was essential to examine the differences between secondary schools *after* statistically equating the schools with respect to their intakes. In order to do this it was necessary first to determine the associations between children's scores (on tests or questionnaires) at ten and their scores at fourteen. Thus, it was found that boys with high scores on the teachers' questionnaire at ten were twice as likely as other boys to show behavioural problems at fourteen. On this basis it was possible to construct a standardisation formula to adjust school scores for differences in intake (see Rutter, 1977). When this had been done it was found that there were still substantial and statistically significant differences between schools even after taking into account what the children had been like at age ten prior to admission to secondary school (Yule and Rutter, 1979).

The differences between schools in their intakes did not explain the differences between them at fourteen because the schools with the most advantaged intakes were not necessarily those with the best outcomes. Furthermore, schools with very similar intakes sometimes had very different findings at fourteen. This is illustrated in Table 2.1 which shows the results for two schools 'A' and 'B' with rather similar intakes of behaviourally difficult boys which were about average for the inner London borough they served. However, in terms of the follow-up results at age fourteen years, school A had about *half* as many boys as the average with high scores on the teacher questionnaire, whereas school B had *twice* as many – a *five-fold* difference between the schools.

	No. in Intake	'Cohort' Children Proportion with Behavioural Difficulties	
		Prior to Intake	At 14 Years
School A	65	30·8%	9·2%
School B	50	34·0%	48·0%

Table 2.1 *Behavioural intake and outcome measures for two schools*

School differences after controlling for intake

When this sort of approach was applied to the fourteen year old findings for the twenty schools as a whole, it was found that the school rates of behavioural disturbance for boys on the teacher's questionnaire varied from 19 per cent *below* expectation to 30 per cent *above* expectation, and for delinquency from 8 per cent below expectation to 21 per cent above expectation (see Yule and Rutter, 1979). The rates of behavioural disturbance for girls ranged from 20 per cent below expectation to 38 per cent above. The school differences on girls' delinquency rates were not examined in view of the fact that so few fourteen year old girls were delinquent.*

The analyses showed that the variations between schools in children's behaviour and in their delinquency rates could *not* be explained in terms of the children's test or questionnaire scores at the end of their period in primary school just prior to secondary transfer. Also, they could not be accounted for in terms of the children's family characteristics or the primary school they had attended (see Yule and Rutter, 1979 for details). It seemed that children's development during the secondary school years might well be influenced by their experiences there. The findings suggested that some schools were able to exert a positive and beneficial influence on their pupils' progress, to some extent protecting them from difficulties. Other schools were less successful in this. It seemed that we would need to look at the features of the schools themselves, if we were to understand why this was so.

At that stage we had only fairly crude administrative data about the schools – in terms of rates of teacher turnover, numbers of pupils eligible for free school meals and so forth. These factors fell a very long way short of explaining the variations in the children's performance. Clearly, it was going to be necessary to study the schools in much greater depth if the features associated with variations in children's behaviour and scholastic progress were to be identified.

Shift of focus from individuals to schools

At this point the study changed its focus from individuals to schools. In order to investigate the functioning of each school in as much detail as we felt was required it was necessary to reduce the number of schools to twelve. These were chosen to represent the range of outcomes in terms of the findings in 1974 for third year children; and also to be representative of other obvious differences among the original twenty London schools. Thus, the twelve included both large and small schools, mixed and single-sex schools, voluntary aided (i.e. Church) and maintained schools, as well as some on single and some on split

---

* There were also substantial but lesser differences between the schools with respect to absenteeism during the second year at secondary school and to reading scores at fourteen years. The findings are given in detail in Yule and Rutter (1979) but are not described here as they were analysed later and so were not used in the decisions taken in proceeding to the next stage of the schools' study.

sites. All were non-selective and none had been academically selective in the past. All served London's inner city population. The schools themselves and the areas they served are described in greater detail in the next chapter.

3

The schools and the area they serve

The area served by the twelve schools

The twelve schools we studied served a large area of inner London extending outwards from the river Thames. The schools themselves lie within a radius of half a dozen miles although the pupils attending them came from homes in six different London boroughs. The majority of the children, however, lived within a smaller central area which is described in this chapter. Like most parts of large cities it is not geographically separate from its neighbouring boroughs and in no sense does it constitute an identifiable community.

During the course of the nineteenth century an enormous pressure of population growth in London destroyed the old pattern of market garden estates. In the districts nearer to the river, small plots of land were sold in piecemeal fashion to speculative builders who created a warren of small streets of poor quality terraced houses for rent. Further from the centre of the city, semi-detached and detached houses with accompanying gardens predominated and population density remained far below that of the districts nearer to the river.

Nowadays much of the area is either rather run down and drab or has recently been rebuilt by the local authority. Much of the newer housing consists of blocks of flats, some in buildings of just three or four storeys but others in tall 'tower blocks'. Many of the yellow brick terraces were pulled down to make way for these developments but others still remain showing the Victorian origins of the area. Many of the public buildings (such as libraries, town hall, and police stations) are typically Victorian and, as is evident from their glazed brown tiles and coloured glass doors, numerous pubs are also survivals from the same era. In some streets destruction of decaying property continues with houses deserted and boarded up while they await demolition. In immediately adjacent parts of the area attractive and well built Regency houses which had been allowed to decay are being carefully restored by new owners. In addition, especially further away from the river, modern estates of more closely packed 'town houses' and a few blocks of luxury flats have been established.

The result is a great heterogeneity of buildings and tremendous variation in housing conditions. Over two-fifths of the population live in local authority flats or houses with subsidised rents; a similar proportion live in privately rented accommodation; and less than a fifth own their own homes. The conditions of the privately rented housing are particularly poor, with over half not possessing or having to share a bath and inside WC (see Quinton, 1979).

The type and quality of housing is rather mixed in all parts of the area but there are major differences between different sections, as exemplified in the 1971 census statistics for the separate electoral wards. For example, the ward rates for owner occupation range from 3 to 44 per cent, for households in shared dwellings from 5 to 26 per cent and the proportion sharing or lacking a bath from 4 to 40 per cent.

There is no highway which passes through the area but there are many main roads which carry goods and people into the city from the suburbs. There are also numerous railway lines which provide commuter services from the more prosperous outlying areas. Often these have been built on viaducts at roof top level so that the smaller streets are crossed by brick arches supporting the railway track. However, within the area itself almost all the public transport is provided by buses. There is considerable traffic congestion on the roads with much accompanying noise. Delays are the rule and traffic jams occur each morning and evening rush hour.

Many of these roads also serve as the main shopping area with both large multiple stores and small privately owned corner shops. There are also several flourishing street markets and a few new shopping precincts with covered areas for pedestrians. There are very few places of entertainment such as cinemas or theatres; most have closed down or been converted into Bingo halls. As in many parts of London there are numerous small parks scattered through the working class suburbs and also one large park in the more prosperous residential area. However, in common with other facilities, the parks are very unevenly distributed with scarcely any in the poorest sections nearer to the river.

Towards the end of the last century business premises increasingly displaced private homes from the middle of London and there was an exodus of the poor to the inner suburbs. At that time the number of paupers in the borough trebled and the area still has a large visible population of vagrants and alcoholics.

Unlike other parts of London which have been noted for specific industries this area has always been known for the variety of its employment. Since the second world war there has been a steady decline in manufacturing work, due both to national and local employment policies and to firms voluntarily moving out of London to less cramped and congested sites. Work in the docks has greatly declined and whole areas of dockland now lie derelict awaiting redevelopment. On the other hand, loss of jobs has been compensated for by the creation of a variety of new jobs in non-manual employment and by a net outflow of skilled manual workers moving to other parts of the country. As a result, unemployment rates have been generally fairly low compared with the rest of the country. Nevertheless, even though the change has been less than that in the country as a whole, the proportion of people out of work has risen considerably in recent years and black school leavers have had particular difficulty in getting jobs (OPCS, 1973 and 1974).

There is a tradition of married women working outside the home and the 1971 census showed that three-fifths of those aged under sixty years of age had regular jobs. Full time day care is available for only 15 per cent of preschool children and parents have to make arrangements of varying quality for their children to be looked after.

By the turn of the century the population had begun to decline and it has continued to fall up to the present day. At first the trend arose largely as a result of people moving out of the area but in recent years the large fall in birth rate has made an even bigger difference. The number of children in primary school has dropped dramatically and the same is now happening in secondary schools.

The area has always included a substantial minority of immigrants from other parts of the country, from Ireland and from abroad. Since the second world war these have included many people from the new commonwealth. The 1971 census showed that these accounted for 8.3 per cent of the total population living in the area. The largest immigrant group comes from the West Indies but there are also a number of Cypriots and a few from Africa and the Asian sub-continent. Because most immigrants are young adults with growing families, the proportion of *children* whose parents come from abroad is very much higher than the proportion of immigrants in the total population. Thus, among ten year old children in 1970, a quarter came from immigrant families and 17 per cent had a father from the West Indies (Yule *et al.*, 1975). On the other hand, at that time half the children from immigrant families were themselves born in the United Kingdom. Since 1970 this proportion has risen greatly and now the great majority of schoolchildren with foreign born parents were born and brought up in London.

Families

Information on the families of ten year old children living in the area is available from the 1970 survey (Rutter *et al.*, 1975c). This showed quite high rates of various different kinds of family adversity. Nearly a quarter (23%) of the children had fathers who held an unskilled or semi-skilled job, over a third (38%) came from families with at least four children, and over half (51%) were living in overcrowded homes (defined in terms of more than one person per room usable for living – i.e. bedrooms and living rooms of any kind but excluding bathrooms and toilets).

Over a quarter (28%) of the mothers had some kind of currently handicapping psychiatric disorder (mostly depressive conditions), although few of these were receiving specialist treatment. This figure is very similar to that obtained in other surveys of mothers living in inner London (Brown *et al.*, 1975) and it is clear that emotional difficulties are a common burden among parents living in inner London. Over a quarter (28%) of the fathers had been convicted of some offence and eight per cent had been in prison. Eleven per cent of the children were living in homes broken by death or divorce, another seventeen per cent were part of families characterised by severe marital discord, and official statistics show that the rate of children in the care of the local authority was 12.5 per 1000.

All of these features of family adversity were very much commoner in inner London than on the Isle of Wight. Moreover, they are characteristics associated with higher rates of behavioural and educational difficulties in the children (Rutter *et al.*, 1975c). It is clear, then, that teachers in the twelve schools we studied had to deal with children many of whom came from homes which were in one way or another deprived or disadvantaged. It is important, of course, not to get the figures out of perspective. Although the *rate* of family adversity was particularly high in the area, nevertheless it was still true that the *majority* of children came from ordinary happy homes which were fairly unexceptionable.

Children

As already outlined, the twelve schools were chosen because they took many of their pupils from the primary schools included in the 1970 survey. That survey provides a picture of what the children in the schools were like just before they transferred to secondary school.

The results of group tests of non-verbal intelligence and of reading at age ten years showed that on both measures the children scored at well below the national average. Thus, the indigenous children had a mean non-verbal intelligence score of 92 and a reading score of 95 in comparison with an expected national norm of 100. These figures *exclude* the children from immigrant families who tended to have rather lower levels of attainment (Yule *et al.*, 1975), and if they are included the mean scores are lower still. The reading levels were in keeping with the earlier ILEA Literacy Survey (ILEA, 1970) and it is evident that although the children's attainments tended to be on the low side compared with Britain as a whole, they were much the same as those of children living in other inner London boroughs.

The mean scores, of course, refer to the average for the total populations of children, and a different aspect of the same picture is seen by considering the proportion of children with particularly severe educational problems. The findings showed that *one child in five* at age 10 years had a reading age below the 7 year 8 months level. This proportion is *twice* that found on the Isle of Wight.

It should be borne in mind, too, that all these results apply to the total population of ten year olds in local authority primary schools. Many of the more able pupils did not transfer to comprehensive schools, going instead to selective grammar schools* and independent

---

* Since the 1970 survey, the local authority has phased out all the grammar schools so that now the secondary school system is completely comprehensive, in terms of all schools taking children of all levels of ability. However, the area is served by some half a dozen prestigious independent schools which continue to take some of the most academically able children.

schools. Thus, of the 75 'cohort' children with an IQ of 120 and above on the group test of non-verbal intelligence, only 20 (29 per cent) went into comprehensive schools. The remaining 55 all went into selective schools, either state or independent. Even in the group of 210 children with an IQ of 110 and above, only 44 per cent went into comprehensive schools. In the twelve schools we studied, only 10 per cent of children were in the top ability band, which constitutes 25 per cent of the total population of all children in inner London. It is clear that the twelve non-selective schools contained very few children with superior scores on these tests.

The 1970 survey indicated that the children also had a high rate of emotional and behavioural difficulties. Nearly one in five (19 per cent) of the children had high scores on the teacher's questionnaire – a rate twice that on either the Isle of Wight or in Aberdeen but about average for inner London (Rutter *et al.*, 1975a). By age ten years some $3\frac{1}{2}$ per cent of children had already been referred to a psychiatric clinic, and by eighteen almost one-third of the boys had been either formally cautioned by the police or found guilty of committing at least one offence.

The schools

There are over one hundred primary schools and more than thirty secondary schools serving the area. The primary schools take children from five to eleven years and the secondary schools from eleven onwards. Schooling is compulsory until the children reach sixteen years of age but a substantial minority of young people remain at school for another one or two years, almost all secondary schools having small sixth forms catering for this oldest age group. The secondary schools are administered by one authority which deals with all education within the twelve inner London boroughs; this is known as the Inner London Education Authority (ILEA). Within the Authority, however, the organisation is based on ten geographical divisions. The twelve schools in our study serve three such divisions.

In the ILEA the children are allocated to a particular secondary school by a system which aims both to meet parental wishes and to ensure a reasonable balance of children of all levels of abilities at each secondary school. At the age of ten, during their last year of primary school, children are assessed on their abilities in Verbal Reasoning, Mathematics and English. They are allocated to secondary school on the basis of parental wishes and the location of their home, but their attainment in the primary school is also taken into account in order to balance the intake to the schools.

Both the primary and the secondary schools present contrasts in buildings. Some schools date back to the turn of the century and consist of 'Victorian three-deckers'. These are rather tall brick buildings, always having three floors and staircases at each corner, each floor having a large central hall with classrooms leading off it. The rooms are large with high ceilings, and the windows are generally set high in the walls so that it is impossible to see out. These schools frequently have tiled walls and stone floors and are rather gloomy if not decorated imaginatively. Other schools have been built more recently and reflect changes in educational philosophy as well as in architectural style. The modern schools have more windows, the ceilings are lower and they do not have the institutional atmosphere of many of the older buildings. Some of the primaries have been built to 'open plan' designs but the new secondary schools still have traditional classrooms. In addition, some have walkways or covered sports areas. Both the new and the old schools have expanded from time to time over the years, extensions being added to cope with increasing numbers of pupils resulting from the rising birth rate in the 1950s and by the raising of the school leaving age from fifteen to sixteen in 1972. These modifications often give the secondary schools a rather unimposing appearance with a variety of different styles and building materials. Playground space is generally rather limited and what little is available is paved, with virtually no grassed areas.

While many of the secondary schools have had to make do with rather old buildings designed for a different educational era, the provision of equipment and resources generally has been very generous. National statistics (see Pratt, 1978) show that the ILEA spends more per child, in both the primary and secondary sectors, than any other educational authority in the country. The estimated per capita expenditure in secondary schools for 1977–78 was £632 in the ILEA compared with a national average of £459. Of course, there are difficulties in interpreting these figures, as high spending may reflect higher local costs or the need to repair buildings left dilapidated from earlier years. However, this is unlikely to be the whole explanation as the ILEA also spends more per child each year on books, educational equipment and materials (£35 for secondary schools in contrast to as little as £11 to £16 in the eleven authorities with the lowest expenditure). Moreover, the pupil-teacher ratio of 14·5:1 in secondary schools is the second lowest in the country – compared with 23·3:1 for Liverpool, the city with the highest ratio.

This good provision of resources is obvious inside the schools in the form of well-equipped science, technical and craft rooms, libraries, the number of television sets, tape recorders, and slide projectors. Many of the schools also have trained personnel to deal with this equipment and to assist in the duplication of materials and preparation of teaching aids.

During the period that the 'cohort' children went through their schooling, there tended to be a rather high rate of teacher turnover in inner London schools. Thus, 43 per cent of primary school teachers had been teaching at their present school for three years or less, compared with 26 per cent on the Isle of Wight (Rutter *et al.*, 1975b). Even more important is the fact that their period of secondary education was one of exceptional difficulty for London teachers and children. Teacher shortages and industrial disputes led to part-time schooling for some children. Education cuts, though less marked than in many areas, imposed certain limitations. For some schools, too, the phasing out of academic selection required reorganisation and, for all, the decrease in the numbers of pupils expected to enter secondary school in the next five years is already causing anxiety. All these disadvantages need to be borne in mind when considering the 'outcome' findings for the 'cohort' age group which we studied most intensively.

Curricula and examinations

Most of the secondary schools have a very similar curriculum for all children during the first three years. Pupils usually study English, mathematics, science, a modern language, history, geography, religious studies, art, music, technical studies and physical education. Very few schools have playing fields on their own site, so that the children have to be taken by coach to outer London for games lessons. Most provide extra tuition for children with learning difficulties, either by putting the least able children in a special class for much of their week or by withdrawing individuals or small groups from some lessons for extra teaching in reading. Little provision is made for remedial mathematics.

The curriculum for pupils during the next two years (when they are aged 14–16) is rather different. The emphasis at this stage tends to turn to the preparation of children for public examinations, and the fourth and fifth years are mainly spent studying the examination syllabus. Usually, pupils and their parents are involved in choosing subjects from a selection of courses available, although English and mathematics are generally compulsory. Most schools permit their pupils to follow approximately seven or eight subjects during these two years, although the choice of courses may be restricted in varying ways (e.g. all pupils have to choose either history or geography or social studies). These two-year courses lead to public exams at the age of sixteen when pupils have been in the secondary school for five years.

Two main types of examinations are taken: the General Certificate of Education (GCE) leading to 'O' (ordinary) levels; and the Certificate of Secondary Education (CSE). The GCE is the accepted examination for children of above average intelligence and it aims to cater for approximately 20 per cent of the total age group. In this examination, each subject is tested separately, usually by two written papers; in certain subjects there is an additional practical exam. These exams are then marked on a five point scale from A to E. Certain careers, and admission to most further education, demand passes of grade C or higher in at least five separate subjects.

The CSE is a newer type of examination which was designed to cover a wider range of ability than the GCE – about a further 40 per cent, so that between them the two exams are intended for some three-fifths of the population. Like the GCE, the CSE is subject based and grades are awarded on the basis of pupils' performance; in this case with a range from 1 to 5. Under both examination systems an 'unclassified' grade may be given although there are no failures as such. However, until recently, the GCE grades of D and E would have been classified as failures.

The existence of this dual system (with different curricula) provides obvious difficulties for teachers and pupils in deciding which examination to enter, and hence which courses to follow. However, there is an accepted equivalent between the two systems with a grade 1 CSE being seen as equal to at least a grade C pass in GCE. The future development of the examination system is currently being considered and it may be that the present arrangements will be replaced by a single examination system for all fifth year pupils.

As is obvious from the description of these examinations, a substantial proportion of pupils leave school without having been entered for either GCE or CSE. Many schools have experienced some difficulties in knowing how best to cater for these pupils and it is striking that throughout the country, as well as in London, the absenteeism rate tends to rise sharply during the fifth year, the last year of compulsory schooling (see Galloway, 1976).

Finally, it should be noted that there is a more advanced examination ('A' levels) which is taken at eighteen years after two years in the sixth form. This constitutes the entry requirement to universities in Britain. It will not be discussed further because very few pupils in the sample took 'A' levels (none in some of the schools) and the results of this examination are not included in our analyses. Some of the pupils also took the CEE (Certificate of Extended Education) at the end of the first year of the sixth form. This is a more advanced form of the CSE and in this case grades 1, 2 and 3 are equivalent to a CSE grade 1.

Similarities and differences between the twelve schools

The twelve schools shared all the features described above for schools in the area as a whole. They also showed a number of other similarities. Thus, all were fairly comparable with respect to the kinds of regulations reported as imposed on the pupils. All required the wearing of some kind of school uniform, although there was variation in whether this meant a precise description of prescribed items to be obtained from a named shop or, rather, a flexible approximation to certain styles and colours. In addition, all sought to establish fairly formal relations between staff and pupils, so that in no case was it usual for pupils to address teachers by their first names.

The twelve included boys' schools, girls' schools and co-educational schools. The boys' schools had mainly male teachers and, similarly, the girls' schools were largely staffed by female teachers. However, unlike those in some other parts of the country, all contained teachers of both sexes. The average time teachers had taught at each school varied

from just over five years to nearly ten, but the total teaching experience
(i.e. including that spent at other schools) was rather greater than that.
At the time of the study two schools were committed to mixed ability
teaching but most grouped their children according to their ability into
sets or streams (tracks).

The 'traditional' academically-oriented sixth form pattern of 'A'
level study was relatively uncommon in the twelve schools. Instead a
'new sixth' approach was more usual. Pupils across the whole ability
range stayed on beyond the statutory leaving age to re-sit
examinations, to convert subjects taken at CSE to 'O' level, or simply
to extend their general education for another year. The majority,
however, left at the end of the fifth year with the intention of going
directly into work.

While the twelve schools were fairly comparable in these respects,
there were also marked differences between them. They varied in size
from approximately 450 pupils to just under 2000. The space available
to schools also varied greatly from 80 to 200 square feet per child.
Some schools had to work on several different sites, so that teachers
were required to travel from one to the other. Within the group of
schools on split sites there was variation in what provision was made
for travelling and in what educational use was made of the two sites.
However, all made deliberate use of the opportunity to organise the
two parts of the school along somewhat different lines for different age
groups. The schools also varied in whether sports facilities were
available on site and in how much travelling was involved for games.
The age of the buildings extended from practically new to over a century old. Regardless of age, there were also striking differences in the
care with which the buildings (new or old) were maintained. In some,
great care was taken to provide attractive decorations, pictures and
plants, and to keep the building in good order by ensuring that any
graffiti were rapidly removed and that damage was immediately
repaired. In others, decorations were allowed to become dirty; there
were delays in repairing broken windows and furniture; the walls were
devoid of pictures and posters, and graffiti tended to be ignored.

Some of the schools were maintained directly by the local authority
whereas others were 'voluntary aided' schools which were run by
either the Church of England or the Roman Catholic Church. As a
result of their voluntary-aided status, these Church schools had
somewhat more autonomy in what they did and were able to exercise

selection on the basis of religious affiliation. However, all took (and had to take) children of all levels of ability.

The schools differed in the style of leadership employed by the head teacher and in the responsibilities of the senior staff. Some heads acted as the chairman of the senior staff group with decisions being taken jointly, whereas others followed a more traditional pattern in which they acted as the main policy maker for the school. The pastoral or welfare side of the schools was organised along a variety of lines. Some favoured a year-based system in which one teacher was responsible for all children of a particular age; in others the organisation was based on houses, with a house teacher responsible for a group of children of varied ages.

The schools differed considerably in their educational aims, as expressed by the teaching staff. Some were firmly committed to the development of children's personalities as the most important goal whereas others saw the passing of examinations as the first requirement. In some, teachers tended to emphasise the teaching of moral codes; in others more stress was laid on making school an enjoyable and rewarding experience for the children.

During the last year of primary schooling, parents are asked to select a particular secondary school as the one they want their child to attend. It is possible to assess the relative popularity of the twelve schools in our study by looking at the proportion of children who entered the school of their first choice. At some of the schools all the children had chosen it as their preferred secondary school whereas at others only half had done so.

It should be added that this description of the schools (and also our findings described in later chapters) refers specifically to the period of study. It will be appreciated that several of the schools were changing during this time (four of the twelve schools had new head teachers) and our findings do not necessarily apply to the particular schools as they are today. Nevertheless, there is every reason to believe that the associations we found and the conclusions we derived from our findings are still applicable to schools as a whole.

Conclusions

Of course, it should not be thought that any of the schools were homogeneous institutions. They were not. All schools had a range of teachers in terms of age, experience and quality (as far as could be judged by our observations). In no school were the teachers all agreed on their educational aims and often there were quite marked contrasts between the views expressed by different departments or between the views of probationary teachers and established staff. Teachers also differed in the ways they taught and in the ways they treated pupils. Some were quite formal, others much less so. Obviously, too, a certain amount of variation depended on the characteristics of each particular school class, or the age and sex of the pupils, on the position of the class in the streaming hierarchy and in the individual reputations of the children. All these differences are important and worthy of study in their own right.

However, as will be evident in the results that follow in later chapters, there tend to be quite distinct and marked differences between schools in their overall style, approach, aims and ethos. It is these differences *between* schools that we have sought to investigate and, as we shall see, the differences have very important implications for the pupils in the schools.

4

Research strategy and tactics

Overall strategy

Our principal concern throughout the research has been to investigate the reasons why there are differences between schools in terms of various measures of their pupils' behaviour and attainments; and to determine how schools influence children's progress. As we have seen in our discussion of other comparable studies, any evaluation of this kind must involve assessments of at least four rather different features.

First, measures are needed on the characteristics of individual pupils at the time they enter secondary school. There are important individual differences between children with respect to their social background, cognitive abilities and behaviour which may be relevant to their later development and progress. These individual differences must be taken into account in any study of possible school influences on children's progress. We will refer to these measures of what the children were like at the time they were admitted to the twelve schools under the general heading of *intake*.

Secondly, measures must be developed for the particular facets of the *process* of schooling which are to be studied. In our case, the focus here was on the social organisation of the schools and on the types of environments for learning which they provided for their pupils.

Thirdly, the *outcomes* of schooling for these pupils must be examined to assess the extent to which they have met their relevant educational goals. In this way, the performance of a school is reflected in the attainments and behaviour of the children who went there. The basic strategy of the research involved an evaluation of the ways in which outcomes are affected by school processes, after making due allowance for the effects of individual intake characteristics.

This approach to the analysis of our data provided an essential basis for the study of possible school influences on children's development. However, as a model of schooling it greatly oversimplifies the many influences at work. What we have termed school processes are likely to be influenced not only by the teachers and by the policies of the school, but also by the pupils themselves. Schools are not self-contained institutions, and what happens within them will be affected by the communities they serve. Eggleston (1977) has described this set of interactions between the school and its environment under the title of 'The Ecology of the School'.

Our fourth set of measures concerns some of these *ecological* influences. In our analyses we were concerned to determine both how far these ecological factors were associated with variations in outcome, and also how far their effect was mediated through an influence on school processes.

Intake measures

As described in Chapter 2, we already had systematic measures on the characteristics of the 'cohort' of children which had entered the twelve schools from the primary schools included in the 1970 survey. Also, we had shown that in the twelve schools as a whole the cohort children were closely similar to others of their age. Furthermore, a school by school comparison showed that, with a few exceptions, this similarity held within each of the individual schools. Because there were exceptions, however, it was necessary to obtain data on the total intake of the twelve in order to recheck whether the outcome differences could be accounted for in terms of variation in intake. We also needed to determine how far the 1971 intake (including the cohort) was typical of the intakes to the same twelve schools in other years.

For both these purposes we used data routinely collected by the ILEA at the time of secondary transfer. Three main measures were relevant: a) the pupils' Verbal Reasoning scores at the age of ten; b) parental occupation; and c) children's scores on a behavioural questionnaire completed by teachers. We also looked at whether the child's parents were immigrants to Britain, although as it turned out this did not relate to outcome once the first three measures had been taken into account.

Ability grouping at the end of primary school

Before the 'cohort' children transferred to secondary school in September 1971 they were each given 'primary profile' scores on their ability in maths, English and verbal reasoning. These scores ranged from 1 (most able) to 7 (least able). Subsequently children transferring to secondary school were assessed in terms of three much broader categories. The new categories are considered to be directly equivalent to the old system, so that scores 1 and 2 become band 1; scores 3, 4 and 5 become band 2; and scores 6 and 7 become band 3. Over London as a whole, the most able 25 per cent of children come into band 1, the middle 50 per cent into band 2, and the least able 25 per cent into band 3.

a) *At 10 years*

| VR Group | Reading Mean Score | |
	Boys	Girls
1	111·20	106·33
2	107·18	103·03
3	101·36	102·52
4	95·10	97·61
5	86·60	90·61
6	78·28	83·64
7	71·64	74·56

b) *At 14 years*

| VR Group | Reading Mean Score | |
	Boys	Girls
1	113·76	111·50
2	110·13	106·54
3	105·79	103·74
4	99·32	98·18
5	93·06	93·62
6	84·37	86·20
7	76·50	76·33

Table 4.1 *VR Score and group reading test scores*

Before using these verbal reasoning (VR) scores* to examine intake variations it was necessary to determine how well they agreed with our

* Wherever we refer to VR scores this means the 7 category system. References to 'banding' and to 'VR bands' mean the 3 category system.

own group test measures of non-verbal intelligence and reading. The upper half of Table 4.1 shows the comparison between the seven verbal reasoning grades and the group test measures for the 'cohort' children at age ten years. The lower half shows the comparison between the VR scores at ten and the group test scores at fourteen for the total group of pupils of that age at the twelve schools. The results clearly show a very strong association between the VR scores and the group test scores as obtained both at the same age and also four years later. It was justifiable, therefore, to use the VR scores as a baseline intake measure against which to judge the performance of the twelve schools.

Parental occupation

The second intake measure available to us was parental occupation. The twelve schools provided information for the whole cohort age group on the occupation of the main family breadwinner. Occupations were coded according to the Registrar-General's (1970) criterion into five categories: a) professional and managerial (RG classes I and II); b) skilled non-manual; c) skilled manual; d) semi-skilled manual; and e) unskilled and unemployed. For almost all purposes we grouped the occupations into three broader categories in which '1' included (a) and (b); '2' was equivalent to (c) and '3' included (d) and (e).

Teacher questionnaire

The third intake measure consisted of the teacher questionnaire previously described in Chapter 2. The questionnaire provided not only an overall measure of possible emotional or behavioural difficulties but also a categorisation of the main type of difficulty. It was the conduct-type designation which showed the strongest association with later delinquency.

Variations in intake over time

Using these measures we were able to look at possible variations over time in the intake to the twelve schools. The findings are summarised in

	1969	1971	1974	1976
1969	—	0·91	0·74	0·87
1971		—	0·73	0·83
1974			—	0·83
1976				—

(The table shows the rank correlations between the twelve schools).

Table 4.2 *Proportion of children in band 3 admitted to the twelve schools*

Table 4.2. The data show that there had been some minor shifts in the balance of intake since 1970 (in the direction of reducing the more extreme inequities in balance), but the overall pattern had remained closely similar. The schools with the most disadvantaged (or advantaged) intakes in 1971 also had the most disadvantaged (or advantaged) intakes in other years.

Outcome measures

The study of twelve schools was based on the earlier analyses, summarised in Chapter 2, which showed that there were marked differences between schools in children's behaviour even after taking variations in intake into account. For these comparisons, delinquency figures and teacher ratings of the children's behaviour were used as measures of 'outcome'. However, these outcome measures were severely restricted in three rather different ways. First, they referred only to a very limited aspect of school outcome. Second, the data applied only to the first three years of secondary schooling and not at all to differences at the end of compulsory schooling. Third, the measures concerned just one age group of children at one particular point in their school career.

For all these reasons we needed to greatly broaden and extend our measures of outcome. In deciding how best to proceed with this, the first issue was the question of how school 'success' might be reflected in different measures of outcome. This posed some difficulties in that educational goals are usually broadly conceived and, of course, schools differ somewhat in their principal aims. It was essential to have measures which encompassed these differences and which reflected what the schools in the study saw as their main tasks. In the end we settled on five measures of outcome: a) the children's behaviour in school; b) attendance; c) examination success; d) employment, and e) delinquency.

Attendance was included for the obvious reason that if schools are going to have any kind of impact on their pupils it is necessary that they attend with a fair degree of regularity. It seemed reasonable to suppose that good attendance should be considered as a necessary (but clearly far from sufficient) prerequisite for success.

Secondly, all schools considered that it was important for the children's behaviour in school to reach certain standards. They often expressed this in rather different ways and certainly there were important differences between the schools in the kinds of behaviour they expected of their children. Accordingly, we tried to devise a behavioural measure which encompassed the expectations *shared* by all twelve schools. As well as including measures of good behaviour we have also included some measures of poor behaviour in order to cover as wide a range as possible. Thus, we used items such as truanting and absconding, arriving late for lessons, damage and graffiti, pupil violence, disruptive behaviour in the classroom, as well as adherence to the prevailing school rules on uniform and being on task in lessons. Full details of these items are given in Appendix A.

Thirdly, we obtained measures on the children's success in the public examinations taken at the end of the fifth year of secondary schooling. For the more able children this provided an important criterion of scholastic achievement, and good examination grades are an essential entry requirement for both further education and also certain jobs. We also looked at the examination achievements of those pupils who stayed at school into the sixth year.

However, as we have described earlier, these examinations are not devised for the least able 40 per cent of the general population of school children. As a result it was essential to have some other indicator which would be relevant for them, and hence we obtained measures on the ex-pupils' employment one year after leaving school.*
The features of work being examined include length of time to obtain the first job, number of jobs in the first year, dismissal from jobs, in-

---

* This part of the study is being undertaken by Grace Gray. The findings on employment are not included in this book as the young people are still being interviewed and therefore data analysis is incomplete. The results will be fully reported elsewhere.

volvement in further training, level of work, and job satisfaction.

Finally, we looked at levels of delinquency. The reduction of delinquency can scarcely be considered an educational goal and it is well known that most delinquency takes place off school premises and out of school hours. Nevertheless, our own earlier findings as well as those of other investigators (see Chapter 1) showed marked differences between secondary schools in rates of delinquency. The implication was that in some way some schools managed to exercise a protective effect by which delinquency rates were kept lower than those at other schools. It was important to examine this possibility in more detail.

Obviously, these five measures* do not reflect the whole range of aims and objectives of schooling. Nevertheless, they do provide important indicators of some crucial aspects of the outcome of the educational process. Also, they reflect areas in which some degree of success is necessary if less tangible aims are to be achieved. Thus, while we have not been able to tap many vital aspects of personality development it would seem unlikely that a school was being successful in meeting objectives of this kind if absenteeism and delinquency rates were high and if attainments and behaviour were poor. Similarly, children can be successful and show achievement in many different skills and many different facets of life, but examination success and job satisfaction are two useful indicators of attainment in areas of particular importance in the educational process.

Ecological measures

In any investigation the choice of sample is crucial in determining which variables can be studied. In our case we deliberately chose a sample of schools which were similar in many ecological features in order that we would be in a better position to examine the importance of differences in internal school processes. Thus, all twelve schools were similar in being in the same local authority (the ILEA), in being academically non-selective, and in serving an ethnically and socially mixed inner London area. As a result of this choice of sample, we were unable to compare the merits and demerits of selective and non-selective systems of education; we could not examine the effects of

* Details of the construction of the measures are given in Chapter 5 on School Outcomes.

differences in the ideology or resource provisions of local education authorities; and we could not assess the consequences for either children or schools of being in an inner city area rather than a small town or a country village. Obviously, these are important issues worthy of investigation in their own right. However, our own earlier findings had shown major differences between secondary schools even when all these external socio-political factors were constant. The main purpose of our study was to determine the nature and meaning of these differences within a group of non-selective secondary schools in our local authority serving an inner city population.

Of course, these overall ecological similarities did not mean that the schools functioned in exactly the same ecological context. They did not. In particular, they differed somewhat in the areas they served within inner London; they also differed markedly with respect to their balance of intake and in their popularity with parents.

Geographical area

In examining the possible effects of differences between schools in the geographical areas they served it was essential to have some means of classifying areas. Fortunately, this is provided by the OPCS/CES classification (Webber, 1977) which uses a set of forty demographic variables (such as occupation of head of the household, proportion of multiple-occupancy dwellings, levels of unemployment, serious over-crowding, etc) to derive a scale which categorises areas in terms of their social status. They provide designations for each electoral ward (the most convenient sized geographical area for these analyses) throughout England and these classifications have been examined in relation to our own data.

The addresses of all the boys* in the sample were classified into wards. Using these data, it was possible to determine the proportions of children in each school coming from each type of area on the OPCS/CES classification. This information was then examined in relation to our outcome measures of delinquency, exam pass rates and attendance.

* This analysis was confined to boys (and hence to the nine schools which took boys) because previous studies had indicated that area influences were most important with respect to delinquency in boys.

Balance of intake

The balance of intake to each of the twelve schools was assessed in terms of the data available at the time of school entry. Individual characteristics of the children have already been considered with respect to *intake* (see Chapter 2). There, however, we were concerned to examine associations in *individual* terms. That is to say, we examined the extent to which, for example, the average examination success of a child in VR band 1 differed from that of a child in VR band 3. We were looking at individual predictors and using these as a means of taking variations in intake into account when looking at school differences in outcome.

However, the same variables may be used in a different way as indicators of possible group effects. Let us again use the VR banding and examination success to illustrate the point. Here we are asking whether the performances of (say) a child in band 3 is influenced by the *proportions* of other band 3 children in the school. In other words, does a largely disadvantaged intake to a school depress scholastic attainments in some overall way, over and above the effects of a disadvantaged background on the individual pupil? Conversely, are there benefits to the school as a whole in having a relatively high concentration of pupils in the upper ability groups – benefits that is to say on *other* pupils? This might occur as a result of peer group influences, or perhaps through the cumulative effects of the balance of intake on teacher expectations which might in turn influence school process variables.

We looked at the balance of intake in terms of VR bandings (i.e. pupils' measured abilities at school entry), parental occupation, behavioural questionnaire scores and ethnic background. The last variable was considered in terms of the proportion of pupils whose mother or father was born outside the British Isles.

Parental choice

We have already outlined the procedures for allocating pupils to secondary schools within the ILEA and have noted the emphasis placed on ensuring that as many children as possible should attend the school of their first choice. However, inevitably, this could not be achieved in every instance and some pupils had to attend schools which had not been their parents' first preference. As schools varied in their public image and popularity, so their proportions of 'first-choice' pupils also varied. Within our sample, some schools were always over-subscribed, whereas others had difficulty in recruiting their full intake and often had to admit fairly large numbers of children who had originally opted to go elsewhere.

It seemed possible that variations of this kind might add yet another dimension to the ecology of schooling. The motivation of children might vary considerably according to whether they had gained a place in the school of their choice. It also seemed possible that the popularity of the school in the eyes of parents could affect staff morale. We were able to obtain data on the subscription rates of ten out of the twelve schools and these figures are analysed in relation both to the outcome measures and to the school process variables.

School process

During the three years in which we made a detailed study of the twelve schools our main emphasis in the development of measures was on establishing a variety of ways of assessing school process. This was necessary because, unlike the situation with respect to intake, outcome and ecology, no satisfactory measures for our purposes were available from previous investigations. A wide range of measures, both self-report and observational, were used to provide indicators of the nature of school life for staff and pupils.

It was important that knowledge of the results of the 1974 survey should not in any way bias our observations of the twelve schools. Accordingly, three new researchers were appointed to undertake the planning and fieldwork for the detailed study of the twelve schools. None had been involved with any of the previous research in the schools and in order that they should undertake the new study free of preconceptions they were kept unaware of the findings of the earlier survey until after collection of data in schools was complete, some $2\frac{1}{2}$ years later.

It was decided at the beginning of the detailed study of the twelve schools that each research worker should be principally attached to four schools, so that the staff in each school would be able to get to know the research worker well. This was essential if the school staff was to learn to trust the researchers sufficiently to allow them to make detailed observations in the classrooms and elsewhere. It was, of course, necessary for each person to visit all schools at various times throughout the study, but we found that this method of working was very acceptable both to the schools and to the research workers. As far as possible, each of the fieldworkers also had a range of schools, church and non-church schools and mixed and single-sex schools. It also became apparent later when the data had been collected that each researcher had both more and less successful schools. Throughout the research all observation schedules were regularly used by pairs of workers so as to ensure that the observation categories were used in a comparable way. These checking procedures will be described in more detail later, along with detailed descriptions of the observation schedules.

Data gathering in the schools

Within this overall strategy for the research, particular techniques and measures had to be selected or devised to provide the data which we needed in each of the areas. For the majority of the outcome measures, and for all the data relating to school intakes, information could be collected from already existing records, either in the schools themselves, or from the relevant administrative sources. The school process data, however, and the information on the children's behaviour in school, all demanded quite different approaches to data collection. Although a number of other studies had looked at different aspects of the school processes which we were interested in, and indeed a few measures have been devised to assess school climate or atmosphere generally (e.g. Halpin, 1966), none of these seemed entirely appropriate to our particular focus in the present study. We thus decided at the outset of the study that we would need to devise our own methods and research tools, and make the necessary tests to ensure that, as far as possible, they were valid and reliable. A wide range of school processes seemed potentially relevant to the pupils' progress; we needed to devise detailed ways of tapping these, so that we emerged with as comprehensive and rounded a picture of school life as possible.

Our emphasis was on those aspects of school life which applied to the pupils as a whole rather than to those which were applicable only to smaller groups with special needs or special problems. Accordingly, we did not make any detailed examination of the special units for difficult children available in some schools, or of remedial classes, or of the work of staff (such as school counsellors) which mainly concerned individual children, or of sixth form work. Clearly, these specialist facilities and resources were important but they fell outside our focus on the social organisation of the school as it impinged on the main body of pupils.

Our observations and interviews in schools were all directed to the kinds of environments provided by the schools for teaching and learning. We were not concerned with details of the curriculum in the narrow sense but rather with the broader curriculum of the social environment within which lesson teaching takes place. Clearly, what children learn will be determined by the nature and quality of the teaching they receive. This constitutes a most important topic in its own right. However, as we have shown in Chapter 1, previous studies suggest that what can be achieved by classroom teaching may be greatly influenced by the overall characteristics of the school itself as an organisation. This side of school life may be as important as the more obviously educational issues of the teaching of reading, mathematics or history. The comparative design led to an emphasis on aspects of policy and practice which were common to all twelve schools but yet on which the schools varied substantially in the ways in which they implemented their policies. In this way we sought to develop measures of crucial aspects of school life which would provide quantitative scores which could be placed on some kind of continuum.

We set about developing our research instruments by spending a fairly extensive period of time at the beginning of the study in informal observations and discussions in three of the schools. These three schools had agreed to act as 'pilots' in this respect, and also helped us when we came on to the more detailed work of developing particular techniques. In the initial stages, however, our aim was a more general one, of learning directly from the teachers and children which aspects of school life seemed most important and influential to them, and blending in these concerns with our own interests, and the suggestions raised by earlier studies. This period of informal observation and discussion was invaluable both in pointing up areas for us to pursue, and in suggesting the sorts of research methods we would need to use to follow up these areas.

We developed a series of guiding principles in all our work in the schools. The first of these concerned the role of the research workers in the schools, which we saw as something rather different from the participant-observer pattern which has been used in many other studies of institutions. Although we did a great deal of observation in the schools, we did not 'participate' in the usually accepted sense. We did not ask to become members of the teaching staff, but instead remained very clearly independent research workers, with quite distinct roles in the schools. We decided on this approach for a number of reasons. First, perhaps most important, we needed to be able to approach all levels of staff, and the children, during the course of the research, and it seemed essential to us that we should not become particularly identified with any one group within the school. By maintaining a rather distinct role, where we were not identified by the pupils as members of the staff, nor by the staff as attempting to become part of the pupils' sub-culture, we hoped that we would be able to maintain open contacts with all groups in the school. Secondly, we were anxious that our presence, and the fact of the research itself, should have as little effect on the usual pattern of school life as possible. Although we realised that some effects were inevitable, we attempted to minimise these as much as possible by maintaining this relatively independent role in our work in the schools, and by providing no feedback at all until the whole of the data collection was completed. Thus, although the schools were undoubtedly affected by being involved in the project, we hoped that whatever influences were at work would be rather similar in all of the schools, and would not affect our comparative analyses to any serious extent.

As we have already mentioned, the three research workers were each principally attached to four schools during the data collecting, so that effective patterns of liaison could be built up with the majority of the staff. This division of the schools meant that it was especially important that checks should be made to ensure that the methods of data collection were similar in all the schools, and details of these checks will be given later. For the most part, the data we collected relate to specific events or behaviours, although we did ask some questions on more general attitudes and values. It seems likely that in many cases individual actions are less important in their own rights (because of some specific effect), than in the part they play in contributing to a broader school ethos or climate of expectations and modes of behaving. Nevertheless, we make no apology for concentrating on particular happenings and behaviours. The impact for the pupil may derive from the overall ethos, but our concern was equally with the sorts of actions which teachers and pupils could take to contribute towards the establishment of an ethos which would enable all those in the school to function well. This concern necessitated a focus which is at least as much on the specific actions taken by teachers and children as on the more general attitudes which may lie behind them.

Results from earlier investigations, both in schools and in other institutions, suggested a number of areas which it might be important to pursue here, and our informal observations and discussions with teachers and pupils rounded these out considerably. At the end of our initial period of informal observation in the schools, we had developed a series of areas we were anxious to pursue, and we had decided that we needed to collect data from three principal sources: staff, pupils, and from our own observations. In this way, we hoped to be able to build up comprehensive and thorough pictures of life within the schools, and use each of these different sources of data as checks on the validity of the others. The main part of the data collection then fell into three broad phases, the first concerned with staff interviews, the second with a questionnaire for pupils, and the third with observations of various sorts.

Our observations in schools were undertaken over a period of two school years and they covered children of different ages and abilities. Similarly our interviews with teachers and pupils covered many aspects of school life as they affected children from the first year to the fifth year. We have no direct way of knowing how stable our school process measures are over time but their wide span provides an effective assurance that they reflect enduring school characteristics.

Interviews with staff

The first main phase of data collection involved a series of semi-structured interviews with staff. This began with an extensive interview with the head teacher, covering a wide range of aspects of policy and practice within the school, and a good deal of basic data on items such as staffing levels and allocation of resources. This interview provided, as it were, a basic 'map' of life in the school, and the more detailed material collected later was fitted into this overall framework. A somewhat shortened version of the interview with the head teacher was repeated towards the end of the study, to take account of any major administrative or policy changes which might have occurred during the two and a half years period of data collection.

The initial interview with the head teacher was then followed in each school by a series of interviews with staff at all other levels of seniority. All members of the senior hierarchy (deputy head teachers, heads of upper and lower schools, and so forth) were interviewed, together with four heads of departments (selected randomly from different subject groupings), three heads of year or house, a random sample of one in four teachers, and one in two probationary teachers. In all, this provided us with responses from 219 members of staff at the twelve schools – 76 teachers, 34 probationers, and 109 more senior members of staff.

The interview schedules included a series of pre-coded reply categories for each question, and the great majority of the questions focussed on specific occasions or events. If, for example, we asked about staff meetings, questions would relate to the topics discussed at the last such meeting attended by the teacher being interviewed.

The interviews were designed to last for about forty minutes, so that they could be completed within one school lesson. Apart from the interview with the head teacher, all the remaining interviews in this particular series were undertaken within one week in each school, during the autumn term of 1975.

The interviews covered a range of topics, varying to some extent according to the roles of the staff concerned. For all teachers except newly appointed probationers, the interview began by covering basic details of their teaching experience, their time in the present school, their current teaching and other commitments, and the general conditions and facilities for teachers in the school. For senior staff, the central section of the interview then related to their particular role, and how either departmental, pastoral or senior functions were carried out. Questions were included here on facilities specific to these particular roles, on patterns of organising the work of the pastoral or academic group, on the oversight of other staff, meetings with them, and the use of specialist resources both inside and outside the school. Information was also collected on contacts with individual pupils and their parents, as well as with outside groups and agencies.

The central section of the interviews with 'basic grade' teachers was used in part to complement the senior staff interviews, and covered aspects of the academic and pastoral organisation of the school, this time approached from the point of view of the ordinary teacher. Where previously a head of department would have been asked if he or she, for example, checked on the setting of homework, teachers would now be asked if their own work was checked on in this way. By including complementary questions of this kind in the interviews with different members of staff, we were able to build up a fairly comprehensive picture of the predominant practices in each school, and gauge the extent to which departments or pastoral groups functioned in autonomous, or relatively similar ways, across the school as a whole.

The remaining sections of the teacher interviews were taken up with questions relating to classroom management, and methods of dealing with a variety of problems which might be presented by the pupils. All of the interviews, with each grade of staff, concluded with a section on the goals of the school. Ten possible goals were derived from those used in the Schools Council project (Schools Council, 1968), and these were presented to the staff twice (see Appendix B for details). On each occasion, respondents were asked to select four of these goals; their first choices related to the goals which they considered were currently being pursued within the school, while their second choices referred to the aims which they personally would select as most important in working in a school of that kind. The interviews with the newly appointed probationary staff also included the section on school goals, but otherwise were briefer than the other interviews, and related almost entirely to the facilities and supports available for the new staff, and the sorts of problems they faced.

In addition to this main series of interviews, a number of other interviews were held with different members of staff at various points in the study. Those with heads of sixth forms and remedial departments, and with specialist counsellors, were complementary to the initial series. Others were of a rather different kind, and took place later in the study. One small set of these was designed to look specifically at methods of dealing with problem behaviour within the school. This presented respondents (all of whom were basic grade teachers) with a standard series of ten brief descriptions of difficult behaviour of various kinds. Full details of these are given in Appendix C, but the examples ranged from a first year child who had been found stealing small items, to a senior pupil who used abusive language to a teacher. In each case, staff were asked to explain how an incident of this kind would typically be dealt with at the school, by whom, and whether a clearly laid down policy existed for dealing with these particular kinds of behaviour. These interviews were carried out with fifty-four teachers in all and were used to complement our other information on rules and sanctions, which had been gathered from the main series of interviews. The teachers involved in this exercise were all drawn from the group whom we had observed (see below) in each of the schools. This was also the case with the staff who took part in a further brief series of interviews focussed more specifically on curriculum matters. These interviews, held with maths and English teachers only, provided us with some background on the curriculum being followed by the classes we observed, and also provided further and more detailed information on the academic sides of school life – on the planning of the curriculum, the use of homework, and teachers' expectations for their pupils.

Material from all these interviews was eventually included in the pool of process items which we were developing throughout the data collection. The different interviews gave us a variety of approaches to our basic concerns with the staff: to gain information on their conditions and ways of working, on the management of both staff and pupils in the schools, and on the degree of consensus which seemed to exist within the staff group on these issues.

Pupil questionnaire

Once we had completed the main series of interviews with staff, we turned our attention to collecting information on the pupils' experiences of schooling. We had held a number of discussions with groups of pupils during the informal pilot work in the schools, and we had learned a good deal from these about the issues which seemed most pressing to the children. We had also explored the possibility of using groups of this kind for our main data collection, but it soon became clear that they tended to be dominated by a vocal minority, so making it difficult to gain views from all the pupils present. We thus decided that we would need to use a questionnaire approach but that this would have to be rather specially devised, in order to overcome reading difficulties which might be experienced, especially by the younger pupils. Our solution, which was developed after a number of pilot versions had been tested with small groups of pupils, was a questionnaire where each child had his or her own copy, but where the questions were also read out by one of the researchers. In this way, whole classes could be given the questionnaire at the same time; the children were taken through the questions together, using terminology appropriate to each school, and dealing with any problems as they arose. The majority of the questions were designed to require only Yes/No answers, which were pre-coded on the form; the pupils simply selected and ringed the appropriate response. Other questions required a 'number of times' answer and here the pupils entered the answer in a box. Appendix D presents a series of specimen questions, and the layout used.

The questionnaire covered a wide range of aspects of the pupils' experiences of schooling, and was designed to provide information both about their behaviour, and about school process factors. The topics covered under this second heading included stability and changes in teaching and pastoral groups, and the teaching staff involved; the pupils' participation in a range of academic, sporting, social and charitable activities, most of which would fall outside basic school requirements; their involvement in positions of responsibility within the school; the numbers and kinds of rewards and punishments they had received within a specified period; the amount of homework they did; the extent to which they would consult staff about problems; and the numbers of outings and journeys they had been taken on.

The questionnaire also included a number of questions on rule-breaking behaviour, interspersed at various points amongst these other topics. The children were asked, in relation to specific periods of time, whether they had worn correct school uniform, written any graffiti on school property, and had been involved in various types of truancy, from skipping occasional lessons to taking whole days off school. To ensure that these questions would be answered as frankly as possible, the pupils were all assured of complete confidentiality for their replies, and the questionnaires were filled in anonymously, the only identifying information being the school class and sex of the child. No teachers were present while the questionnaires were completed, and the pupils were told that they could omit any questions which they preferred not to answer. In the event, this happened very rarely, and in almost every class we visited the children responded very positively.

The final main section of the questionnaire was concerned with the goals of the school, and was designed to parallel the final section of the teacher interviews. The same ten goals were presented to the pupils, with minor changes in wording to make these appropriate from the pupils' point of view. The children were asked to select firstly the four goals which they thought teachers in their school were principally aiming at, then secondly the four which they themselves considered to be most important. Finally, two short sections were provided at the end of the questionnaire where pupils were asked to write in their own words what seemed to them to be the three best, and the three worst, aspects of school. Although we could not use these data in our quantitative analyses, we hoped that they might provide further interesting insights into the pupils' view of schooling.

We were anxious to gain responses from as wide a sample of children as possible, so that our information would not be biased by reflecting the experiences of only certain groups of the pupils. We thus decided to give the questionnaire to classes in each of the first, third and fifth years at each school, and we chose three classes in each year group, from the top, middle and bottom of the ability range in schools organised on a streamed or banded system. We returned at least once to all the classes where any children were absent on our first visit, and we eventually achieved a response rate of 92 per cent overall. This provided us with information from 2730 pupils (948 year 1, 932 year 3 and 850 year 5).

As we could not repeat the questionnaire with any groups of pupils, we needed to make an alternate check on its reliability. As our main interest was in comparing responses between schools, we divided the replies from each school into two halves on a random basis, then compared the relative positions of the schools for these two sub-groups of children. We used rank correlations (see page 69) to test the levels of agreement, and found that for the great majority of the fifty questionnaire items the reliability was entirely acceptable. Any items which were not reliable were excluded from the subsequent analyses, and the details of particular items which were included in our later analyses of the children's behaviour, and the school processes, are given in Appendix E.

Observations

As a complement to the staff and pupil reports on school life, we ourselves made systematic observations as outside researchers. We needed these to record more detailed information on the day-to-day life of the schools, and, in particular, to look at events in the classroom. The self report data could give us information on the broader sweep of events in school, but it was crucial also to look at the classroom interactions and approaches to teaching that varied between the schools. We were not concerned with the complex problems of teaching style per se, nor indeed were we interested in the approaches of individual teachers. As with all the data in the project, our aim was to focus on school-wide practices, and on the general tenor of classroom activity and interactions in the twelve study schools.

A great deal of observational research has already been undertaken in classrooms, and an almost bewildering range of observation techniques has been developed, extending from participant methods to more structured event and time-sampling approaches. Since we were aiming to collect fairly simple descriptive data about lessons, we decided to use the time-sampling techniques. This requires that each lesson is divided into a series of much shorter time periods so that the principal activity of particular individuals may be recorded for each of these short periods. In our own case, we observed for ten seconds, then recorded our observations for five seconds, and continued observing and recording alternately, throughout each lesson. By summing data from all these brief observation periods, we could then derive a fairly clear picture of the predominant activities taking place.

We gradually developed a recording schedule which enabled us to collect data about the activities of both teachers and pupils in each lesson. The very short observation periods were grouped into sections, which focussed first on the teacher, then on selected individual children, and finally on the whole class. Each section lasted five minutes, and this pattern was repeated throughout the lesson. As we developed the schedule, we also developed a series of very detailed definitions of the activities we wanted to record, and we tested the levels of agreement between the different researchers in using the schedule before we started collecting the data, and at intervals during the period of data collection. Appendix F gives sample category definitions, and the procedure for testing inter-observer agreement. Definitions of the particular items which we used in our later analyses are given as they occur, together with the details of the reliability checks for each of those items.

In observing the teacher's activities, for each 10-second period we recorded whether his or her main focus was on the subject matter of the lesson, was dealing with pupils' behaviour, or was concerned with some other, perhaps administrative, activity. In addition, we noted whether the teacher was interacting with the children, and if so whether this was with the whole group or with individuals. Finally, we noted any examples of praise or punishment, and any marked expressions of warmth or negative feelings towards the children.

In looking at the pupils' behaviour, we were interested both in the extent to which they appeared to be engaged in tasks set by the teacher, and also in the levels of other, perhaps less acceptable, behaviour. As we expected, rather different kinds of behaviour seemed to be acceptable in the different schools, and indeed at different points in any one lesson. Fairly quiet chatting, for example, was often allowed whilst pupils were working on some activities but not on others. In view of these variations, we decided that our recording categories should simply relate to various types of behaviour, whether or not these appeared to be acceptable at any particular time. This would allow us to make direct comparisons between schools, and our analyses might suggest the extent to which different sorts of distracted or disruptive behaviours appeared to be associated with more work-oriented ones.

We found that we needed to focus on individual children if we were to make reliable ratings of 'on-task' behaviour, so we selected five pupils at random for this purpose at each lesson, and recorded whether they were working, together with a series of other behaviours which they might be engaged in. These were comparable with the ratings which we made on the class as a whole, which included chatting, shouting out, a category for very severe disruptions, and two further classifications of what we came to describe as 'informal' behaviours. We divided these into 'mild' and 'severe' groups, the first of which included possibly distracting behaviours such as tapping on the desk with a ruler, combing hair, or chewing gum, while the second was more clearly disruptive, and included throwing items across the room, loud swearing, fighting and the like. For each of these categories, we recorded not only whether they had occurred but also the proportion of the class involved in them, from one or two children to the majority of the group. In this way our final data provided information both about the frequency and extent of these behaviours. These detailed recordings constituted the main part of the observation schedule. We developed rather different sections, using a check-list, to record aspects of the beginnings and endings of each lesson and basic details such as class size. Appendix F gives details of these.

Our main series of observations, from which the majority of the data was drawn, consisted of one whole week's observation of this detailed kind in each school. We chose middle ability third year classes for this exercise, and spent a complete week with each class, making recordings in all their lessons. In this way, we hoped to obtain information in classes which were comparable between schools, to see a variety of lessons in different subjects, and to give both children and teachers an opportunity to become acclimatised to our presence.* We observed a total of 402 lessons in all, the majority of which (312) were in academic subjects, the remainder being taken up in art, craft and sport. The data to which we refer in later chapters are drawn exclusively from these academic lessons, once again to ensure comparability between schools.

Our main interest, as in the whole study, was in variations between schools in these lesson observations, and in later chapters we discuss the very considerable variations which we found. At this point, however, it is appropriate to mention some of the more general features which emerged from the observations as a whole. The first of these was the fact that by far the majority of the third year academic lessons used a fairly traditional, group based, approach, with very few individually based. Art and craft lessons used individualised approaches to a much greater extent. The atmosphere in the academic lessons was often informal, with chatting and movement around the room as the children worked, but teacher-child interactions were predominantly group based. A fairly high proportion of the teacher's time in each lesson (about 10 per cent on average overall) was spent in setting up equipment and distributing books or resources to the children, with an

* We made efforts to be as inconspicuous as possible during our observations, and did not speak to, or interact with, either teachers or children during the lessons unless it was absolutely essential. Our informal impressions of the weeks in the schools were that the children came to accept (and indeed ignore) our presence very quickly, and analysis of the data according to different days of the week showed no significant differences between them. There was, however, a tendency for lessons to be generally quieter and more work oriented at the beginning of the week than at the end. This pattern was the same in all the schools, so we assume that although our presence almost certainly did alter events to some extent, the effects were rather similar in all the schools, and would not invalidate our comparisons between the schools.

overall average of about 75 per cent of his or her time spent on the subject matter of the lesson. For the pupils, the average of 'on task' behaviour was 81·5 per cent of each lesson (although, as we shall see, schools vary considerably in this). Although there was a good deal of 'informal' behaviour, relatively little fell into our 'severe' category and there was only one incident during all of our twelve weeks' observation so serious as to stop the course of a lesson completely. While teachers clearly experienced difficulties with some of their classes, the 'blackboard jungle' image of city schools was definitely not the predominant impression which emerged from our observations.

We used the same observation schedule to observe a small number of lessons with first year children immediately on entry to secondary school, and then six months later. The aims here were to examine the teaching approaches used with new entrants to the school, and also to assess the children's behaviour both just after intake, and subsequently after an initial period of acclimatisation to their new setting.

In addition to these highly structured, time-sampled, observations we made a series of other recordings at various points during the study. During our week's observations with the third year pupils, we spent time in the playgrounds at break, recording the pupils' activities then and noting in addition any incidents of physical violence between children or unofficial sanctions by staff. On every occasion when we visited classrooms (both when we gave the questionnaire and in the series of lesson observations), we also recorded additional material about the children, and the use and conditions of the school buildings themselves. As far as the children were concerned, we recorded the proportions late, not in the correct uniform, and without pens or pencils, on all these occasions. Our observations of the classroom included measures of damage and graffiti, the state of the decorations, and the amounts of information and children's work which were displayed on the walls. Appendix F provides a copy of the schedule used. Similar measures were also taken in the 'public' areas of the schools, such as entrance areas, halls and corridors.

This wide range of observations enabled us to get quite detailed measures of many aspects of school life. We collected data from both senior and junior staff and from children of different ages with the intention of developing school-wide indicators of process. The relationship between these measures and the outcomes will be discussed in detail in Chapter 7.

5

School outcomes: children's attendance, behaviour and attainments

As we have said, we used four main measures of outcome: attendance, pupil behaviour, examination success, and delinquency. In devising appropriate measures of outcome it was necessary to ensure that the measures were reliable and accurate: that they applied to children throughout the school; and that they reflected as wide a range of behaviours as possible. To do this we repeated measurements on several occasions and obtained measures on several different groups of children. In addition, where appropriate, we used several sources of information and we combined data of various different kinds.

Two further steps were taken to check that the measures were indeed a reflection of school experiences. First, we determined whether the outcome measures were similar for different age groups of children and were stable over periods of several years. In so far as they were, it made it less likely that the results were just a function of one particular atypical group of pupils, and more likely that they truly reflected the usual outcome for that school on that measure.

Secondly, we undertook a variety of analyses to find out how far the children's behaviour and attainments were merely a continuation of characteristics already evident at primary school. In order to show a school influence, it was necessary, in the first instance, to study *changes* in behaviour or attainment while at secondary school in children who were substantially comparable at the time they entered secondary school. To examine this we considered the children's intake characteristics at each school. Only if the outcome measures for secondary schools differed markedly after taking into account what the children were like when they entered the schools at eleven years of age could we conclude that the outcome differences were likely to be due to experiences while at secondary school. The findings on these various steps are now discussed with respect to each of the outcome measures in turn.

Of course, in looking at outcome differences between schools after controlling for variations in intake, it was crucial to choose the most appropriate intake variable or variables. In this connection, 'most appropriate' means that the individual measure used had the strongest statistical correlation or association with the relevant outcome. This means that the intake measures will not necessarily be the same for each type of outcome. With each outcome measure, the first step which was needed was a series of analyses to determine which intake variable or combination of variables provided the best prediction of outcome. The best predictor was then used for all further analyses. It will be appreciated that the best statistical predictor does not necessarily directly tap the causal mechanisms involved in the association. The procedure is simply a statistical means of obtaining the best possible control for variations in intake.

One further criterion had to be applied to the choice of intake variables — that the measure was available on the maximum number of children, with very few for whom data were missing for any reason.

Finally, in selecting which outcome measures to use we placed most reliance on those where we had the best possible control for variations in intake. This was essential if we were to be sure that any differences in outcome we found were not artefacts of intake variation.

Attendance

The main attendance measure was based on the recorded attendance of all fifth year pupils at the twelve schools during two particular weeks in September and January. The average attendance in each school over these two weeks varied from 12.8 to 17.3 out of a possible maximum of 20 attendances.

An analysis of variance of these data (see Table 5.1 in Appendix G) shows that both VR band at ten and parental occupation were significantly related to fifth year attendance.* There was also a strong relationship between children's attendance and the school they attended.

* The analysis of variance is a statistical technique used for determining whether the average (mean) level of some characteristic varies between several different groups within a sample to a greater extent than would be expected by chance alone. To a large extent, this depends on how far apart the group means are from one another and also on the extent to which scores vary or spread about their mean. If there is a lot of spread the

However, the analysis also showed a small but significant interaction between school and band (see the footnote for an explanation of interaction), and between school and occupation. This means that the pattern of associations was not quite the same for each of these groups in each school. The differences were quite small and only just significant but in controlling attendance for intake variations it seemed safer to restrict the analysis to the middle VR band children only. This includes the middle 50 per cent of the ability range and is by far the largest group of children in the school.

The analysis was therefore repeated using only the 1262 children in the middle VR band (see Table 5.2 in Appendix G). Again there was a highly-significant* difference between schools in their rates of fifth year attendance ($F = 4.18$; df 11; $p < 0.001$). The difference according to parental occupation was much smaller. However, this small difference was used to adjust the school rates of attendance for differences between the schools in occupational distribution. The adjusted school attendance rates were then found to vary from 11.85 to 16.80 out of 20. The ranking on this measure was almost identical with the original ranking (only two schools changed places) showing that the school differences in attendance were *not* a consequence of variations in intake.

Thus, when the analysis was restricted to pupils of similar ability,

---

means must be further apart for the difference to be significant – simply because a large spread (that is a high variance) implies a substantial degree of overlap between the groups. In this case, the analysis of variance is designed to deal with several different variables (schools, VR band and parental occupation) and the analysis determines whether each variable varies significantly between the groups when considered independently of the effects of the other variables. In this and subsequent analyses of variance an hierarchical approach was followed in which the school variable was always put in last. A significant effect for schools then means that the effect is present even after taking account of the effects of all variables previously put into the analysis earlier in the hierarchy. The findings on 'interaction' are concerned with the question of whether the relationship with respect to one variable works in the same way *within* some other variable. That is, for example, is the association between ability level and attendance the same within all schools? The fact that some interaction was found indicates that it was not. In order to be sure that this last difference was not merely a reflection of intake differences it was necessary to control for both VR and occupation.

* The conclusion that some statistical result is 'significant' means that the finding is unlikely to have arisen just by chance. The 'p' value gives a more precise indication of this probability. Thus, in this case the p value of less than 0.001 indicates that the result would arise by chance less than once in a 1000 times. If the p value is greater than $.05$ the result has possibly arisen by chance, and is considered non-significant. This is shown in the text as NS (not significant).

and when the effects of parental occupation had been taken into account, there were still substantial and statistically significant differences between schools.

Instead of considering school differences in terms of average levels of attendance, an alternative measure is provided by the proportions of children who were *very poor attenders*. The same attendance data were used for this purpose, with very poor attendance defined as less than 8 attendances out of a possible 20. The proportion of poor attenders in each school varied from 5·7 per cent to 25·9 per cent, and as might be expected there was a very high correlation ($r_s = 0·93$)* between a school's rank position on this measure and its position on the mean attendance measure already described.

Attendance by age group

In order to determine how far school attendance varied according to the child's age group, data for the academic year 1975/76 were obtained from the school registers for first, third and fifth year children in all twelve schools. Again, the two sample weeks utilised for fifth year attendance were employed. The findings are shown in Figure 5.1.

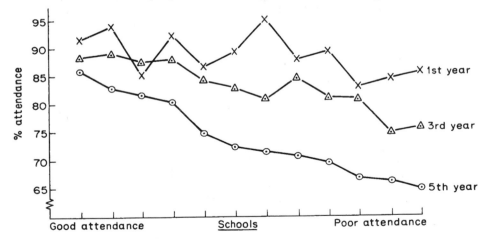

Figure 5.1 *Attendance by school for first, third and fifth years*

* The correlation coefficient is a mathematical expression of the strength of association between two variables. A correlation of zero indicates no association at all whereas a correlation of 1·0 indicates perfect agreement. Intermediate values represent intermediate degrees of association. As the calculations are based on rank orders of schools, rank correlations are used. The term r_s is used to refer to the rank correlation coefficient (see Siegel, 1956).

As other investigators have found (Galloway, 1976), attendance tended to be much worse in the fifth year. However, it is also clear that there were considerable differences between the schools. While these were most marked for the fifth year pupils, somewhat similar trends were evident for the first and third years. A few schools maintained relatively high rates of attendance across all age groups. In other schools, particularly those with lower rates of attendance in the earlier years, there was a marked fall off in attendance among older pupils.

Stability of school differences in attendance

The stability of school differences in attendance was examined both over age groups and over time. In addition to the sample weeks' data for first, third and fifth year pupils in 1975/76, the attendance of all second year pupils had been recorded for the complete school years of 1972/73 and 1975/76. Table 5.3 shows the rank correlations between' schools for the attendance of the four age groups studied in 1975/76. The intercorrelations between years 2, 3 and 5 are all at least 0·86, indicating very strong stability across age groups. Those with the first year attendance are somewhat less but all are in the 0·60s.

| | | Age Group | | |
		Yr. 1	Yr. 2	Yr. 3
	Yr. 1			
Age Group	Yr. 2	0·60		
	Yr. 3	0·69	0·90	
	Yr. 5	0·68	0·86	0·87

Table 5.3 *Intercorrelations between age groups on attendance*

The stability of school attendance rates over time was determined by comparing the second year figures for the 1972/73 and the 1975/76 years. The rank correlation between the two was 0·90, indicating considerable stability over a three year period, at least for these younger pupils. Not only were the rankings very similar, but so also were the absolute levels. In 1972/73 the school averages ranged from 79 per cent to 92 per cent; three years later the range was from 75 per cent to 91 per cent. The maximum drop in any individual school was only 5 per cent.

Association with self-report data

A strong association between the school register attendance data and the self-report data from the anonymous pupil questionnaire would not be expected, if only because the most persistent truants were unlikely to be present to complete the questionnaire. However, it seemed worthwhile to determine just how well the two did agree in terms of school rankings. The correlations between the fifth year register data and self-reported truancy (0·32) and absconding, i.e. leaving school after being registered as present (0·43), were both positive but not statistically significant.

Easter leavers

Schools also varied greatly in the proportion of pupils who left school at the very first legal opportunity – at the end of the spring term of their fifth year and before taking any public examinations. All pupils who had reached their sixteenth birthday by the end of the January of their fifth year (rather less than half the total group) were eligible to leave at Easter. But the proportions of these pupils who actually left

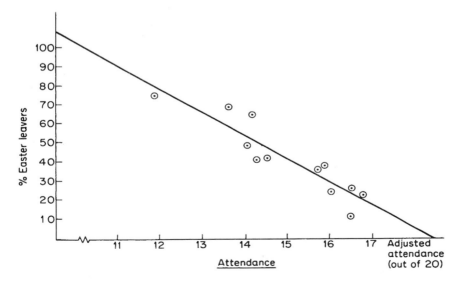

Figure 5.2 *School attendance and percentage Easter leavers*

ranged from 10·7 per cent to 75·0 per cent in different schools (representing 5 to 35 per cent respectively of the total fifth year roll).

There was a very high correlation ($r_s = 0·94$) between a school's score on the adjusted fifth year attendance measure and the proportion of Easter leavers. This is shown graphically in Figure 5.2.* The finding indicates that schools which maintain good levels of attendance also tend to keep a majority of their pupils at least up to the end of the fifth year. It was also found that they tended to have a higher proportion of pupils staying on into the sixth year. The correlation between the fifth year attendance measure and the proportion of children remaining at school into the sixth year was 0·81.

Summary of attendance findings

Pupils of below average intellectual ability or from families of low occupational status were the ones most likely to show poor attendance records. However, even after controlling for school variations in intake on VR band and occupation, large and statistically significant school differences in levels of attendance remained. These school differences in attendance were rather consistent both over time and over age groups. Schools with good levels of attendance in the fifth year tended also to have a high proportion of pupils staying on into the sixth year.

Pupil behaviour

The measure of pupil behaviour in school was rather different from the other outcomes in that it was not based on individual data. It con-

---

* Similar graphs will be used throughout the book to illustrate correlations between two measures. Each point represents the scores for one school on both measures (one on the vertical and one on the horizontal axis). Where the rank correlations are statistically significant the graph includes a 'regression' line based on the correlation between the scores. In Figure 5.2 a negative association is indicated by a diagonal going from the top left corner to the bottom right corner. The extent to which the points cluster closely or scatter widely about the regression line gives a visual impression of the strength and consistency of the association; the closer the clustering along the line the stronger and more consistent the association.

sisted, instead, of a scale combining both self-report and observational measures for several different age groups of children. We decided on this approach to achieve the broadest possible picture of day to day behaviour in the schools, and the scale included all the available measures of pupil behaviour which discriminated between the schools. The scale was made up of twenty-five items in all,* each one based on the school average for that particular measure (thus, for items derived from the pupil questionnaire the school average took account of first, third and fifth year responses to each question).

*Mis*behaviour tends to be more readily observed or asked about than does *positive* behaviour, so that items of this kind inevitably predominated to some extent in the scale.

At the most detailed level, our direct observations of first and third year lessons were used to assess late arrival at lessons, the extent of off-task behaviour, disallowed chatting and calling out in class, and instances of overtly disruptive behaviour. Classroom observations during the administration of the pupil questionnaire provided information on the proportion of pupils in correct uniform, the wearing of overcoats and anoraks in class, and the proportion of children coming to class without pens or pencils. Indirect measures of children's behaviour were obtained from our observations of the amount of damage to school property and the extent of graffiti. Finally, self-reports from the pupil questionnaire tapped aspects of behaviour which could not easily be observed such as truanting, absconding and skipping lessons.

Most of the twenty-five items correlated highly with one another, and the Kendall coefficient of concordance (reflecting the overall rank correlations between all 25 items) was highly significant ($W = 0.53$; $x^2 = 146.2$; 11 df, $p < 0.001$). In order to obtain an overall score on this measure, each school was ranked on each of the twenty-five items (thus giving each item an equal weighting) and an average score calculated. This mean rank score ranged from 1.94 (worst) to 10.56 (best) indicating the very great variations between schools with respect to pupil behaviour. The scores for all twelve schools are shown in histogram form in Figure 5.3.

---

* See Appendix A for details.

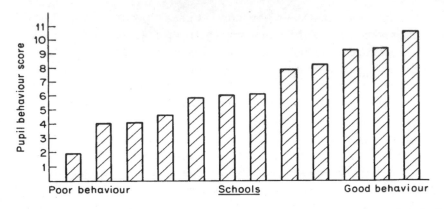

Figure 5.3 *Pupil behaviour score by school*

Controlling for intake differences

Because this measure of pupil behaviour in school was not derived from individual data, it was not possible to control for intake differences on a child-by-child basis. The question could be approached, however, in terms of whether the secondary schools with much problem behaviour (as reflected in the behaviour scale score) were the same as those with a particularly high proportion of difficult or disruptive children in their intakes from primary school.

We were able to look at this question directly by comparing the rank order of the schools according to the proportion of children in their intakes with high scores on the primary school teacher questionnaire, and their rank order on this secondary school pupil behaviour scale. The rank correlation between them was only 0·27, indicating that the secondary schools with the worst behaviour in the classroom and on the playground were *not* necessarily those with the 'worst' intakes of difficult pupils at the age of ten years. The very considerable differences between schools in their pupils' behaviour could *not* simply be seen as a continuation of patterns previously established in primary schools.

Stability over age groups

In that the measure was deliberately constructed to span all age groups, it was not relevant (or possible) to examine stability across ages using the overall scale. In addition, because our measures of behaviour had been made 'in situ', we could not of course examine the extent to which children's behaviour at the schools while we were undertaking the study was similar to that in the same schools during previous years. However, some indication of stability could be provided by examining the extent to which the pupil questionnaire findings for the first, third and fifth year pupils produced similar rankings. When we asked pupils about whether they had ever deliberately missed any lessons, there was good agreement between the replies of those from year one and those from year three (0·65) and also between the replies of the pupils of year three and year five (0·62). For one of the other questions concerning the writing of graffiti on classroom walls, corridors, etc., these relationships were less marked. The correlation between first and third year pupils was 0·38 whilst between third and fifth it was only 0·23. However, there was a significant correlation of 0·52 between the replies of first and fifth year pupils, showing that there was a certain amount of agreement between members of the same school. Thus, overall there was a moderate (but not very strong) consistency across age groups for those pupil behaviour measures where this could be tested.

Delinquency

Delinquency data were collected in the spring of 1977 (when the pupils were in their eighteenth year) from the Metropolitan Police Juvenile Bureaux for all pupils who had been on roll at any of the twelve schools at age fourteen years (2352 pupils in all). The information included all incidents which had been recorded up to that point, and for the purposes of the study a pupil was termed 'delinquent' if he or she had been officially cautioned or found guilty of an offence in a Juvenile Court on at least one occasion. Note was taken of how many convictions each child had received and a separate analysis was made of school differences according to the proportion of children committing multiple offences. In fact it was found that the schools with the lowest or highest rates for *any* delinquency were also the ones with the lowest (or highest) rates for *repeated* delinquency. As a result, attention will be confined here to comparisons according to the proportions of

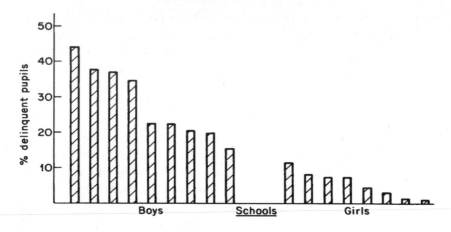

Figure 5.4 *School rates of delinquency*

delinquent pupils (irrespective of number of offences).

The data for boys and girls have been treated quite separately in this part of the analysis, because their rates of delinquency differ so greatly. Figure 5.4 shows the proportion of 'delinquent' pupils at each school, with the mixed schools represented twice, once for their boys and once for their girls. School rates for boys varied from 16 per cent to 44 per cent, and for girls from 1 per cent to 11 per cent.

Stability over time: delinquency rates

These school delinquency rates all refer to the age group of pupils who entered secondary school in 1971, and who have been followed through to about age seventeen years. In order to find out how far the delinquency rates were similar for other groups of young people attending the schools, we collected information on the rates of offending for all the other age groups of pupils in the schools for the two years 1974 and 1976. (One school had to be omitted from these tests because the necessary data were not available.) It was then possible to compare the school delinquency rates for the main sample with these two samples of other pupils in 1974 and 1976. The Kendall coefficient of concordance was once again used to examine the relationships between these three sets of data. It showed very close relationships both for the girls

(W = 0·81, x^2 = 17·01 with 7 df, p < 0·05), and for the boys (W = 0·78, x^2 = 18·72 with 8 df, p < 0·05). The variations between schools which had emerged in the delinquency figures for the main sample of pupils were clearly echoed in these data for a wide range of other age groups. Once again, it seemed that school variations on this outcome also showed considerable stability over time.

Controlling for intake differences

Before we could proceed to analyses of school delinquency rates which controlled for intake differences, it was necessary to determine which factors (measured prior to secondary school entry) best predicted delinquency. We have already noted the marked sex difference in rates; because of this we have analysed the findings separately for boys and girls throughout.

In the earlier analyses concerned with delinquency up to the age of fourteen years (see Chapter 2), the behavioural ratings made by primary school teachers had constituted the best predictor, and this was used to control for intake variations. However, we were now concerned with a time span of seven years from the point when the questionnaires were completed, and it was not obvious that they would still provide the best controls. As it turned out, the questionnaire was still an excellent predictor of delinquency in girls, but its predictive power for boys was rather poor (see Table 5.4 in Appendix G).

Previous research has often shown connections between verbal reasoning skills and delinquency, and between occupational status and delinquency. Both associations were examined with respect to our own data – in this case for the whole age group of children in the 1971 intake. The results, summarised in Tables 5.5 and 5.6, show strong and statistically significant associations between both variables and delinquency for both boys and girls. It was clear that a combination of VR grade and parental occupation was likely to constitute the best predictor of delinquency, and hence that these would be the most suitable variables to use in controlling for intake differences.*

---

* Analyses were also undertaken to determine whether the fact that a child came from an immigrant background was associated with variations in delinquency rates. There was only a very small difference in rates of delinquency for boys between the indigenous group (28·3 per cent delinquent) and those with one or both parents born abroad (31·4 per cent delinquent) and this factor added nothing to prediction.

VR score	Girls % delinquent	(total)	Boys % delinquent	(total)
1	0·00	(21)	11·54	(26)
2	5·13	(78)	7·14	(98)
3	2·70	(148)	19·15	(188)
4	4·87	(226	29·54	(237)
5	5·56	(162)	34·18	(237)
6	6·92	(159)	30·56	(216)
7	11·11	(99)	37·98	(129)

Girls
  Mean VR – Non delinquents = 4·44
           Delinquents = 5·07
           $F = 8·26$ $p < 0·005$

Boys
  Mean VR – Non delinquents = 4·41
           Delinquents = 4·92
           $F = 32·10$ $p < 0·001$

Table 5.5 *Delinquency and verbal reasoning score*

Occupational group	Girls % delinquent	(total)	Boys % delinquent	(total)
1	1·32	(76)	16·28	(86)
2	1·72	(58)	17·81	(73)
3	3·98	(377)	27·45	(601)
4	6·05	(314)	33·51	(388)
5	16·33	(49)	46·39	(97)

Girls
  Mean Occupational Level – Non delinquents = 3·12
                       Delinquents = 3·72
                                $F = 11·88$ $p < 0·001$

Boys
  Mean Occupational Level – Non delinquents = 3·17
                       Delinquents = 3·47
                                  $F = 26·09$ $p < 0·001$

Table 5.6 *Delinquency and parental occupational group*

    The statistical techniques used in dealing with the attendance data were not appropriate in this case, as the delinquency data concerned the distribution of *individuals* rather than the distribution of *scores*. It was necessary instead to use some kind of standardisation approach which, in effect, would compare school delinquency rates *within* each

VR and occupation grouping; in other words to compare like with like. The particular standardisation method we had used with the fourteen year old data (see Chapter 2) was less suitable here where we had to deal with two variables in addition to schools. Instead we used a log linear modelling technique (Everitt, 1977 — see also Appendix H for details of this approach). In essence, what this does is to test out different 'models', using all the available variables in different combinations, to determine which combination best accounts (statistically speaking) for the observed distribution on the 'outcome' being considered — in this case delinquency. The minimum number of variables and interactions (i.e. statistical combinations between variables) to obtain a good 'fit' to the observed data is determined. If, in the present analysis, the school variable does not significantly 'improve' the model then it can be concluded that the 'school' does not exert an effect on delinquency which is above and beyond that of verbal reasoning and parental occupation.

This was done separately for boys and girls. The analysis showed that the 'delinquency by school' term *was* required for boys ($G^2 = 32 \cdot 50$, with 8 df) but that it did not result in any significant improvement in fit for girls. This meant that there did not appear to be any substantial school effect on delinquency in girls, once due allowance had been made for the differences between schools in intake. As there were so few delinquent girls in our sample, it is not possible to be sure whether this result means that schools truly have no effect on delinquency in girls, or rather that the effect was too small to be shown, given the number of delinquent girls we studied. We have no means of taking the question any further in connection with our own data.

However, the same analyses did show a substantial school effect on delinquency for boys. As a consequence, all further analyses of possible school influences on delinquency rates are restricted to boys.

The data for boys from the log linear model are shown in Figure 5.5. At first sight the graph looks complicated, but the principle it illustrates is basically quite straightforward. Each line represents one specific school, with respect to the children within a particular occupational and VR group. The points on the line show the probability of delinquency for a boy at that school within that particular VR band and occupational group. The data are plotted on a logarithmic scale so that they fall on parallel lines.

From the graph it is possible to read off comparable probabilities.

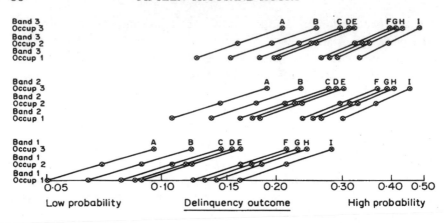

Figure 5.5 *Delinquency by band and occupational group (boys only)*

Thus, it may be seen that at school 'I' a boy in the *top* VR band and top occupational group is as likely to be delinquent as a boy in the *bottom* VR band and top occupational group at school 'B'. These probabilities are all adjusted to take account of the different numbers of children in each group at each school. The differences in delinquency rates between schools are indicated by the *distance* between the various parallel lines. Thus, it can be seen that for comparable groups of boys in the same VR band and occupational group the delinquency rate at school 'I' is *three times* that at school 'A'. All the graphs in later chapters of this book which deal with delinquency use the figures for band 2, middle occupational children. However, the picture would be the same with any of the subgroups since the *relative* difference between schools remains the same.

Academic attainment: public exam results

Our fourth measure of outcome was that of academic attainment in public examinations. Here once again we will largely be concerned with the main sample of pupils, who took their first public examinations in June 1976. As discussed in Chapter 1, results in public examinations appear to have considerable advantages over scores on standardised intellectual tests as indicators of academic progress at secondary level. Because they focus on subjects in the curriculum which are specifically taught, they are likely to provide rather better guides to the effects of schooling. The complexities of the examination system, however, do present considerable difficulties in any attempt to compare results in different schools.

Within the twelve schools candidates were entered for 'O' levels with a number of different examination boards and schools varied in their policies on which children were entered for CSE and which for (the more academic) GCE 'O' levels. Many schools offered Mode 3 CSE exams (which are based on courses designed by the teachers at each particular school) in addition to the standard Mode 1 CSE papers. A few schools also offered some subjects in the experimental CEE examinations. At the time the study was undertaken few pupils took 'A' levels, so that for the vast majority of children the CSE, GCE and CEE results constituted their main school-leaving qualifications. But, as we noted earlier, it was fairly usual for pupils to stay on one year into the sixth form to re-sit some examinations, to take extra ones, or to move from a CSE to an 'O' level syllabus.

All of these variations raise obvious problems of comparability. We could not hope to tease out all the possible combinations so we dealt with the data in two different kinds of ways. First, we followed the generally accepted conventions about comparability to combine the exam results into an overall measure of academic achievement. Second, we re-analysed the results separately for particular examinations and ability groups. As it turned out, these multiple ways of analysing the findings gave closely comparable results with respect to differences between the schools.

Exam comparisons

Our main interest was in the numbers and grades of passes gained by the pupils, rather than the particular subjects taken. Accordingly, we gave all subjects an equal weight but we divided the pass grades into several different categories.

The first constituted all passes which are equivalent to an 'O' level. This includes 'O' level grades A to C, CSE grade 1, and CEE grades 1 to 3. The second constituted all passes which are equivalent to a good CSE grade. This includes the lower graded 'O' levels (D and E), CSE grades 2 and 3, and the lowest grades of CEE (4 and 5). The final group consisted of the lowest grades of CSE (4 and 5).

Thus, we had information for each pupil in the age group on the number of passes he or she had gained in each of these categories. Results were available at two points in time: firstly at the end of the fifth year, and secondly by the end of the first year sixth. As many pupils re-sat examinations during their sixth form year, we used their best grade in any repeated exam as their grade for that subject. But when pupils transferred from a CSE to an 'O' level syllabus in the same subject area, we treated any 'O' level pass as a separate, additional pass grade. This was because, although the subject was the same, the syllabus (and hence the body of knowledge to be mastered) was substantially different.

Overall levels of achievement

Before examining patterns of attainment by school, it may be helpful to consider the overall levels of attainment for the whole sample of pupils in the twelve schools in order to put things into perspective. In this connection, it is important to emphasise that the populations of children in the schools were heavily skewed towards the middle and bottom of the ability range (see Chapter 2). Very few pupils were in the top ability band (10 per cent, compared with 25 per cent in London as a whole). Since examination success is closely related to measured ability, this point is of obvious importance.

By the end of the fifth year, a third of the children (33·5 per cent) had gained some kind of 'O' level grade, whereas two-thirds (68·5 per cent) had achieved a CSE. The policy of entering candidates for 'O' levels in the sixth form is reflected in the rise to 38·9 per cent for children with at least one graded pass by the end of the first year sixth. There was no comparable increase in the figures for the CSE.

As shown in Table 5.7, the pupils may be grouped into a number of broad categories according to the grades of results obtained, by the end of the fifth and separately by the end of the sixth year. The major gains during the sixth form year are evident in the almost doubling of the proportion of children with five or more 'O' level equivalents.

It is difficult to compare these results directly with nationally available figures because the Department of Education and Science

Exam Category	Total Sample	
	By end of 5th yr % Pupils	By end of 6th yr % Pupils
Easter leavers	14·6	14·6
No graded pass	14·8	14·7
CSE 4 or 5 only	12·3	11·2
CSE 2 or 3, 'O' D or E only	29·7	27·1
1–4 'O' level equivalents	24·8	25·8
5 or more 'O' level equivalents	3·7	6·6

Table 5.7 *Exam grades in total sample at 12 schools*

Exam Grades	DES Figures			
	All England % Pupils	Greater London % Pupils	'Modern' Schools % Pupils	12 Schools % Pupils
No pass	19·6	23·2	23·0	29·4
Lower CSE or 'O' level	39·6	39·7	44·6	38·2
1 to 4 'O' level equivalents	30·7	28·2	27·8	25·8
5+ 'O' level equivalents	10·1	8·9	4·8	6·6

Table 5.8 *Comparison of exam results with national statistics*

statistics are calculated differently.* Moreover, it is necessary to take into account geographical area and types of school. However, Table 5.8 provides the best available comparison (in which 'A' level passes have been excluded and the categories collapsed into the groupings used by the DES).

The only figures available for London concern Greater London (which includes the more prosperous outer suburbs) and all schools (including the academically selective). In view of the ability distribution in the twelve schools, a comparison with secondary modern schools (which exclude the more able children going on to academically selective schools) may also be appropriate.

---

* The DES statistics refer to all school leavers in one calendar year and so include pupils from at least three different groups, some of whom have taken 'A' levels. Our figures relate to only one age group and do not include 'A' level passes.

Compared with the secondary modern schools, the twelve study schools included rather more pupils with at least five 'O' levels but also rather more without any passes. Compared with all schools in Greater London (selective and non-selective) exam results in the study schools were generally not quite so good.

Combining exam grades for school comparisons

In order to assess how far schools differed in their levels of academic attainment we needed to reduce this rather complex picture of different types and levels of exam pass to some simpler 'score'. In doing this we had two main concerns. First, it was important that the academic outcome measure should reflect the attainments of the majority of the pupils (and not be too dependent on the grades of the most able children). Second, it was necessary that we took proper account of the ways in which the examination entry policies of the twelve schools might affect comparisons.

To meet the first of these points, our main school comparison was based on results from the fifth year examinations only with all pupils regarded as potential examination candidates. We also decided that our measure should incorporate some of the lower grades of pass.

Our second concern, over entry policies, raised rather more complicated issues. We have already seen that only about one-third of the pupils gained 'O' level grades at the end of their fifth year. However, when we looked at this on a school by school basis, we found that the proportions varied quite considerably. The explanation seemed to lie in the fact that, in some schools, much more emphasis was placed on the CSE exams in the fifth year (so that at this stage, perhaps, only one or two 'O' level subjects were taught). This suggested that we could not make any kind of meaningful comparisons between schools by looking at each of these examinations separately. Rather, we needed to find some means of equating them.

A second kind of difficulty arose over the CSE exams. In some schools, almost all pupils were entered in some subjects, so that a very large proportion of the children would gain at least some lower graded passes. In other schools, by contrast, entries were rather more restricted, and were only made if it seemed likely that pupils would attain a reasonably high grade.

In order to take account of these differences, it was necessary both to combine GCE and CSE grades and also to weight passes according to the grade obtained. One point was allocated for each grade in the top category of 'O' level equivalent and half a point was given for each pass grade in the middle category of good CSE equivalent (see above). No points were given for passes in the bottom category of CSE grades 4 and 5. By summing each child's points for each subject an overall attainment score was obtained for each child.

Controlling for intake variations in verbal reasoning

As would be expected, the children's measured ability on verbal reasoning at age ten proved to be the best overall predictor of exam results (using the combined score system just described). The average score ranged from 0·35 for VR grade 7 through 1·50 for grade 4 to 3·99 for VR grade 1 (F = 147·56, 6 df, p < 0·001).

Accordingly, the next step was to compare exam scores in the different schools, within each VR group. The analysis of variance results (see Table 5.9 in Appendix G) indicated that both the differences between schools, and those between VR groups, were statistically highly significant. Schools differed in their levels of exam results (mean score 1·39 with range from 0·62 to 2·58) even after taking account of variations in the ability of their children as measured at intake.* Figure 5.6 presents the same findings graphically (except that the 7 VR groups have been collapsed into three bands for ease of presentation). The data refer to all fifth year pupils at the schools, and relate to mean pass rates on the weighted pass measure. Across the twelve schools, the average number of passes for VR band one was 3·18, for band two it was 1·53, and for band three 0·46. Thus, examination success is strongly correlated with the assessment of intellectual abilities prior to entering secondary school.

Even so, the same data also show marked variations between schools such that, at the extremes, the average score for band 3 children in the most successful school was as good as that for band 1

---

* Table 5.9 presents the statistical results as given by a hierarchical analysis of variance. The results were found to be closely similar and highly significant, however, if instead a standardisation approach or an analysis of covariance was used.

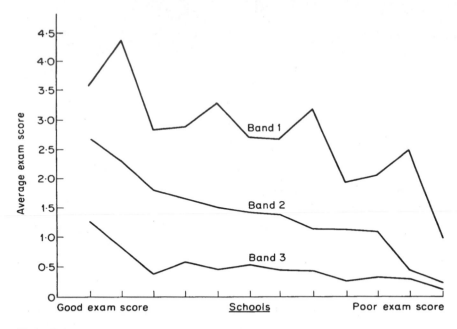

Figure 5.6 *Average exam score by school and band*

children in the least successful school! It is also evident that the pattern of results for each school was broadly similar in all three bands. The schools are ordered on the graph according to their scores for band 2 children. But it may be seen that, in general, in schools where band 2 children are doing better than average, the band 1 and band 3 children tend also to be getting better than average examination results.

The extent of the school variations is shown graphically in Figure 5.7. This uses the overall weighted exam score for each school, adjusted for VR distribution, to express the findings in terms of percentage above or below the average figure for the sample as a whole. The school results range from 71·2 per cent better than expectation to 55·4 per cent below expectation – large differences indeed. The exam score, after adjusting for VR, of the most successful school (2·38) was nearly four times as high as that of the least successful (0·62).

Controlling for intake variations in VR and parental occupation

The analyses so far have used verbal reasoning, as the best single predictor of academic attainment, to control for intake variations.

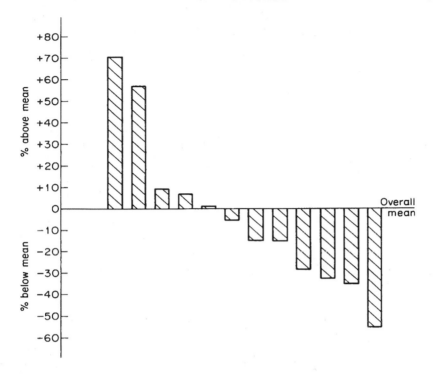

Figure 5.7 *Adjusted exam scores by school compared with overall mean*

However, other studies (e.g. Douglas, 1964; Douglas *et al.*, 1968) have found that, even after controlling for IQ, parental occupation is also associated with attainment. We found the same.* Thus, within the middle ability band the average exam score was 2.1 for children whose fathers held clerical or professional jobs, compared with 1.1 for children of unskilled manual workers. The differences according to occupational status were highly significant ($F = 7 \cdot 24$; df 4; $p < 0 \cdot 001$) for this band, less so for the upper VR band ($F = 2 \cdot 93$; df 4; $p < 0 \cdot 052$), and were not statistically significant for the lower VR band.

In view of this effect of parental occupation, we used the hierarchical analysis of variance to take account of both VR band and parental oc-

* We also found, as have other studies (see Yule *et al.*, 1975), that, on average, children from immigrant families tended to have lower levels of scholastic attainment than children from indigenous families. However, ethnic background showed no significant association with exam success after the children's verbal reasoning score and parental occupation had been taken into account.

cupation. There was still a highly significant school effect ($p < 0.001$), but also there were band by school and occupation by school interactions which were just significant at the 5 per cent level. As these complicated any interpretation of findings, the analysis was repeated for the middle VR band children ($n = 1104$) only, with occupation and school as main effects.

There was still a highly significant school effect ($p < 0.001$, see Table 5.10 in Appendix G). The rank order on this analysis, using the exam scores for middle VR band children only, adjusted for occupational status, was almost identical (a correlation of 0·97) with the one previously obtained for the whole sample in which the scores were adjusted solely on the basis of VR scores at age ten. The findings showed large differences between schools in academic attainment (mean 1·60 with range from 0·35 to 2·80) even after making full allowance for variations in intake.

Stability of school differences over time: exam results

As with the other outcome measures, it was necessary to check how far the differences between schools in exam results were similar from year to year. To examine this, we collected similar intake and examination data on a group basis for pupils two years older than our main sample, namely those who reached school leaving age in 1974. Once again, highly significant differences between schools were found, after adjusting for variations in intake. Moreover, with one exception, the relative positions of the schools in the two years were closely comparable. Only one school had changed its position to any substantial extent, giving an overall rank correlation of 0·69 (or 0·82 if that one school is excluded). The findings show a reasonable degree of stability over time for schools' examination performance.

Exam results for the least able and most able children

As a final check on school differences, we needed to test whether our use of weighted exam scores had led to results which were very different from those obtained by considering different exams separately according to particular groups of pupils. To look at this possibility, we first focussed on the least able group of children – those in the bottom VR ability band – and considered their exam results solely in terms of CSE grades 4 and 5 (i.e. the lowest grades, which had been excluded from the weighted pass measure). It could reasonably be argued that the exam score cut-off was too stringent for these pupils, and that the lower CSE grades would represent considerable levels of achievement for them. As with the other measures, we found highly significant differences ($p < 0.001$) between schools once more (mean score 1·25 with range from 0·55 to 2·17 – see Table 5.11 in Appendix G). Moreover, the rank ordering of schools on this lower exam pass measure correlated very highly (0·83) with that on the examination score.

We then turned our attention to the other end of the VR ability spectrum, and the schools' performance on the 'O' level equivalent passes alone. For this analysis we selected the top 3 VR groups only and repeated the hierarchical analysis of variance (see Table 5.12 in Appendix G). Again, there were highly significant ($p < 0.001$) differences between schools (mean score 1·57 with range from 0·15 to 2·36), and a ranking of schools which was broadly similar (0·70) to that obtained with the overall weighted pass measure.* Two schools obtained rather different results (one better and one worse), suggesting some differences in emphasis. However, by and large, it seemed that the schools' exam performance was much the same regardless of which academic outcome measure was chosen. The exam score seemed to provide a very acceptable indicator of attainment which reflected fairly closely the results for the much smaller groups of pupils for whom it was possible to use particular exam results directly. We have thus used this score, taking the rank ordering of schools on the analysis controlled for VR, as our main measure of academic outcome in all later analyses.

Exam results, school attendance, Easter leavers and delinquents

It is clear from all these analyses that there were major school differences in scholastic attainment. However, three further factors needed to be taken into account. We have seen already that there were

---

* The same applied to school differences with respect to academic attainments in the sixth form (see Appendix I). The school ranking for the exam scores of the more highly achieving pupils who stayed on into the sixth form correlated 0·87 with that on the overall weighted mean pass score.

also large differences between schools in rates of attendance, in the proportion of Easter leavers, and in rates of delinquency. Could these explain the differences in exam success? Were the differences in attainment simply a result of differences in the percentage of children attending sufficiently regularly for them to benefit from the teaching? Could it be that the school variations in achievement were merely a consequence of the varying proportions of children who remained in school to take the examinations? Or was it just that the delinquent pupils were employing their talents in fields other than school work and that differences in the proportion of delinquents accounted for variations in exam scores?

To examine these questions we needed to carry out a series of further analyses. We began by considering the factor which might have the most confounding effect, the variation in Easter leaving. The initial comparisons of exam scores had included all fifth year pupils, on the grounds that they were all *potential* examination candidates, and that the scholastic performance of each school should be assessed on this basis. However, obviously the pupils who left at Easter added nothing to the exam scores, as they took no exams. In order to determine what effect this had had on the findings, we repeated the analyses of the school exam scores controlling for VR, but this time excluding all Easter leavers. This had the expected effect of raising the overall levels of attainment (most markedly for pupils in the top ability group) but it made almost no difference to the rank ordering of schools; the correlation with the original order was 0·99.

To study the effects of variations in attendance, we began by analysing the exam scores of different ability groups according to their levels of fifth year attendance.* As anticipated, this showed that exam scores varied significantly by attendance ($p < 0.001$). In each ability group, children who attended at least 75 per cent of the time in the fifth year obtained significantly better exam scores than those with poor attendance records ($p < 0.001$ for all three bands). We then made a further analysis of school differences, controlling for VR, but excluding both Easter leavers and poor attenders, in order to focus on pupils who might seem to have taken the best advantage of their school opportunities. School differences remained highly statistically significant

---

* The attendance data used here once again relate to the selected weeks in the September and January terms of the school year 1975/76 discussed with respect to the attendance outcome.

(p < 0·001) and the rank ordering of the schools was almost exactly the same.

Figure 5.8 combines these findings to show the adjusted scores for each school, firstly for the sample as a whole, then after excluding

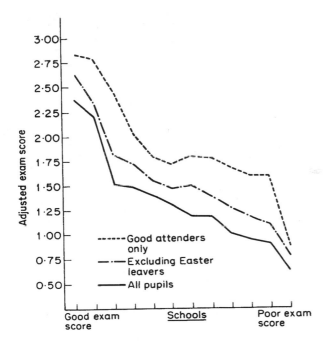

Figure 5.8 *Adjusted exam scores by school*

Easter leavers, and finally after excluding both Easter leavers and poor attenders. In all three cases the patterns are closely comparable.

Our final query in this part of the analysis concerned the possible relationship between delinquency and academic attainment. Many other studies have suggested that children who get into trouble with the police also score rather poorly on attainment tests (see Rutter, Tizard and Whitmore, 1970; West and Farrington, 1973). To see whether this was also the case among the children at the twelve schools, we examined the exam scores of children (boys and girls separately) in each ability band according to whether or not they were delinquent. As anticipated, the 'delinquents' of both sexes scored significantly less well than their peers. The differences were highly significant for both boys and girls in all three bands, except for band 1 boys where the difference fell just short of statistical significance ($p = 0.07$).

The next step was to determine whether this association might account for the school variations in exam success. This was done by testing the exam scores once again, after the exclusion of all delinquent pupils. School differences remained large and statistically significant ($p < 0.001$) and the rank order of schools was virtually identical (correlation of 0.97) with that in the original analysis of the total sample.

The final step was to examine the school difference after excluding poor attenders, Easter leavers *and* delinquents (see Table 5.13 in Appendix G). The sample size was much reduced by these exclusions (from 2200 to 1087) but the pattern remained much as before. There were still important and statistically significant differences between schools ($p < 0.001$) and the rank order was similar (0.92) to that first obtained. We may thus conclude that there were substantial differences between schools in scholastic attainment, even after eliminating the effects of poor attendance, early leaving and delinquency.

The four outcomes

Taking all these findings together, we have now seen that there were large and statistically significant differences between secondary schools with respect to levels of attendance, children's behaviour in school, delinquency and academic attainment — differences which still remained even after controlling for the relevant intake variables. The last issue to consider in these connections is how far each of these separate outcomes produced a similar pattern of school variation. Table 5.14 sets out the rank orders of the twelve schools on the attendance, behaviour and academic outcome measures. It can be seen that the picture which emerges is a rather consistent one, with the exception of the one school with a good behaviour score, but otherwise poor outcomes. On the whole, schools which have high levels of attendance and good behaviour tend also to have high levels of exam success. The delinquency rankings can only be considered with respect to boys' schools but, again, there were substantial correlations between the

different types of outcome (correlation for delinquency and attendance $= 0.77$; for delinquency and academic outcome $= 0.68$; for
delinquency and behaviour $= 0.72$). We have shown that the marked
school variations in each different type of outcome could not be accounted for in terms of individual intake characteristics on any of the
measures available to us. As such measures included not only pupil
behaviour and attainments at primary school, but also social
background, it seems likely that the school variations in outcome are
linked with characteristics of the schools themselves. In short, it
appears that in a part of inner London known to be disadvantaged in
numerous ways, some schools were better able than others to foster
good behaviour and attainments.

Attendance	Academic	Behaviour
1	1	1
2	2	4
3	6	3
4	5	5
5	8	10
6	4	6
7	10	11
8	9	9
9	3	8
10	7	7
11	12	12
12	11	2

(NB rank 1 = 'best')
   rank 12 = 'worst')

Table 5.14 *Comparison of different outcome measures:
       attendance, behaviour and academic attainment in 12 schools*

However, it is necessary to appreciate that our analyses which 'control' for intake differences cannot by themselves show that the
variations in outcome are due to school characteristics. All that they
demonstrate is that the outcome differences were *not* due to differences
in any of the intake measures, and that they were due to 'something
else'. The inference that that 'something else' concerned schools would
be immensely strengthened if it could be shown that the school
variations in outcome were consistently associated with measured

differences in school structure, organisation or functioning. Such evidence, of course, would also indicate *which* features of school life were most likely to influence children's development. The remainder of this book is concerned with our findings on these crucial questions.

6

Physical and administrative features of schools: associations with outcome

In this and the following chapters, we will be reviewing all our information about the schools themselves, and about life within them, in the search for factors which might further our understanding of the differences in pupil outcomes. The emphasis will be upon organisational or process variables which also differed between the schools*, and we will be considering in turn three broad sets of factors, each of which might be expected to have a bearing on pupil progress. The first concerns the most publicly available, and perhaps the most immediately obvious, ways in which the schools differed – that is with respect to their physical features and administrative structure. Under this heading we will consider items such as their size, the sex composition of their intakes, the age of the buildings in which they were housed, the space available to them, and the administrative aegis (either voluntary-aided or local authority maintained) under which they operated. We have chosen to treat this rather heterogeneous group of factors together for several rather different reasons.

First, unlike some of the later features we will be discussing, factors of this kind all represent relatively permanent characteristics of any individual school, which would only be likely to change as a result of major administrative reorganisations. The size of the intakes to a number of the schools fluctuated somewhat from year to year during the course of the study, and some schools had extensions or changes to their buildings. Nevertheless, by and large, these factors could be regarded as relatively stable characteristics of the schools. Secondly, these are all features which most previous studies have found *not* to be related to outcome. It was important to determine how far our findings were in keeping with previous comparable research in this respect

---

* We will comment in passing on some of the more interesting characteristics which the schools had in *common*, but obviously these are of no help in understanding the variations in outcome within the group of twelve schools.

before going on to break new ground with variables not much considered in earlier investigations. Thirdly, although our sample of twelve schools was well suited to the study of many aspects of school functioning, it was clearly too small for an investigation of differences in overall educational policies (indeed, as already noted, we deliberately chose a sample which was homogeneous in many of these aspects in order to better focus on individual styles of social interactions and organisation). Accordingly, our main concern with physical and administrative features was to check how far we would need to take their effects into account when examining other aspects of school processes.

The second set of school features, which we will discuss in Chapter 7, concerns the social organisation of schools, and draws on the wide range of data we had collected to examine school 'processes'. These include factors such as academic emphasis, rewards and punishments, pupils' responsibilities and participation in school life, working conditions, and staff supervision. By comparison with the physical and administrative characteristics of schools, these are much more open to change of direction within each school. The study was specifically designed to explore features of this kind, the sample was well chosen for this purpose, and a good deal of confidence can be placed on this set of findings.

The third set of factors, discussed in Chapter 8, is concerned with ecological variables. Schools function as part of a socio-political environment, and what any school is like will be determined in part by that environment. The subject raises a wide range of issues, including questions of resource allocation, the distribution of power in society, educational ideologies, conflicts both within schools and between schools and political administrators, attitudes to social control, and the values attached to education by the public at large (see Eggleston, 1977, and Karabel and Halsey, 1977, for thoughtful introductions to these topics). Most of these questions are outside the scope of our study and, as discussed earlier, we deliberately chose a sample of schools homogeneous with respect to many of these external factors in order to better focus on 'internal' school processes. However, there are crucial ecological differences even within a single local authority, and between schools all serving a disadvantaged inner city area. These include the social circumstances of the particular districts from which each school draws most of its pupils, the characteristics of the balance of intake to each school, and the popularity of the schools in the eyes of parents.

This three-fold distinction between administrative arrangements, internal school practice, and ecological influences is, of course, a rather simplified schema for examining the influences at work in schools. It provides a useful device for highlighting points of possible interest at each of these rather different levels of influence, but necessarily it presents only a partial view of a much more complex reality. At various points in the discussion, we will consider how factors of each of these kinds might interact together, but inevitably our conclusions must be tentative here, pointing to the possible interconnections between some variables and the apparent independence of others. No single study can hope to answer all of the questions raised by its subject matter, and we will be satisfied if some of our findings can suggest valuable avenues for other investigations to pursue.

Statistical analyses and presentation of findings

Throughout all our analyses examining possible associations between school features and outcome variables, we have used one of two main types of statistical technique. When the school variables could reasonably be considered in terms of some kind of continuous distribution (as for example with pupil-teacher ratio or frequency of punishment), we *correlated* these variables with the outcome variables. Because most of our measures did not constitute a standard scale with equal intervals between points, we have always used Spearman's rank correlation (see Siegel, 1956) in the first instance. The tables in this and the next two chapters give the rank correlations for the various school features we examined. When rank order correlations are made with twelve schools, a correlation of 0·5 would be obtained by chance only once in twenty times – that is to say there is a 19/20 or 95 per cent probability that the association is a 'real' one. We have followed the usual convention of taking any association with a significance level of 5 per cent or less ($< \cdot 05$) as indicating the likelihood of a 'real' association. When only nine schools are involved, as in the case in any comparison concerning the delinquency outcome, a correlation of ·58 is required in order to reach a 5 per cent level of statistical significance (the figure is higher because with smaller samples rank orders will coincide by chance more often than is the case with large samples).

The second main type of statistical analysis was used when the school variable concerned broad groupings which differed qualitatively (rather than quantitatively with respect to degrees on the same variable). Thus, split and single site schools provided two groups, and sex composition three (boys, girls and co-educational). In these cases we have used the Mann–Whitney 'U' test or the Kruskall–Wallis one-way analysis of variance (see Siegel, 1956). The aim of these tests is basically the same as with the rank correlation, the main difference being that they deal with groups rather than ranks on the school variable. Thus, for example, we were able to test whether the schools in one group (say those in Victorian buildings) differed in outcome from those in another (say those in modern buildings) – the difference (if there was one) would be evident in the average outcome rank (say on pupil behaviour) in the two groups. Once again, as with the rank correlations, we have taken a significance level of 5 per cent as our cut-off point.

One last point to note is that in all our subsequent analyses relating school variables to outcome, the school outcome measures have *already been adjusted for intake variations* (as described in the previous chapter). Having cleared the way in terms of how we dealt with the data we can now turn to the substantive findings.

Status and sex composition of schools

The twelve schools differed on only two main overall administrative features: voluntary-aided or local authority maintained status, and sex composition. The voluntary-aided schools were those with religious affiliations (Roman Catholic or Church of England) and which, because of this, had a degree of autonomy. There were only four such schools in the sample, far too few for any adequate examination of the importance of this distinction in status. However, it did not appear to be a crucial variable within our sample. The voluntary-aided schools tended to have slightly better outcomes than the other schools but the groups overlapped considerably in outcome, and the differences fell well short of statistical significance.

There were no significant differences, either, with respect to sex composition. Delinquency rates, of course, were very much lower among girls than boys, and girls had been excluded from the delinquency out-

(a) *School status and outcome ranks*

	Mean Ranks		Mann–Whitney U Test	
	Voluntary Aided	*Local Authority*	*U*	*p (2-tailed)*
Attendance	4·0	7·8	6	NS
Behaviour	5·8	6·9	13	NS
Academic	5·8	6·9	13	NS
Delinquency	3·8	6·0	5	NS

(b) *Sex composition and outcome ranks*

	Mean Ranks			Kruskal–Wallis one-way analysis of variance	
	Girls	*Boys*	*Mixed*	*H*	*p*
Attendance	7·3	8·3	4·6	2·42	NS
Behaviour	3·7	8·3	6·8	2·83	NS
Academic	4·0	8·3	6·6	2·39	NS

				Mann–Whitney U Test	
				U	*p (2-tailed)*
Delinquency	—	6·8	3·6	3	NS

Table 6.1 *Status and sex composition*

come measure. However, there were no major variations between boys', girls' and mixed schools on any of the other outcomes. There was a trend, which fell short of statistical significance, for better behaviour (on the pupil behaviour scale) in girls' schools than boys' schools. There was a similar non-significant trend for boys in mixed schools to be less delinquent than boys in boys' only schools. A much larger sample than ours would be required to determine whether these slight trends represented real, even if small, differences in outcome. Nevertheless, it was clear that, within these twelve schools, sex composition was of negligible importance in accounting for variations in outcome.

Size and space

As we have seen in Chapter 3, the twelve schools varied in size from about 450 to about 2000 pupils. We classified those with three to five form entries as small, those with six form entries as medium, and those with seven to twelve form entries as large, but size proved to have no significant associations with any of our outcome measures. It was thought that this lack of association might be misleading if the 'psychologically effective' size of schools on two sites would be one of these separate units, rather than the school as a whole. To test this possibility we reclassified all split-site schools as 'small' and re-examined the associations. Again, no significant relationships were found. It may well be that the size of a school does have an impact on its character and style but, at least within our sample, small schools were neither more nor less likely to have favourable outcomes, however it was measured.

(a) *School size and outcome ranks*

	Mean Rank			Kruskal–Wallis one-way analysis of variance	
	Small	*Medium*	*Large*	*H*	*p*
Attendance	7·8	5·7	6·0	0·737	NS
Behaviour	6·5	5·0	7·4	0·831	NS
Academic	8·5	6·0	5·2	1·939	NS
Delinquency	7·5	3·7	4·8	2·411	NS

(b) *Floor and site space and outcome ranks*

	Rank Correlations			
	Floor Space		*Site Space*	
Attendance	−0·45	NS	·06	NS
Behaviour	−0·19	NS	·16	NS
Academic	−0·54	<·05	·30	NS
Delinquency	−0·57	NS	−·07	NS

Table 6.2 *Size and space*

The possible relevance of space was examined using figures made available to us by the ILEA. These dealt with space in two different ways. First, there was the number of pupils per 100 square feet of total floor space. This figure included corridors, offices, halls and gymnasia and hence did not directly reflect teaching space, but it did give a fair indication of the degree of overcrowding of the buildings. The twelve schools had ratios on this formula which ranged from 0·994 to 2·448 – indicating that several were much more crowded than the average of 1·39 children per 100 square feet for London as a whole in 1976. Curiously, this measure of density of occupation emerged as having *negative* relationships with both the academic and delinquency measures – meaning that overcrowded schools tended to have somewhat *better* outcomes. Of course, we would not wish to suggest that overcrowding was actually an advantage, but certainly spacious buildings did not seem to be any kind of prerequisite for successful outcomes.

The other measure of space concerned the number of pupils per 100 square feet of total site (i.e. including playgrounds and the like). This ratio varied from 0·459 to 0·960, and showed no significant associations with any of the four outcomes. Interestingly, this measure did not coincide with the first (the correlation between them was only −0·03). Some of the schools which were best endowed with space within the buildings were rather restricted in terms of overall site area and vice-versa.

Age of buildings and number of sites

The school buildings varied in age from about ten to over a hundred years old. Some of the old buildings were decidedly unattractive and not well designed for contemporary approaches to secondary schooling. Nevertheless, the age of the buildings showed no significant associations with any of the four outcome measures. It is important to mention in this connection that the schools varied greatly in how they responded to the physical conditions available to them. It was striking how very different essentially similar buildings could be made to appear. Some of the older buildings had been made pleasant and attractive places through the imaginative and well planned use of decorations. They appeared smart and well-cared for; other schools, by contrast, had done little to transform their surroundings. Much the same applied to the modern buildings. Some schools had capitalised greatly on the advantages these provided, while others seemed hampered by the limitations of modern architecture. As we will see in the next chapters, these variations in the care and decorations of buildings did prove to be related to outcome, although age, considered alone, did not.

(a) *Age of school buildings and outcome ranks*

| | Mean Ranks | | Mann–Whitney U Test | |
	Old	Modern	U	p
Attendance	7·2	5·8	14	NS
Behaviour	5·2	7·8	10	NS
Academic	6·8	6·2	16	NS
Delinquency	4·8	5·2	9	NS

(b) *Split and single sites and outcome*

| | Mean Ranks | | Mann–Whitney U Test | |
	Split Sites	Single Sites	U	p
Attendance	5·5	7·0	12	NS
Behaviour	3·0	8·3	2	< ·05
Academic	5·5	7·0	12	NS
Delinquency	1·5	6·0	0	<·001

Table 6.3 *Buildings*

The findings concerning split site schools were unexpected. There were no differences between single and split site schools in terms of either attendance or academic attainment, but on both the pupil behaviour and delinquency outcomes split site schools had better results. We would not wish to place too much reliance on these findings, particularly as our sample of schools included only four on split sites. Nevertheless, the results were interesting and thought-provoking, especially in view of the manifest *dis*advantages of split sites from the teachers' point of view. Our findings on school size (see above) suggest that the effective reduction in size of each unit in split site schools was not the crucial factor. Perhaps, instead, the findings mean that with careful planning, separate sites can be turned to advantage by using them to create separate environments, particularly adapted to the needs of specific age groups of children. Whatever the explanation, split sites had clearly not prevented our schools from achieving good outcomes for their pupils.

Staff provision and class size

We examined staffing ratios to determine how far a favourable

| | Rank Correlations | | | |
	Pupil/Teacher Ratio		Class Size	
Attendance	−0·38	NS	−0·24	NS
Behaviour	0·16	NS	0·33	NS
Academic	−0·01	NS	0·01	NS
Delinquency	−0·18	NS	0·11	NS

Table 6.4 *Pupil/Teacher ratio, class size, and outcome ranks*

pupil:teacher ratio might predispose to better outcomes. The ratio in all twelve schools was generous by comparison with national figures (see Pratt, 1978) and the variation between schools was quite small. The number of children per teacher at different schools (averaged over the three years 1975/6, 1976/7 and 1977/8) ranged from 14·02 to 16·30. School rankings on this measure showed no significant association with outcome. What minimal trend there was indicated that attendance tended to be better in schools with *more* children per teacher − but this relationship fell well short of statistical significance.

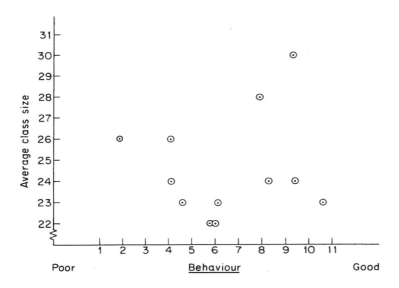

Figure 6.1 *Class size (third-year academic lessons) and behaviour score*

Of course, these analyses were concerned with staff provision for the school as a whole, and there is no necessary link with the size of teaching groups. To examine the possibility that the size of individual classes might be important, we looked at the association between pupil behaviour and the size of the class in third year academic lessons (see Figure 6.1). No significant association was found (rank correlation of 0·14) in spite of variations in class size from 22 to 30.

Internal organisation

Before leaving these questions of physical and administrative features, it is convenient to discuss some further variables which fall between the broad externally imposed factors we have been discussing up to now, and the more detailed aspects of school life we will be concerned with in the next chapter. These relate to the systems of pastoral care in the schools, and the groupings of the children for teaching purposes.

Our sample of twelve schools included both year and house based systems for the organisation of pastoral care. No differences were found between these two systems with respect to any of the four outcome measures; it appeared that either system could be operated successfully as a general framework, and neither appeared to have any particular over-riding advantages.

(a) *Pastoral organisation and outcome ranks*

	Mean Ranks		Mann–Whitney U Test	
	House systems	Year systems	U	p (2-tailed)
Attendance	6·3	6·6	13	NS
Behaviour	7·3	6·2	11	NS
Academic	6·7	6·4	13	NS
Delinquency	4·7	5·2	8	NS

(b) *Academic organisation and outcome ranks*

	Streamed	Banded	Mixed Ability	Kruskal–Wallis one-way analysis of variance	
				H	p
Attendance	6·71	6·67	5·50	0·18	NS
Behaviour	5·86	7·00	8·00	0·63	NS
Academic	7·43	4·67	6·00	1·28	NS
Delinquency	5·40	5·50	3·50	3·78	NS

Table 6.5 *Pastoral and academic organisation*

We had less variety within our sample in terms of academic groupings. The majority of the schools operated some form of streamed or banded system, and only two had developed mixed ability teaching to any major extent at the time of the study. Such variations as we did have within the twelve did not discriminate in terms of any of the outcome measures.

We must, of course, reiterate the point that our study was *not* designed to focus specifically on factors of this kind, and our sample could not allow us to draw any detailed conclusions about them. A comparison of schools with more widely differing pupil: teacher ratios, for example, might well find this to be a very important variable. Our concern in the present chapter has simply been to establish whether the outcome variations between the schools directly followed the lines of any of these broad administrative or physical differences. With the possible exception of the split site question, the findings clearly show that they did not, and suggest that it was possible for schools to operate effectively using a variety of administrative arrangements, and in spite of apparently unpromising premises. The most immediately obvious factors which differentiated between the schools had thus failed to offer any pointers to account for the outcome variations. In the next chapter we will discuss the more detailed school process measures, and the relationships which they showed with the outcomes.

7

School processes: associations with outcome

As outlined earlier, the term 'processes' is used to refer to those features of the social organisation of school life which create the context for teaching and learning, and which seem likely to affect the nature of the school experience for both staff and pupils. We explored many aspects of these features, examining first the extent to which schools did vary in the kinds of environments they provided for their pupils, and secondly whether these variations were associated with the differences between schools in outcome, described in Chapter 5.

The data on school processes derive from the interviews with teachers, pupils' responses to the questionnaire we had given them, and our systematic observations in classrooms, playgrounds and other parts of the school. The majority of individual questions or observation categories were treated as separate process items (although in a few cases small numbers were combined to form short scales). This produced a large pool of items, each of which had to be tested in a number of different ways to establish whether it might contribute to our understanding of school influences.

The first stage in this procedure involved the elimination from the pool of any items which were not reliable, in the sense that two observers or two raters could not agree on the score for each school.

Secondly, we discarded items which were the same or closely similar in all schools. As our aim was to examine the reasons for outcome *differences* between the schools, process items which failed to differentiate between them were not relevant.

Thirdly, we checked the extent to which *different* measures of what appeared to be the *same* variable produced similar findings. This was done in two ways: by looking at intercorrelations between variables (see Appendix E), and by determining whether the correlations with outcome were similar.

The fourth, and principal, stage consisted of examining the associations between each process item and each of the four outcome measures. We used rank correlations for this purpose, once again taking the 0·05 (5 per cent) level of significance to indicate which associations were unlikely to have arisen by chance alone. This chapter will be primarily concerned with those items which *did* prove to be significantly associated with outcome, but we also draw attention to all important variables which did *not* correlate with outcome (as it is often as important to know what is not relevant as what is). In this way we could begin to build up a picture of the features of school practice and functioning which distinguished between the more successful and less successful schools. We could not, of course, take these significant associations as implying causation. Firm conclusions on causative influences can only come from experimental studies. Nevertheless, by considering associations between process and outcome only after controlling statistically for intake differences, and by examining the patterns of correlations, it is possible to suggest how and why the process items *might* be important in the school context.

The study was not designed to test any one particular theory about schooling, nor was our analysis based on any preconceived ideas about which particular aspects of school process *should* be important. Instead, we used a rather wide ranging approach including and testing many items relevant to a variety of theoretical notions.

For ease of presentation the findings are discussed in terms of seven broad conceptual areas: academic emphasis, teacher actions in lessons, rewards and punishments, pupil conditions, children's responsibilities and participation in the school, stability of teaching and friendship groups, and staff organisation. However, the decisions on which items go under which heading were occasionally rather arbitrary and in a few instances, where it seems particularly appropriate to do so, the same item is considered under two headings. Full details of all the items are given in Appendix E.

Academic emphasis

Although we did not attempt to study the curriculum or the content of classroom teaching as such, we were concerned to assess the extent to which schools placed an emphasis on academic matters. We examined this issue both by determining what was actually done, and by asking teachers about their attitudes and values. Table 7.1 summarises the

		Correlations with outcomes*		
Item	Att.	Beh.	Acad.	Del.
1. Homework observed during the 1st year lessons	0·40	*0·76*	0·41	0·42
2. Homework as reported by 3rd year maths and English teachers	0·49	0·46	*0·61*	0·32
3. Teachers' setting of homework checked	0·49	0·16	*0·52*	0·50
4. % of 3rd year class expected to gain 'O' level in English and maths	*0·57*	0·18	*0·55*	0·22
5. Children's work displayed on walls	0·34	0·17	*0·50*	0·42
6. Total teaching time per week	*0·63*	0·06	0·35	0·46
7. Head teacher's reported pastoral emphasis (negative relationship)	0·38	*0·60*	0·20	0·45
8. Children's reported use of school library	*0·52*	0·43	*0·64*	0·55
9. Group or supervised course planning	*0·66*	0·14	0·35	*0·78*
10. Teachers teaching own subject only (negative relationship)	0·40	*0·67*	0·28	*0·67*

Table 7.1 *Academic emphasis and outcome*
* Significant correlations are shown in italics

correlational findings with respect to the main ten variables which emerged in this area of academic, or 'instrumental' emphasis.

In some respects, the most obvious indication of a school's attitude to academic work is provided by its use of homework. We had

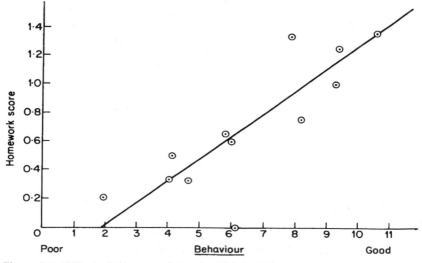

Figure 7.1 *Homework (first-year lessons) and behaviour score*

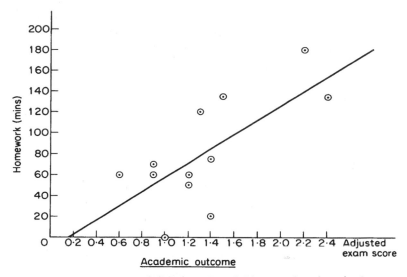

Figure 7.2 *Third-year homework (Maths and English) per week and academic outcome*

measures on this from our own observations, from teacher interviews and from pupil questionnaires. The results from all these sources gave much the same picture and, therefore, we have included only three measures here. The findings show that schools which set homework frequently and where there was some kind of check on whether staff did in fact set it, tended to have better outcomes than schools which made little use of homework. The relationship with outcome was evident with both pupils' behaviour in school (as shown in Figure 7.1 which uses our classroom observations on whether homework was either set or returned), and with scholastic attainment (as shown in Figure 7.2 which is based on the reports of the third year Maths and English teachers on how many minutes of homework they gave the class each week).*

The average time spent on homework (as reported by the pupils themselves) was not very great in any of the schools; for the fifth year

---

* One of the drawbacks of rank correlations is that, by definition, they can provide no indication of the size of the *actual* differences between schools on any particular measure (because all differences are treated as equivalent in the procedure of ranking them). To provide this information we have used graphs which give the actual scores of each school on both the process and the outcome variable. The way to read these graphs was described on page 72 in Chapter 5. In this and subsequent figures, a regression line from bottom left to top right indicates a positive association.

pupils the amounts of time spent on homework per evening ranged from an average of a quarter of an hour in one school to thirty-five minutes in another.

The findings, of course, do not show how and why homework is associated with better outcomes. But it may well be that in addition to its practical value in providing opportunities for the consolidation of the learning of work introduced in school time, homework may also be of symbolic importance in emphasising the school's concern for academic progress, and its expectation that pupils have the ability and self-discipline needed to work without direct supervision.

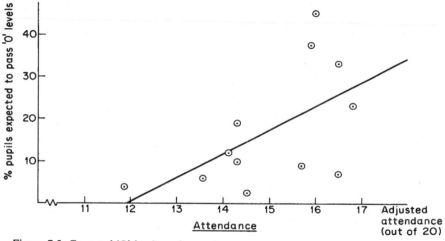

Figure 7.3 *Expected 'O' levels and attendance outcome*

Another aspect of academic emphasis concerns teachers' expectations for their pupils. We asked the Maths and English teachers of the third year middle ability class we observed to tell us how many of these children they expected to get either 'O' level passes or CSE grade ones in each subject. Schools varied markedly in the proportions of children expected to gain these qualifications (from 2·5 per cent to 45 per cent) and school scores on this measure were found to correlate significantly with both attendance and academic outcome (see Figure 7.3). Of course, it could be suggested that this was no more than a reflection of the fact that teachers are good judges of children's abilities. This could not be the whole explanation, for when we compared teacher expectations with the intakes in the schools, we found that two of the schools in the *bottom* third with respect to academic expectation were in the *top* third with respect to the children's measured abilities at intake. It is perhaps difficult for teachers to know how their pupils compare with children at other similar schools, and as a result they may develop inappropriate expectations as to what children can achieve. It seems probable that these expectations will be transmitted to the children who will then show some tendency to conform to their teachers' views of their expected attainments.

We also found that schools which displayed a lot of the children's work on the classroom walls tended to have a better academic outcome. It seems likely that this practice could influence pupils in several different ways – by stressing the academic side of the school, by encouraging children to work well and rewarding them by displaying their work, and by making the school a more visually attractive place. Secondary schools are often a striking contrast to primary schools in this respect. It is also interesting to note that we found an *inverse* relationship between the amount of pupils' work and other material on display in school, and the amount of graffiti we observed in the buildings (correlation of −0·61). Anxieties are often expressed that any material displayed in schools – pupils' work, pictures or posters – will quickly become damaged or defaced. The findings here suggest that this need not be the case, and indeed that visual displays of various kinds were positively related to outcome (see also section on Pupil Conditions, p. 126).

A further measure under the heading of academic emphasis concerned the proportion of the school week devoted to teaching. There are many other activities (such as assemblies, registration and form time), and the total *teaching* time per week in the twelve schools varied between 21·9 and 24·2 hours. This showed a positive relationship with pupil attendance.

The proportion of children who reported using the school library during the previous week related to both attendance and academic outcome. This may indicate that the school had encouraged the children to read for their own pleasure, but also to be responsible for and trusted with school property. All the schools had good libraries and some went to considerable expense to ensure that they were open after school and in the dinner hour. On average one child in three had used the library during the previous week but this varied from 17 per cent in one school to 56 per cent in another (see Figure 7.4).

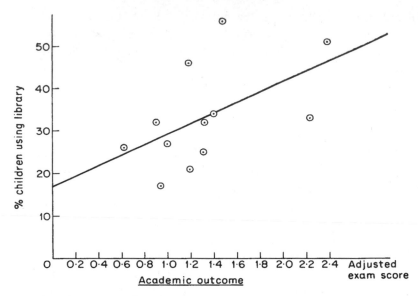

Figure 7.4 *Library use and academic outcome*

One possibly paradoxical finding which emerged from this analysis was the negative relationship between pupil behaviour and the head teacher's pastoral emphasis as reported at interview. This finding might be explained in two ways. First, it is possible that schools which put a great deal of emphasis on pastoral care did not have sufficient resources left to put an equal emphasis into the academic side of the school. Hence the positive benefits which a concern with academic matters brings were lost. Alternatively, the negative association could relate to the fact that the less successful schools generally had more day to day behavioural difficulties with their pupils. This might mean that they were quite justified in putting more emphasis on pastoral matters, as they had more pastoral problems to solve than did the more successful schools.

The final topics to be considered under the heading of academic emphasis concern the planning of courses and teaching of lessons. The teachers in the schools which were more successful in terms of good attendance and low delinquency were much less likely to report that they had absolute freedom in planning their course (see Figure 7.5). In these schools, planning was a group matter, generally based on departments, with the head of department both monitoring and ad-

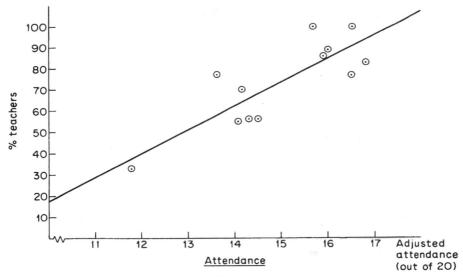

Figure 7.5 *Teachers reporting 'group' planning and attendance outcome*

vising on the department's curriculum planning. In the less successful schools, teachers worked on their own to a much greater extent, with the consequence that often there was little coordination between teachers in the same department. The second finding, that teachers in schools with better outcomes on behaviour and delinquency tended to teach more than one subject is interesting, and might be a reflection of the greater coordination between teachers in these schools. Some schools taught integrated programmes which demanded that all teachers taught a range of related subjects. However, in other successful schools this was not the explanation, as teachers taught two subjects just because of timetable problems or an imbalance in the expertise of the staff group. It should be noted that this relationship was with pupil behaviour rather than with the academic outcome. A lack of specialised teachers at the top of the school might well lead to poor academic attainment. In the twelve schools these 'general' teachers usually only taught the younger children.

A small number of other measures which might be thought to be associated with academic emphasis did not relate to any of the outcomes. The proportion of children who reported that they would consult (or had consulted) a teacher about a work problem did not vary greatly between schools, and was unrelated to outcome. Teachers' reports on their hours of work preparation, on problems with the timetable, and on the checking of their record books also did not correlate with outcome.

The findings as a whole, however, suggest that children tended to make better progress both behaviourally and academically, in schools which placed an appropriate emphasis on academic matters. This emphasis might be reflected in a well planned curriculum, in the kinds of expectations teachers had of the children they taught, and in the setting and marking of homework. It is also relevant, perhaps, that when we asked pupils what they thought were the most important goals or functions of schooling, they consistently selected 'instrumental' goals such as examination success and preparation for jobs. Evidently, schools which organised their approach to ensure some emphasis on academic matters not only achieved better results but also were more likely to be fulfilling their pupils' expectations.

It should be noted, however, that the 'academic emphasis' items were intercorrelated only to a rather weak extent (see Table E.1 in Appendix E). This may imply either that the concept is not a very cohesive one, or that there are many different ways to emphasise academic concern, so that it matters less which *particular* method is used, than that the emphasis is provided by some means.

Teacher actions in lessons

This leads on to a more detailed consideration of teacher actions as assessed during our systematic observations of one week's lessons with a third year class in each school.

Measures	Att.	Correlations with Outcomes Beh.	Ac.	Del.
11. Teacher on 'topic'	0·39	0·72	0·14	0·50
12. Teacher on 'equipment'	0·30	0·62	0·20	0·47
13. '% lessons ending early – 3rd yr.	0·58	0·58	0·57	0·52
14. Disciplinary intervention – 3rd yr. lessons	0·10	0·66	0·18	0·13
15. Disciplinary intervention – 1st yr. lessons	0·06	0·55	0·41	−0·05
16. Silence – 3rd yr. lessons	0·37	0·60	0·19	0·23
17. Interaction style – 3rd yr. lessons	0·50	0·52	0·52	0·32

Table 7.2 *Teacher actions in lessons and outcome*

We recorded the proportion of the teacher's time spent on the subject matter of the lesson (as distinct from setting up equipment, handing out papers, dealing with disciplinary problems and so on). The average time per school spent on the lesson topic itself varied from 65 per cent to over 85 per cent. It was found that pupil behaviour was better in schools with a high proportion of 'topic' time per lesson. It should be noted that the association was with children's behaviour rather than with their scholastic attainment. This suggests that the importance of the item lies in its implications regarding group management, rather than in the scholastic benefits of increased instruction time.

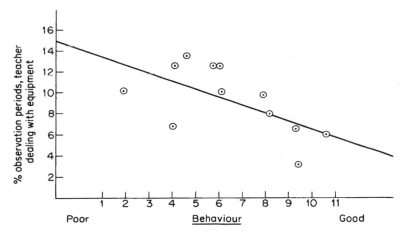

Figure 7.6 *Teacher's time on equipment and behaviour score*

Of course, it might be argued that the association merely represents teachers' responses to behavioural disruption. If they are having to spend time dealing with problem behaviour, inevitably there will be less time for teaching. This may well be part of the story, but it certainly does not constitute the whole explanation. Figure 7.6 illustrates a further point.* This shows the significant association between the proportion of teacher time spent setting up equipment or handing out materials and pupil behaviour. School averages here varied from 2 per

---

* In this figure, unlike previous ones, the regression line runs on the diagonal from top left to bottom right. This simply indicates that the correlation was significantly *negative*, rather than positive. In this case the figure shows that the *less* time spent on equipment, the *better* was pupil behaviour.

cent to 13 per cent of the teacher's time, and behaviour was worse when the proportion was high. This is probably because when teachers spend a lot of time distributing resources or organising things *after* the children are all assembled and the lesson should have begun, they are likely to lose the attention of the class. This may then make disruptive behaviour more likely to occur.

Interestingly, the measure of time spent on the lesson topic was not significantly associated with academic success. An attentive well-behaved class provides the opportunity for effective teaching and productive learning. What *use* is made of this opportunity, however, will be crucial in determining just what and how much the children learn.

The same consideration probably also applies to the next finding, which concerned one aspect of the style of teaching in the classroom. Most of the academic subject lessons we observed were taught using a fairly formal class-based approach. Within this context, it was found that teachers in the more successful schools spent higher proportions of their time interacting with the class as a whole, rather than with individual pupils (see Figure 7.7). We had several different measures of these differences in interaction style, all of which gave very similar results. The measure shown here relates to the overall rate of interaction with individuals (rather than with groups or the class as a whole),

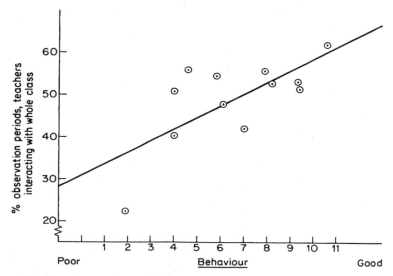

Figure 7.7 *Class interactions and behaviour score*

regardless of the content of the interaction. Higher proportions of time spent with the whole class were associated with better outcomes in terms of attendance, behaviour and academic attainment.

Relatively inexperienced teachers in all schools seemed to have difficulty in maintaining contact with the class as a group, and were particularly likely to concentrate on individuals, either to give specific instructions on work or to deal with disruptive behaviour. The effect of this focus on the individual was often to lose the interest and attention of other members of the class, with adverse consequences in terms of the children's behaviour. The same tendency also seemed to distinguish in a rather more general way between the approaches used by the majority of teachers in the more and less successful schools. In the schools with less satisfactory behaviour and less good exam results even the more experienced teachers tended to focus unhelpfully on the individual to the detriment of overall class management.

In a similar way, lessons in the successful schools more frequently included periods of quiet work when the teachers expected the pupils to work in silence. Once again, these differences could not be accounted for simply by differing levels of experience amongst the particular teachers observed.

It should be appreciated that these findings do *not* mean that an individualised approach to teaching is a bad thing. We observed so few lessons in academic subjects (10 out of 312) explicitly organised in terms of individual rather than group instruction that we can draw no conclusions about the relative merits or demerits of these two approaches to teaching. Certainly, the very few lessons set up for individualised instruction and being taken by experienced teachers worked well, but the sample is far too small for any conclusions to be drawn. What the results *do* show, however, is that *if* the class is set up for group teaching, it is important to teach in a way which keeps the whole group involved. The implications concern the social psychology of groups rather than the style of pedagogy.

It also appeared that frequent disciplinary interventions in the classroom were associated with worse behaviour (see Figure 7.8). Once again, it is difficult to disentangle cause and effect, as the teachers' interventions were designed to deal with behaviour which disrupted the class. Nevertheless, it does seem that a form of teacher response which results in innumerable interruptions to the flow of the lesson and which involves constant checking and reprimand may serve

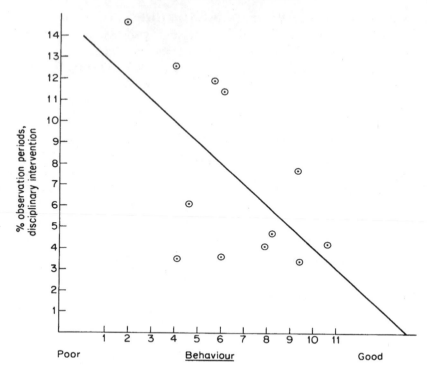

Figure 7.8 *Disciplinary intervention (third-year academic lessons) and behaviour score*

to perpetuate behavioural disturbance. If so, this is likely to be both because the interventions disrupt the attention and interest of the rest of the class, and because of the negative atmosphere they create.

The timing of lessons also proved to be related to pupil outcomes (see Figure 7.9). Schools varied greatly in the proportion of lessons which finished early (the range extended from none to almost half of all lessons in the week of our observations). There was a quite strong tendency for this to be associated with worse outcomes for the children not only in terms of behaviour, but also with respect to attendance and academic attainment. Conversely, schools where most lessons started promptly tended to have better outcomes with better behaviour. This staff concern with timekeeping could be seen both as setting models for the children and expressing school values. Taken together, these items relating to teacher actions in the classroom suggest that even at this very detailed day-to-day level, the schools varied considerably and that many of these variations were associated with much longer-term out-

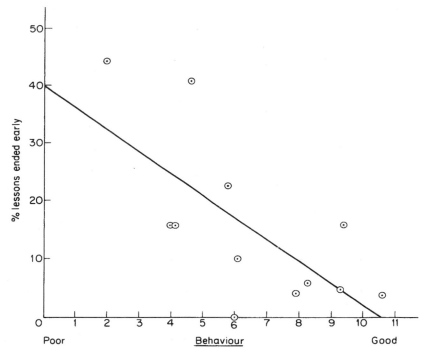

Figure 7.9 *Lessons ended early and behaviour score*

comes. A cooperative and productive atmosphere in the classroom is clearly a crucial starting point for effective teaching and learning, and likely to make an important contribution to positive pupil outcomes. While much obviously rests on the individual teacher here, the findings on the variations between *schools* raise the interesting possibility that the wider organisation of the school as a whole may provide considerable support for the teacher. We will return to this possibility later.

Rewards and punishments

Information on a wide range of incentives and rewards and all kinds of sanctions and punishments was obtained both by asking individual pupils about their experiences and also by systematic observations in the classroom and elsewhere. The particular types of rewards and punishments used varied considerably between the twelve schools;

some had formal systems of detentions or credit marks whilst others had more informal, less clearly defined approaches.

Pooling all these different possibilities together, however, the first striking finding was that, for a similar period of time, pupils across the whole sample reported on average three times as many instances of punishments as of rewards. The classroom observations showed a ratio of about 2 to 1. Thus, in third year classes there was an average of six reprimands per lesson compared with only three instances of praise.

The ways in which rewards and punishments relate to outcome are best considered separately.

Punishment

Most of the associations between levels of punishment and outcome were weak, and not statistically significant. Thus, there was no association between the average number of detentions received by the children and any of the various measures of outcome (see Figure 7.10). Indeed, the schools with the best behavioural outcome included both those with the highest and those with the lowest use of detention. The number of times 'lines' or extra work were given out by teachers as a form of punishment showed no association with behavioural outcome (or attendance or academic attainment), but schools with a high level of 'lines' did tend to have lower levels of delinquency. Schools in which a larger proportion of children were reprimanded by the head teacher tended to have worse outcomes with respect to attendance.

We used a set of examples of difficult or worrying behaviour (the 'Ten Naughty Children' scale – see Appendix C) to assess teachers' at-

		Correlations with Outcome		
Measures	Att.	Behav.	Ac.	Del.
18. Pupils told off by the Head (negative relationship)	0·59	0·26	0·49	0·48
19. Group based discipline standards	0·17	0·47	0·64	0·62
20. No. of detentions	0·15	0·03	−0·27	0·47
21. No. of lines or extra work given	0·41	0·04	0·03	0·62
22. Corporal punishment (negative relationship)	0·04	0·48	0·44	0·22
23. Ten Naughty Children scale	0·11	0·61	0·04	0·50

Table 7.3 *Punishment and outcome*

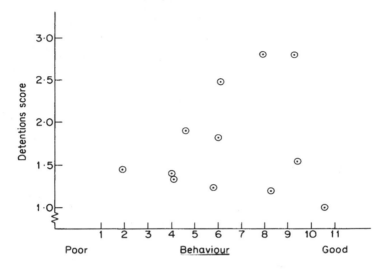

Figure 7.10 *Detentions and behaviour score*

titudes and approaches to discipline. The findings showed that there was a significant tendency for teachers in schools with better behaviour to report a disciplinary rather than a 'welfare' approach to problems. However, very few teachers said that they would take severe disciplinary action and for most of the ten examples the usual report was that their response would be either 'no action' or some minor disciplinary action.

Teachers were also asked whether there were general standards of classroom discipline expected at the school. The proportion of teachers who reported that discipline standards were based on general expectations set by the school (or house or department), rather than left to the individual, varied by school from 30 per cent to 100 per cent. Academic and delinquency outcomes were significantly better in schools where discipline was group based in this way. The particular rules and approaches to discipline may be less important than the existence of some generally recognised and accepted set of standards.

The findings for corporal punishment and pupil behaviour are shown in Figure 7.11. Overall, there was a tendency (which fell just short of statistical significance) for *high* levels of corporal punishment to be associated with rather *worse* behaviour. If the one school with exceptionally high levels of corporal punishment (and a moderate

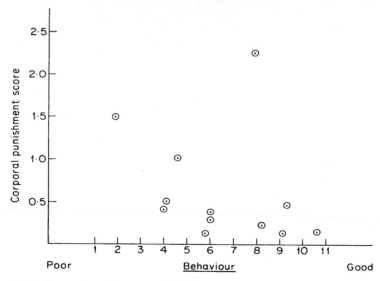

Figure 7.11 *Corporal punishment and behaviour score*

behaviour score) is excluded the correlation becomes statistically significant.

In summary, the pattern of associations between punishment and outcome are generally weak and inconsistent. Insofar as any kind of overall statement is possible, it may be said that these findings (together with those already discussed on disciplinary interactions in the classroom) *suggest* the possibility that children's behaviour is most likely to be good in schools when there is an agreed disciplinary approach, but not too much actual use of punishment. An extensive use of corporal punishment may also carry some disadvantages. However, these tentative inferences are based on uncertain trends and the stronger conclusion must be that variations in levels of punishment were *not* of crucial importance with respect to outcome. On the whole, in schools with particularly high levels of punishment this seemed to have become an institutionalised part of school life with no obvious benefits, but equally no overriding disadvantages.

The one exception to this generally inconclusive pattern of associations concerned teachers' use of *unofficial* physical punishments, such as slaps or cuffing. The rates of these unofficial sanctions were generally very low, especially in girls' and mixed schools, and because of this Figure 7.12 departs from the usual

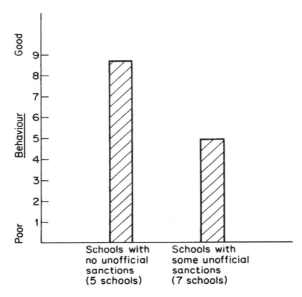

Figure 7.12 *Unofficial sanctions and behaviour score*

pattern, and simply groups the schools according to whether or not unofficial sanctions were observed. It is clear that in schools where they were at all frequent, pupil behaviour was correspondingly worse. We may speculate that teacher actions of this kind might set models of violence for the pupils. Also, unofficial sanctions of this kind may breed resentment in the children just because they are unofficial.

Rewards and praise

While the links between punishment and outcome were rather variable, those between rewards and outcome were more consistent. All forms of reward, praise or appreciation tended to be associated with better outcomes.

We assessed these in several different ways. First, we noted the extent to which children were praised for work in the classroom. The absolute levels of praise observed in lessons were rather low: the average across all schools being only three or four instances of positive comment by teachers in any one lesson. However, in those schools where staff took more opportunities to praise pupils' work, outcomes were substantially better with respect to both behaviour and delinquency (see Figure 7.13).

	Correlation with Outcome			
	Att.	*Beh.*	*Ac.*	*Del.*
24. % pupils named for work in assembly	0·32	*0·76*	0·37	0·30
25. % 'topic' praise in lessons	·0·39	*0·76*	0·34	*0·87*
5. Children's work on walls	0·34	0·17	*0·50*	0·42
26. Pupils receiving prizes for sport	*0·52*	0·08	0·22	0·13
27. Pupils receiving prizes for work	0·02	0·34	−0·06	−0·10

Table 7.4 *Rewards and outcomes*

Frequent public praise for good work or behaviour by commending individual children in assembly or other meetings was also associated with better pupil behaviour (as shown in Figure 7.14). The giving of prizes for sport to a larger proportion of children was associated with better attendance, but not with better outcomes on the other measures. Formal prizes for work showed only a weak and inconsistent association with outcome. It is relevant to note that formal prizes differ from other forms of reward in reaching a smaller proportion of children, in

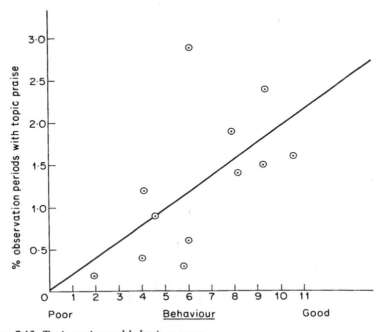

Figure 7.13 *Topic praise and behaviour score*

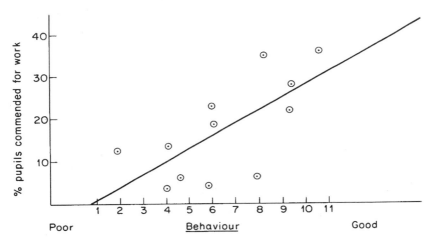

Figure 7.14 *Public commendation for work and behaviour score*

occurring less frequently, and in being given long after the event. All these elements are likely to detract from their values as incentives or encouragements.

Another form of positive feedback to children is provided by the display of their work on classroom walls (as already mentioned with respect to academic emphasis). This could be seen as a means of the school showing appreciation of the value of the pupils' work – and hence an indirect form of reward or encouragement. Schools which

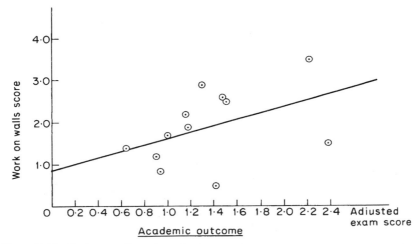

Figure 7.15 *Work on walls and academic outcome*

used much display of pupils' work tended to have a somewhat better level of exam success (see Figure 7.15). The associations with other measures of outcome were in the same direction but fell short of statistical significance.

The use of some sanctions is clearly an essential element in any school organisation, but taking the findings on rewards and punishments together, the results do tend to suggest that the balance between punishments and rewards may be less than helpful in some schools. It may be difficult to design systems of rewards which will maintain their value and appeal to secondary school pupils, and especially to the oldest age groups. Where this had been attempted in the schools we studied, the results appeared to be positive, in contrast to the findings on punishment which suggested low, and generally rather negative, relationships with outcomes.

Pupil conditions

Quite apart from rewards or praise for specific pieces of work or behaviour, schools varied in the extent to which they went out of their way to provide a pleasant and comfortable environment for the children. It might be expected that good working conditions would help to encourage pupils to appreciate the school and hence possibly to identify with its goals. To investigate this possibility we developed a fourteen item scale of general conditions, which included items such as freedom to use the buildings during breaks and the lunch period, access to a telephone, and the availability of hot drinks. High scores on

	Correlations and Outcome			
	Att.	*Beh.*	*Ac.*	*Del.*
28. Proportion of children who would consult teacher about personal problem	*0·52*	0·29	*0·69*	−0·05
29. Number of outings	−0·04	0·44	*0·55*	−0·22
30. Pupil conditions scale	0·21	0·37	*0·59*	0·07
31. School decorations and care of buildings	0·02	*0·64*	0·32	0·12
32. Teachers report seeing children at any time	0·27	*0·64*	0·32	0·29
33. No. of children seen in previous 2 weeks	−0·02	*0·51*	0·28	0·28

Table 7.5 *Pupil conditions and outcome*

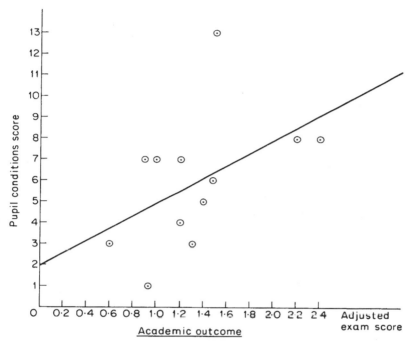

Figure 7.16 *Pupil conditions score and academic outcome*

this scale were associated with better rates of exam success (see Figure 7.16). The associations with other forms of outcome were much weaker and statistically insignificant.

Other aspects of pleasant working conditions were covered by a separate five point scale which dealt with the care and decorations of both the classroom and the school generally. This was based on our own observations of cleanliness and tidiness of classrooms and the use of plants, posters and pictures. It correlated significantly with pupil behaviour (see Figure 7.17) but not to an appreciable extent with other outcomes.

We also considered extracurricular school activities as other possible indicators of conditions for pupils. Most such items (including out of school clubs and other activities) did not differentiate between schools with good and poor outcomes (however measured). However, one, the provision of school outings, was significantly correlated with examination success. Interestingly, once again it showed only low insignificant correlations with other measures of outcome.

Figure 7.17 *Decorations of classroom and behaviour score*

A further indication of pupil conditions, or rather of how pupils felt about school, was provided by their reported willingness to approach staff for advice and help. The pupils were asked whether, if they needed to, they would talk to a member of staff about a personal problem. In the schools with better attendance and academic attainment, a higher proportion of pupils said that they would (see Figure 7.18). On the

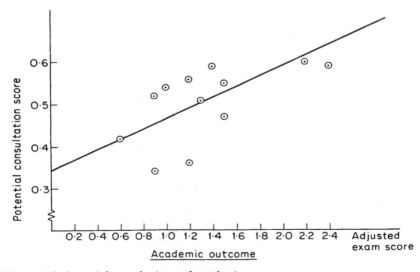

Figure 7.18 *Potential consultation and academic outcome*

whole, children were more willing to consult a teacher about personal difficulties in schools with a counsellor or a teacher with special pastoral responsibilities. However, it is important to note that in these schools children were more likely to approach and talk about their concerns to *ordinary* teachers, as well as to counsellors. In the schools with a better behavioural outcome, a higher proportion of teachers both reported that they would see children about a problem at any time (not just at fixed times) and also that a higher proportion of children had been seen during the previous two weeks. It appears that the schools which make formal provisions for pastoral care (which probably reaches only the small number of children with the most marked problems) are also likely to have teachers who are seen by the pupils as more approachable and who actually do talk to more children about problems.

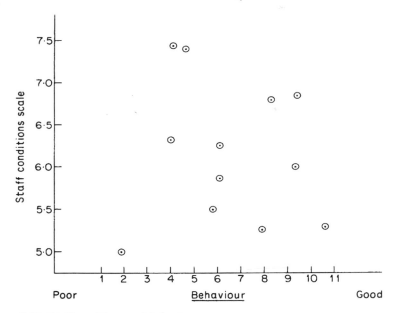

Figure 7.19 *Staff conditions and behaviour score*

It is interesting to note that *teachers'* conditions of work (at least as assessed on the items which we looked at) did not appear to relate to outcomes for the children. We developed a twelve item scale based on features such as the free periods available, adequate equipment and clerical help, own storage space, and the existence of a departmental office or room (see Appendix E). The schools varied considerably in their provision for teachers, although there was also much variation between teachers in the same school in their conditions of work (see Figure 7.19). The *school* differences were generally unrelated to any of the pupil outcomes, but it must be remembered that all the schools in this study were within the same education authority so that variation might not be very great compared with schools in different areas of the country. Also, one item, adequacy of clerical help, considered under staff organisation (see below), did relate to behavioural outcome.

Responsibilities and participation

Another area of school life which proved to be important in relation to outcome was that dealing with children's opportunities to take responsibilities and to participate in the running of their school lives.

		Correlations with Outcome		
	Att.	Beh.	Acad.	Del.
34. Proportion of children who had been form captain (or equivalent)	0·37	0·64	0·78	0·35
35. Pupils caring for their own resources	0·51	0·72	0·27	0·80
36. Participation in assembly or house/year meeting	0·22	0·63	0·62	0·25
37. Contributions to charity	0·52	0·48	0·17	0·38

Table 7.6 *Responsibilities participation and outcome*

We looked at these issues in several different ways. Thus, we asked pupils whether they had ever been form captain or homework monitor, or held a similar position in their class. The proportion of children who had ever held one of these posts of responsibility varied greatly from school to school – the range extended from 7 per cent to 50 per cent and the proportion in each school correlated significantly with both pupil behaviour and academic success (see Figure 7.20). The findings suggest that there are likely to be benefits in ensuring that a high *proportion* of pupils have opportunities to hold some kind of post of responsibility.

Pupils were also asked whether they had ever taken a special part in a school assembly or a house or year meeting. Schools with a higher pupil participation in these activities had significantly better behavioural and academic outcomes (see Figure 7.21). The proportion

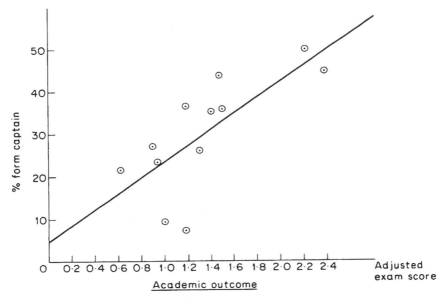

Figure 7.20 *Form captain and academic outcome*

of children who had contributed to a collection for charity organised by the school correlated just significantly with attendance. We also asked about participation in lunch hour clubs, school and house sport, and after-school activities but, although schools varied on these items, the differences did not relate to outcome. It is not clear why this should

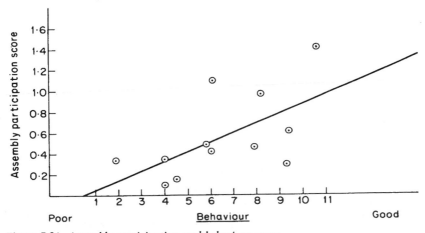

Figure 7.21 *Assembly participation and behaviour score*

be, but possibly these activities tend to be somewhat separated from the mainstream of school life.

In our systematic observations of third year lessons, we made a regular note of whether pupils brought and took away their own books, folders and writing materials. There was an immense variation between schools in the proportion of academic lessons in which pupils looked after their own resources – the range extended from 3 per cent to 79 per cent. It was striking that the schools in which children were expected to take responsibility for their own things had better out-comes with respect to attendance, behaviour and delinquency.

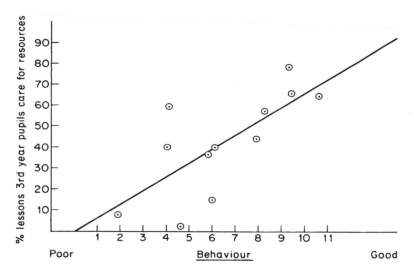

Figure 7.22 *Pupils caring for resources and behaviour score*

Once more, of course, there is the problem of which leads to which. Probably the influences work both ways. Doubtless some of the limitations on participation and responsibility resulted from the irresponsible behaviour shown by pupils. The schools which provided the least opportunity for participation and responsibility were *not*, however, ones with particularly difficult or disadvantaged intakes of pupils. It appears that the schools' giving of responsibility may be in part a reaction to pupil behaviour; but that it also plays a part in developing an overall school climate, which itself helps to shape pupil behaviour.

Stability of teaching and friendship groups

We looked at two rather different aspects of group stability within schools; teacher continuity and stability of peer groups.

Teacher continuity

First, we looked at teacher continuity in terms of the number of English teachers and the number of form (or set) teachers experienced in the school by all fifth year pupils. We focused in the first instance on fifth year pupils as they had been in the school the longest, with the

Measures	Att.	Correlations with Outcome Beh.	Ac.	Del.
38. Stability of 3rd year maths and English teachers (negative relationship)	−0·14	0·54	0·11	0·42
39. 5th year continuity (negative relationship)	0·06	0·53	0·31	−0·13

Table 7.7 *Teacher continuity and outcome*

consequence that any differences between schools in teacher continuity would be most likely to be evident. There were considerable differences between the schools, but the measure showed no association with academic outcome (or attendance or delinquency), although there was a just significant negative association with pupil behaviour. Figure 7.23 shows that there is a good deal of scatter with this association, but it was perhaps surprising that such association as there was indicated that schools with *least* continuity tended to have the *best* behaviour.

This association was supported by a similar finding with respect to the average number of terms that third year pupils had been taught by their current maths and English teachers. These two measures of teacher continuity showed no significant intercorrelations (−0·31) but their association with behavioural outcome was similar.

It would be unjustified to make too much of this finding, especially as the period of study was one of high teacher turnover, so that few of the children experienced much continuity of teachers. But it does show that, at least within the twelve schools studied, there were no observable academic advantages in striving to ensure that children were always taught by the same teacher, and indeed there may have been

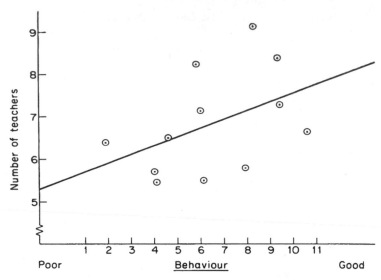

Figure 7.23 *Continuity of teachers (fifth-year pupils) and behaviour score*

behavioural disadvantages. The apparent lack of academic benefits needs further examination since many schools are very committed to maintaining as much continuity as possible in spite of the strains that this imposes on the timetable. Three points may be relevant in this connection. First, the fact that a child does not have the same teacher to teach English or maths for several years in succession does not necessarily imply high teacher turnover in the school as a whole. Second, whether having the same teacher for several years running is a good or bad thing will depend, for an individual child, to a considerable extent on how well he or she gets on with that particular teacher. Continuity can have disadvantages as well as advantages. Thirdly, continuity of teaching style and of curriculum can be maintained through joint planning as well as through keeping the same teacher. We will return to this point in the next section when considering staff organisation.

Stability of peer groups

The second set of questions all refer to the extent that the same group of *children* remained together throughout the school. This was

	Att.	Correlations with Outcome Beh.	Ac.	Del.
40. % of children in same English class	0·29	−0·03	0·12	0·78
41. % of children in same form/set/group	0·39	0·08	0·28	0·88
42. No. of friends in same year	0·46	−0·13	0·08	0·73

Table 7.8 *Peer group stability and outcome*

assessed by asking pupils whether they had remained in the same English class since starting at the school, and whether they had remained in the same form or teaching group. Schools in which a high proportion of children had remained in the same group tended to have lower levels of delinquency. The third question in this group concerned the number of friends, *not* in their set or class, whom children had arranged to meet out of school during the last school year. Schools where children had met many friends outside their class tended to have lower levels of delinquency. It is interesting that these three items, all concerning peer groups within the school, show significant associations only with delinquency. We will take up some of the possible implications of these findings in later chapters.

Staff organisation

The final group of items draws together measures which all refer to staff organisation and the checking of teachers' work. A number of these have been noted earlier, in other contexts, but it seems helpful to reconsider them together here. The variables seem to fall into three subsets. First, there is the matter of planning courses. Teachers were asked how much freedom they had in planning the courses they were teaching that year. The proportion of teachers who said that courses were planned jointly with others varied from 33 per cent in one school

	Att.	Correlations with Outcome Beh.	Ac.	Del.
9. Group planning of syllabus	0·66	0·14	0·35	0·78
43. Pattern of decision making	0·37	0·64	0·57	0·45
44. Representation of views	0·36	0·09	0·51	0·28
45. Other staff aware of teacher lateness	0·53	−0·03	−0·01	0·32
46. Adequate clerical help	0·27	0·61	0·19	0·47
3. Checks on homework setting	0·49	0·16	0·52	0·50

Table 7.9 *Staff organisation and outcome*

to 100 per cent in another. Schools where most teachers planned jointly tended to have better attendance and less delinquency. Of course, the group planning took many different forms – from fully integrated courses to the more usual method of the head of department providing guidance on the general format of the courses from year to year, but leaving individual teachers to plan the details independently. It was striking, however, that in the less successful schools teachers were often left completely alone to plan what to teach, with little guidance or supervision from their senior colleagues and little coordination with other teachers to ensure a coherent course from year to year. Another finding in this area was that the more successful schools were likely to be seen by the teachers as providing them with adequate clerical help. This might either come from the school office or from part-time helpers attached to individual departments. Often, they were financed by the school itself from money provided by the local authority for the schools to spend in whatever way they thought most appropriate.

The second variable concerns checking of the teachers' work. Staff were asked whether there was any check on whether they set homework. Schools varied from 10 per cent to 100 per cent in the

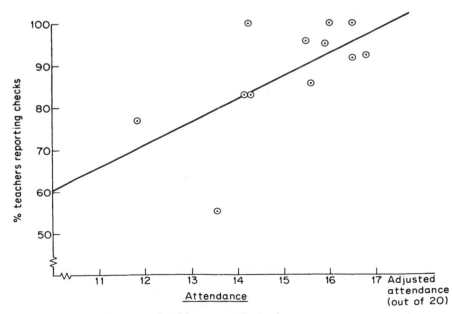

Figure 7.24 *Checks on teachers' lateness and attendance outcome*

proportion of teachers who said that checks were made. A high proportion was associated with a better academic outcome. Teachers were also asked if anyone was aware if staff arrived late for school. Again, schools varied in the proportion saying that people were aware – from 56 per cent to 100 per cent. Lack of awareness of staff punctuality was associated with poor attendance by the children (see Figure 7.24).

The checking of both homework and punctuality was usually an informal process rather than a formal procedure. But in the more successful schools teachers reported that senior colleagues knew what was happening. It may be that group planning also played a role in this – providing support and supervision at the same time. It should be emphasised that the more successful schools were not unduly regimented. Rather, good morale and the routine of people working harmoniously together as part of an efficient system meant that both supervision and support were available to teachers in a way which was absent in less successful schools. In some schools with relatively poor outcomes teachers appeared very isolated, teaching their own syllabus with little interest being taken in what they were doing or how they were doing it.

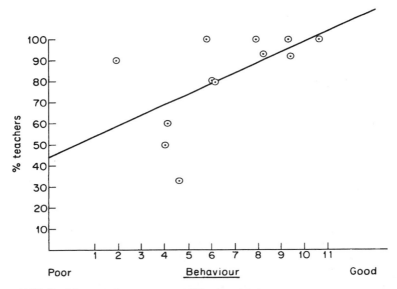

Figure 7.25 *Decisions made at senior staff level and behaviour score*

The third area of staff organisation concerns the pattern of decision-making in the school. Schools varied in the ways in which they were run, but most had some kind of inner cabinet of senior teachers, Heads of Departments and Heads of Year or House which met together, in addition to staff meetings for all teachers. We asked the teachers in each of the schools where they felt that the decisions in their school were made. In the majority of schools most teachers said that decisions were taken at senior staff level – but the proportions per school varied from 33 per cent to 100 per cent. Schools with good outcomes tended to be agreed that decisions were made at a senior level rather than in the staff room (see Figure 7.25).

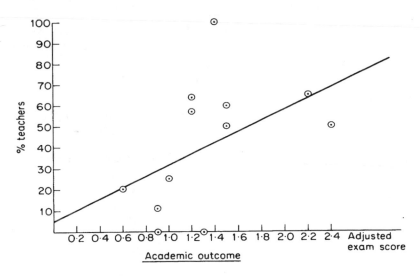

Figure 7.26 *Representation of teachers' views and academic outcome*

On the other hand, when asked whether their own views were taken into account at the appropriate decision-making level the teachers in the less successful schools tended to state that they felt that their views were not represented. We have too few data to draw any firm con-clusions about the most effective styles of school management, but the findings here do suggest that the combination of decision-making by senior staff, after consideration of the views of the whole staff, may be a good one.

Skills of teachers

We have considered many different 'school process' measures in terms of *styles* of social organisation, personal interactions and group management. In making school comparisons and in examining associations with pupil outcomes, we have not dealt with the question of teacher 'quality' or skills.

Could it be that the differences we found between schools were merely a consequence of some schools getting all the 'best' teachers, whereas others had to put up with the 'worst' ones? The implication of such a question, of course, is that there may be some innate quality concerned with teaching ability. If there is, certainly it cannot be measured. Doubtless people do vary somewhat in their 'natural' ability to become outstanding teachers. However, it would be quite wrong to suppose that this is an unalterable characteristic. Our observations suggested that it was very much easier to be a good teacher in some schools than it was in others. The overall ethos of the school seemed to provide support and a context which facilitated good teaching. Teaching performance is a function of the school environment as well as of personal qualities.

Our study findings cannot show whether or not some schools recruited more 'naturally good teachers' than others. Even if this were the case, however, two findings imply that this is unlikely to be the whole explanation for the differences between schools in outcome. First, some of the most important school process variables were not concerned with the actions of individual teachers. Thus, the availability to the children of positions of responsibility, the distribution of rewards, good conditions for pupils, and the pattern of decision-making are all to a considerable extent matters of school policy – and not within the scope of the individual teacher.

	Probationary Teachers	Experienced Teachers
School: 1	34·80	77·00
2	30·60	52·93
3	33·00	45·50
4	38·50	50·06
5	18·60	38·87
6	15·22	12·00

Table 7.10 % *Teacher time spent in class-based interactions: experienced and probationary teachers*

Second, the main differences between schools in teacher effectiveness (insofar as that could be measured at all) related to experienced teachers. In all schools *in*experienced teachers were rather unsuccessful in class management. Table 7.10 shows the findings for group-focused interaction in the six schools where we had systematic third year class observations for both probationary and experienced teachers. It was striking that the classes of probationary teachers seemed rather similar in all six schools. The main differences applied to established teachers. It seems that most people find a lot of difficulty in class management to begin with. However, the extent to which teachers can improve their skills appears to be dependent, in part, on the school they are working in.

Of course, it must be accepted that teacher quality is very important, but school ethos and good teaching should not be regarded as completely independent or separate. Not only does good teaching do much to create a beneficial ethos, but so also does a good ethos help in recruiting experienced and able teachers and in providing the optimal setting to bring out their teaching skills.

Overall school process effect

In a study where a large number of statistical comparisons are made, some significant associations will arise just by chance.* It is necessary, therefore, to take steps to determine as far as possible which *statistically* significant associations are real (in the sense of not arising by chance) and hence *educationally* significant. The strongest test is whether other comparable investigations give the same results. Another test is whether the findings are consonant with what is known about the ways in which children's behaviour may be influenced in settings other than schools. We discuss both these points in the last chapter of this book.

However, there are also 'internal' statistical comparisons which can provide a guide to how far the findings are valid. First, the statistically significant associations are more likely to be meaningful if they fall into

---

* 5 per cent significance level means that the likelihood of the result occurring by chance is 1 in 20. Of course, this also means that out of every 20 results, one may be statistically significant by chance.

an understandable pattern (chance associations would be scattered randomly among the variables). In the present case there *is* a pattern. Thus, findings on physical factors and administrative organisation (considered in the previous chapter) were largely negative, whereas those on school process (considered in this chapter) include many significant associations. Secondly, confidence in findings can be greater when different measures of the *same* variable produce similarly significant findings. To examine this issue, we made comparisons such as between different measures of homework (as reported by teachers and by pupils, and as observed by us), between different types of reward (praise in the classroom, public praise in assemblies, etc), and between different measures of interaction style. On the whole, different measures *did* produce similar findings although, as we have noted, this was not always the case.

However, it was evident that in most cases the intercorrelations between apparently comparable items were rather low, in spite of their having similar associations with the outcome measures. This could mean that the concept of an overall school process effect was a mistaken one, and that many of the correlations had in fact arisen by chance. Alternatively, it could mean that the overall school ethos was indeed crucial but that it could be established in a variety of different ways. In this case, the relatively low intercorrelations between items would be expected as, to a considerable extent, the measures would represent *alternative* means to the same end.

A rather stringent test of these two possibilities is provided by seeing what happens if all the statistically significant process items are summed to produce an overall score. If each of the individually significant associations had actually arisen by chance, their combination would result in a *reduced* correlation with outcome. If the findings were indeed a result of chance, some schools would score highly on one measure but would have low scores on others; when put together, these would to some extent cancel each other out. The result would be 'average process' scores which were very similar in all twelve schools (lying between ranks 5 and 7). In addition, the summed process score would have only a low correlation with the four outcome measures.

In contrast, if the results were truly valid and meaningful, the combination of measures into an overall composite score should show a wide range of average scores, and should *increase* the correlations with the outcomes. Expressed graphically, this would show as a diagonal line with little scatter about it, indicating that a high school process score was associated with a high outcome score.

In order to test this possibility we selected the thirty-nine process items which had significant associations with one or other of the outcomes (excluding the four which related only to delinquency). The separate ranks of the schools on each of these items were then summed to produce an overall scale. The resulting mean ranks showed a clearly differentiated pattern (with a range from 3·85 to 9·46), reflecting the fact that, in general, the schools had achieved rather similar rank positions on each of the conceptually distinct aspects of school processes.

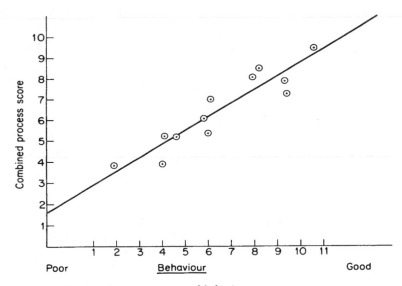

Figure 7.27 *Combined process score and behaviour score*

This more global summary school process measure could then be correlated with the four pupil outcome measures. The findings are shown in Figures 7.27 to 7.30. There was a very strong and highly consistent correlation (0·92) between overall school process and pupil behaviour. The correlation with academic attainment (0·76) was also very substantial indeed, although not quite as strong as that with pupil behaviour. The relationship between school process and attendance was also strong and consistent, apart from one school with particularly

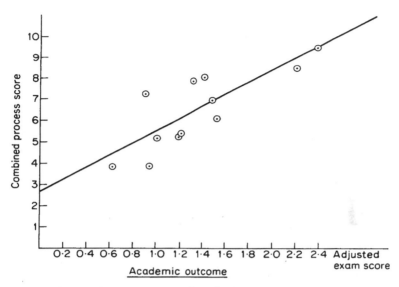

Figure 7.28 *Combined process score and academic outcome*

poor attendance in spite of an average school process score. As a result the overall correlation (0·65) was rather lower although still highly significant. The correlation (0·68) with delinquency was about

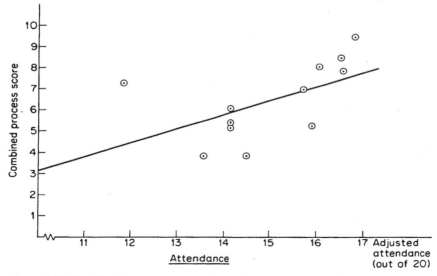

Figure 7.29 *Combined process score and attendance outcome*

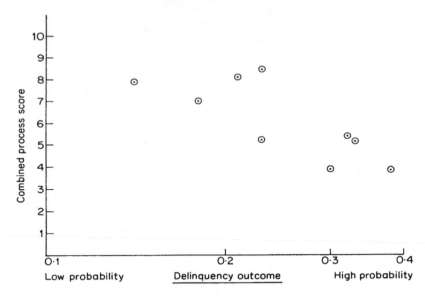

Figure 7.30 *Combined process score and delinquency*

The regression line is omitted from Figure 7.30 as the delinquency outcome is shown on a logarithmic scale.

the same. The somewhat lower correlations between school process and attendance and delinquency suggest the possible operation of other types of influences. These are considered in the next chapter.

8

Ecological influences

In the last chapter we were concerned with *internal* school processes — that is with the characteristics of schools in terms of their social organisation, their patterns of personal relationships and their styles of group management. The findings clearly showed that these school processes were strongly associated with pupil outcomes, as assessed in terms of attendance, behaviour, scholastic attainment and, to a lesser extent, delinquency.

These results, however, raise two further sorts of questions. First, there is the query as to what *other* influences affect children's behaviour and attainments. We have noted that, even when taken together, our measures of children's individual characteristics (with respect to intellectual level and occupational status) and the features of the schools they attended, left much of delinquency unaccounted for. Of course, this is the usual state of affairs in any study of this kind, and it may mean no more than that there were important aspects of schooling or of a child's personal qualities or home circumstances that we did not measure. Undoubtedly, that was the case. However, it is also necessary to examine the possibility that there were *other* factors, of a different kind, which played a part in increasing or decreasing the likelihood that a child would engage in delinquent activities. One of the most obviously important variables in this connection is the area in which a child lives. From the pioneer social surveys in Chicago before the Second World War (Shaw and McKay, 1942) to the present day (see Gath *et al.*, 1977), repeated investigations have shown that delinquency rates tend to vary according to different areas, and to be particularly high in urban areas of low social status. Even within a single city such as London, there are 'pockets' of crime which have remained remarkably persistent over several decades (Wallis and Maliphant, 1967). The twelve schools which we studied all admitted children from inner London, but within this area, they drew their pupils from many different local neighbourhoods. Although these overlapped considerably, it seemed possible that these differences in catchment areas might account for some of the variation in pupil outcome. That was the first question which we had to examine.

The second question was of a rather different kind. We had found marked differences between the schools in their patterns of functioning, but we did not know how these differences had arisen. Why did schools differ so strikingly in the process variables we measured? The answer must lie in part in the policies and practice of the staff of the schools, who decide how they shall be run. Given similar opportunities and comparable resources, there is enormous scope in how these can be used to create a well functioning school. But schools are not only shaped by the actions of heads and teachers, external influences may also limit what they are able to achieve. 'External' factors could include in this context not only matters of geography and buildings, but also the equally (and perhaps more powerful) effects of the mix or balance in the pupil intake, public attitudes to the school, and the political considerations which determine how far schools are in control of their own destinies. These 'external' factors do not act independently of the school. Rather they constitute one set of elements in a complex pattern of ecological interactions. A school is part of its environment, and influences the wider community, just as environmental forces provide constraints and pressures which determine what a school can be like. In this chapter we will consider the evidence on some of the important ecological variables which differentiated between the twelve schools we studied. This latter qualification is important, as obviously there were many ecological factors of very great importance to the functioning of schools which did not differentiate among the twelve study schools, and which we could not study. Our prime focus here will be upon the questions of intake balance, parental choice, and physical and administrative factors.

The implications of the differences in these aspects had to be examined in two rather different ways. First, there was the question of what effects they had on pupil outcome. This could be determined by looking at the associations between these ecological variables, and each of our four outcome measures. Second, there was the question of what effects they had on school functioning. This could be tackled by examining correlations or associations between the ecological variables and our measures of school process. In short, the first question was concerned with the issue of why children were as they were and the second with the different issue of why schools were as they were. Only by making these two separate kinds of assessment could we hope to understand how factors of this kind might operate, and whether their influence would primarily be a direct one on the pupil group, or rather a more indirect one, affecting school functioning.

Area differences

We began by examining the areas in which the children had their homes. A good deal of other research has pointed to the fact that rates of social problems of various kinds differ between geographical areas, but it is very much less clear why this should be so. It may be that differences between areas simply reflect the individual characteristics of the people who live there, but it also seems possible that some kind of independent 'community' influence is at work. Questions of this kind were clearly beyond the scope of our study. We were concerned with a more limited issue: could it be that the differences we had found in school outcomes, and especially perhaps in delinquency rates, were in fact largely accounted for by differences in the home neighbourhoods from which the children came?

Research into questions of this kind faces two particular difficulties: firstly, the size of the areas to be studied, and secondly, the ways in which these basic neighbourhood groupings can be grouped or classified together for any analysis. The solution to the first of these problems is bound to be somewhat arbitrary in densely populated inner city areas, where administrative boundaries will not necessarily coincide with changes in the social characteristics of areas. We selected electoral wards as the basic unit for our analyses.* These are relatively large areas, housing between 10,000 and 20,000 people. However, they had the very considerable advantage that independent information was available about their social and demographic characteristics, based on the 1971 Census.

Statistical analyses can be used to determine the ways in which different areas cluster or group together in terms of their demographic

* Other writers have suggested that the smaller enumeration districts would constitute more appropriate units in analyses of this kind, but limitations in resources prevented us from studying the children's home areas in detail. Our conclusions are thus limited to the particular types of area we were able to study.

and social characteristics. In this way geographical districts may be grouped in terms of their socio-demographic profiles rather than their spatial proximity (see Gath *et al.*, 1977). Then these socially homogeneous (but geographically scattered) population units may be compared with respect to their rates of delinquency (or other outcome variable). The Centre for Environmental Studies, in conjunction with the Office of Population Census and Surveys, has produced just such a classification of residential neighbourhoods (Webber, 1977). Accordingly we used this classification as the starting point of our own analyses.

OPCS/CES classification

As our main focus in these analyses was on delinquency, we restricted our attention to the boys in the sample. The first step was to take the home addresses of the 1289 boys in the 'cohort' age group, and allocate them to the ward in which they were situated (in forty-six cases the ward location of the addresses could not be determined). It was found that the boys came from eighty-four different wards, in six different London boroughs. These wards were then grouped according to the thirty-six clusters in the OPCS/CES classification. As it turned out, the wards fell into only eleven clusters. Overall, the variations in delinquency rate between the eleven clusters were fairly small (range from 16 per cent to 36 per cent) and the differences were not statistically significant ($F = 1.01$, df $= 10$, NS).

However, most of the children came from socially disadvantaged clusters. Over half (723) came from just one cluster described as including 'a very large amount of low status inner London combining high proportions of multi-occupancy, privately rented accommodation, single non-pensioners, immigrants and women at work. The type also includes a fair amount of local authority housing'. The next largest proportion (215 boys) came from a cluster associated with traditional dockland areas 'picked out by their very low levels of skill, their high unemployment and their serious overcrowding'. A small number (53) fell in outlying areas which could not easily be classified in this way, so these have been excluded from the analyses.

Area differences and delinquency

Altogether, only 136 of the boys lived in wards which could in any way be described as relatively advantaged, and only another 116 in wards of intermediate social status. The delinquency rate in the somewhat favoured group of 136 boys was 19 per cent, in the intermediate group with 116 boys it was 36 per cent, and in the disadvantaged remainder it was 28·9 per cent. This showed significant variations between these groups ($x^2 = 9·32$, df $= 2$, p $< 0·01$), but with the highest rate of delinquency falling in the apparently intermediate area in terms of social characteristics. Of course, any discussions on which districts are more 'advantaged' than others are necessarily somewhat arbitrary when the districts vary on forty variables, and when the classification has been undertaken initially in national, rather than local, terms. Nevertheless, it did not seem that this particular classification of areas could be of great value in identifying social or neighbourhood factors associated with delinquency in our sample.

The fact that the groups did vary in their rates of delinquency, however, made it essential to examine whether these differences were accounting for the school variations. We could only examine this question in relation to the largest clusters. In the second largest cluster, of 215 boys, the school rates of delinquency did not vary greatly, but in the largest cluster, of 723 pupils, the school variation was very large, and highly significant ($x^2 = 34·55$, df $= 8$, p $< 0·001$). These differences suggest that the school variations were *not* simply a product of neighbourhood differences. The clustering on demographic variables did differentiate between areas in terms of their delinquency rates (although not in any very easily understandable way), but there were still variations between schools within the largest clusters.

It remains to be determined just what constitutes an area influence and *how* it operates. In particular, it remains uncertain how far 'area' effects are separate from 'family' or 'home' influences. Other studies have shown that the high delinquency areas are *not* congregated together into one neighbourhood. Rather, they are scattered around boroughs (see Gath *et al.*, 1977) and indeed are concentrated in very small areas indeed (Jephcott and Carter, 1954). Opinions are divided (and the research findings are inconclusive) on how far the area variations represent the effects of social groups or communities and how far they just reflect family or home influences. A detailed consideration of these issues would take us a long way from our study of schools. Our own data are in agreement with earlier studies in finding differences in delinquency rates between areas. These did not, however, seem to be accounting for school differences.

Area differences and pupil behaviour

The issue of possible home area influences arises, of course, with respect to the other outcomes also – although they have not been considered in previous studies of area differences. Pupil behaviour may be considered first, as in some respects disruptive behaviour in school might appear to have most in common with delinquency. Because our measure of pupil behaviour consisted of a composite scale for each school, rather than a measure of individual children's behaviour, it could not be studied on a child by child basis in the same way as the delinquency rates. The most appropriate approach was to examine the pupil behaviour scores of schools with the highest, middle and lowest intakes of children from high delinquency areas. In this way, it was possible to assess whether schools with poorer in-school behaviour were in fact admitting larger proportions of pupils from apparently delinquency-prone neighbourhoods. No significant differences were found. Indeed there was not even a consistent trend. The schools with the most favourable intakes (in terms of delinquency areas) had *worse* behaviour than schools with intermediate intakes, although the very worst behaviour was in schools with the least favourable intakes. We may conclude that the school differences in pupil behaviour were *not* accounted for by area differences in intake.

Area differences and academic attainment

As our measures of academic attainment were available for individual pupils, we were able to examine possible area effects in rather more detail here. We began by looking at the examination results of the boys according to the three broad area groupings we had defined previously – the relatively advantaged, intermediate, and disadvantaged areas, according to the social indicators. As would be anticipated, there were significant differences between these areas on the pupils' examination scores ($F = 12.40$, df = 2, $p < 0.001$), and interestingly, once again, the apparently intermediate group in social terms had the poorest academic results.

Our next question in relation to academic attainment was whether these apparent differences between *areas* were in fact representing anything more than different groupings of pupils with varying *individual* characteristics. An analysis of variance (see Table 8.1 in Appendix G) taking account of Verbal Reasoning Band, parental occupation and the three broad home areas showed that all three factors interacted together. The areas in which the children lived did not appear to be having any clearly independent influences, but no very definite conclusions were possible in view of the interaction between the factors. The only way to examine the different influences in more detail was to hold the pupils' ability variable constant by selecting a sub-group of the children, and then test whether home area had any effect. We could then also test whether school variations remained once these area effects had been taken into account.

We selected the Band 2 pupils only, and assessed the effects of home area and school on their exam results. The findings (see Table 8.2 in Appendix G) showed that, once the pupils' ability had been held constant, there was no significant effect for home area ($F = 2.59$; df = 2, NS) but significant variations between schools still remained ($F = 6.19$; df = 8; $p < 0.001$).

The findings for academic attainment suggest that the neighbourhood effects were not independent of individual background characteristics. Focussing specifically on the effects of home area on pupils' attainment, it seemed that these did *not* account for school variations, which persisted even when home area and individual VR band had been taken into account.

Area effects and attendance

Our final analyses in this section concerned attendance; these followed exactly the pattern used for the examination results. A preliminary breakdown of attendance rates for the three broad classifications of areas showed that these did not differ greatly; the average attendance rate for the 136 pupils from the socially most advantaged areas was 15·27 out of a possible 20, and for the 938 boys from the least favoured area, 14·08 ($F = 2·46$, df $= 2$, NS). It nevertheless seemed worthwhile to pursue the questions of whether these small variations affected the school attendance rates, and whether they reflected anything other than the pupils' individual characteristics.

An analysis (see Table 8.3 in Appendix G) to test whether the home area was having any independent effect, once individual VR band and parental occupation had been taken into account, suggested that it was not. As a final check, however, it was necessary to test whether home areas might somehow be influencing the school variations. We again restricted the analysis to Band 2 pupils, and tested whether school effects remained, once home area had been taken into account (see Table 8.4 in Appendix G). The findings for attendance again paralleled those for examination results; home areas had no significant effects ($F = 0·31$; df $= 2$, NS) and significant school differences remained even after these had been taken into account ($F = 2·45$, df $= 8$, $p = 0·013$).

Conclusions on area influences

These various area analyses indicated that, although the home areas of
the pupils might have played some small part in influencing their
behaviour and attainments, the effects did *not* in any way account for
school differences in pupil outcome. Moreover, such differences as
there were between areas appeared unrelated to their relative 'disadvantage' in terms of the social and demographic indicators we had
available, and the area differences overlapped to a considerable extent
with home background factors.

Balance of intake

In our earlier analyses we were essentially concerned to take account
of the individual characteristics of the pupils at the time they entered
secondary school. We will now examine the question of school intakes
from the point of view of their possible *group* effects. As we have noted
throughout in our discussion of school process variables, schools are
social organisations. This means that they are likely to be influenced
by the composition of the social groups in them. Clearly, the
characteristics of the children admitted each year are relevant in this
connection. The ethos or atmosphere of a school may be influenced by
the proportion of its intake which is intellectually less able or is socially
disadvantaged in some way.

The presence of a relatively high concentration of pupils in the upper ability groups may work to the advantage not only of those pupils themselves, but also of their peers. In a similar way, a largely disadvantaged intake might depress outcomes in some cumulative way, over and above the effects of a disadvantaged background on the individual pupil.

As we have been at pains to point out throughout this book, none of the schools in our sample could be regarded as 'favoured' in their intakes in any national, or even perhaps London comparisons, but the extent of the variations even within this limited range warranted further consideration. Despite administrative efforts to ensure that ability groupings should be reasonably comparable across all London schools, there were fairly major variations within our sample.* For example, only one of the twelve schools had the expected 25 per cent of its pupils in the top ability band. By comparison, three schools had less than 5 per cent of their pupils in this ability band, and in a further four schools the proportion was less than 10 per cent. Similar variations occurred with respect to the bottom ability band; the proportions here ranged from under 25 per cent to over 50 per cent of the intake in different schools.

Differences were also found in the occupational balance of the intakes. The proportion of children from homes with parents who held professional, managerial and clerical jobs ranged from 2 per cent to 23 per cent across schools. The comparable figures for children whose parents held unskilled or semi-skilled jobs varied between 24 per cent and 47 per cent. The school proportions of children from immigrant families varied even more widely – from 4 per cent to 53 per cent. Children with known emotional or behavioural difficulties at the end of their primary schooling were similarly unevenly distributed between the twelve schools; the proportions varied between 10 per cent and 40 per cent of the intakes. These figures are all based on one particular year group of pupils, but we found that the relative positions of the schools on each of these different indicators of intake balance were generally similar for the other age groups of pupils on whom we had intake data. For example, the rank correlations between the intakes in

---

* The methods taken by the ILEA to ensure comparability of intakes across schools have changed since our study began and it may well be that the disparities between schools have now lessened.

1971 and 1974 for ability bands, occupational groups and number of immigrant families were respectively 0·73, 0·71, and 0·84. For behavioural difficulties, data were available for 1971 and 1976, and here the correlation was 0·87.

The analysis of how the group composition of a school's intake might affect the pupils' later outcomes is clearly a complex issue. It has received relatively little attention in the past, and our analyses can only represent the beginnings of attempts to unravel the network of interacting influences. We began by using an approach exactly comparable with the ones we had adopted in looking at school processes. Thus, we ranked the schools according to the relative 'balance' in the intake on each of the indicators mentioned above. In looking at ability groupings and social background we also produced separate rankings of the proportions of pupils in both extreme groups on these variables, to give a clearer picture of the extent to which any overall balance effects might be attributed to positive or negative skewing. We then correlated these rankings with the schools' rankings on the four outcome measures, and on the overall process score.

Balance of intake and pupil behaviour

	Correlations with Behavioural Outcome
Academic Balance	
'% Band 1	0·19
'% Band 3	0·09
Occupational Balance	
'% Non-Manual	0·01
'% Unskilled/semi-skilled	−0·01
Ethnic Balance	
'% Immigrant families	−0·01
Behavioural Balance	
'% High scores on teacher questionnaire	0·25

No correlations statistically significant

Table 8.5 *Balance of intake and pupil behaviour*

Table 8.5 summarises the findings on pupil behaviour. There were no significant correlations between pupil behaviour and any of the measures of balance of intake. It appears that the day to day behaviour of the children in the twelve schools bore a very much stronger relationship to the characteristics of the schools themselves, than to any of these features of the pupil group admitted at age eleven years. It might have been anticipated that different intake 'mixes' would lead to the formation of contrasting peer group cultures, which would in turn be manifest in the pupils' behaviour at school. However, our data provided no support for a conclusion of this kind. Instead, it seemed that the pre-existing culture of the school as a whole, which we assessed with our school process measures (but which would of course include the behaviour of the older pupils at the school), was the predominant influence on the behaviour of each new intake of children.

Balance of intake and delinquency

	Correlations with Delinquency	p
Academic Balance		
% Band 1	0·75*	< ·05
% Band 3	0·57	NS
Occupational Balance		
% Non-Manual	0·27	NS
% Unskilled/semi-skilled	0·15	NS
Ethnic Balance		
% Immigrant families	0·73*	< ·05
Behavioural Balance		
% High scores on teacher questionnaire	0·40	NS

Table 8.6 *Balance of intake and delinquency*

The findings with respect to delinquency provide something of a contrast (see Table 8.6). Again, there were no significant correlations with either the behavioural or occupational balances of the intakes. However, there were significant correlations with both the proportion of ability band 1 children, and the proportion of children from immigrant families. School delinquency rates were higher when there was a small proportion of the most able children, or a high proportion of children from immigrant families. The majority of immigrants in the area the schools served came from the West Indies. In view of the evidence from previous studies (see Yule *et al.*, 1975) that children of West Indian background have higher rates of educational difficulties than indigenous children, these two aspects of intake balance are likely to be inter-related. However, there was one crucial difference with respect to outcome. Whereas children of lower intellectual ability had a much increased delinquency rate (see Chapter 5), children from immigrant families did *not*. In so far as the ethnic mix had any effect on delinquency, this must have been indirect, as the children's ethnic background showed no association with delinquency.

Balance of intake and attendance

	Correlations with Attendance	p
Academic Balance		
% Band 1	0·76*	< ·01
% Band 3	0·84*	< ·01
Occupational Balance		
% Non-Manual	0·52*	< ·05
% Unskilled/semi-skilled	0·09	NS
Ethnic Balance		
% Immigrant families	0·45	NS
Behavioural Balance		
% High scores on teacher questionnaire	0·78*	< ·01

Table 8.7 *Balance of intake and attendance*

Attendance also showed significant associations with intake balance factors – with academic balance, as in the case of delinquency, but also with the balance as assessed on the primary school behavioural questionnaire, and with the proportion of children whose fathers held non-manual jobs. The ethnic mix was unrelated to attendance. Of all the outcome measures, this was the one which showed the strongest association with the balance of intake.

Balance of intake and academic attainment

Academic attainment was also related to intake balance with respect to children's ability banding. As with delinquency, the association was stronger with the proportion of band 1 children than with the proportion of band 3 children. The same difference was evident with respect to occupational balance – the proportion of children from non-manual families made more difference than the proportion of children from un-skilled or semi-skilled families. Neither ethnic mix nor behavioural mix showed any significant correlation with examination success.

	Correlations with Academic Attainment	p
Academic Balance		
% Band 1	0·61*	< ·05
% Band 3	0·48	NS
Occupational Balance		
% Non-Manual	0·64*	< ·05
% Unskilled/semi-skilled	0·34	NS
Ethnic Balance		
% Immigrant families	0·21	NS
Behavioural Balance		
% High scores on teacher questionnaire	0·45	NS

Table 8.8 *Balance of intake and examination success*

It is apparent then that the balance of intake was of *no* importance with respect to pupil behaviour, but that it did have significant effects on the other three outcomes. Comparing the four different aspects of intake on which we had information, ethnic mix and behavioural mix seemed least important: both correlated significantly with only one outcome measure. Academic balance was most influential, and showed significant associations with all three outcome measures apart from pupil behaviour. Occupational balance was significantly associated with attendance and exam success but not with delinquency.

These analyses suggest that the various intake balance factors did show some relationships with pupil outcome. What they could not clarify, however, was whether this relationship was a direct one, or whether it was mediated by other factors. It seemed possible, for example, that the balance of the intake might affect school processes, and that certain types of internal school practices would only be possible if the intake was relatively favoured. We then examined this possibility.

Balance of intake and school process

The findings, shown in Table 8.9, are striking in indicating *no* significant associations between any of the balance variables and the overall school process measure. Perhaps surprisingly the results are clear-cut in demonstrating that, however the balance in the intake to a school

	Correlations with Overall Process Score
Academic Balance	
% Band 1	0·44
% Band 3	0·32
Occupational Balance	
% Non-Manual	0·24
% Unskilled/semi-skilled	0·01
Ethnic Balance	
% Immigrant families	0·17
Behavioural Balance	
% High scores on teacher questionnaire	0·39
No differences statistically significant	

Table 8.9 *Balance of intake and school process*

may be associated with the pupils' outcome, it does *not* have its impact on either pupils' behaviour at school, or on school functioning in terms of the process variables we measured. Instead, it presumably has some kind of impact on the children themselves, probably through its influence on the composition and thereby on the attitudes and behaviour of the peer group.

Perhaps the key points here are: first, that the strongest links are with attendance and delinquency and, second, that the most influential balance variable concerns ability groupings (rather than the child's socio-cultural background). The implication is that the outcomes are likely to be most favourable when there is a reasonable balance* of academically successful children who are liable to be rewarded by their good attainments at school and, therefore, who perhaps are more prone to identify with the school goals and aims. When the proportion of less able children becomes too high, this will mean that a *preponderance* of the pupils will fail to achieve examination success

* A reasonable balance, rather than a very high proportion, because none of the schools had a particularly advantaged intake with respect to intellectual ability.

and hence may see themselves as not achieving anything useful at school. In this way contra-cultures within the school may develop (see Hargreaves, 1967). These suggestions, of course, go beyond the immediate factual results and the implications will be considered in more detail in the final chapter.

In the meanwhile, the findings indicate that a school's balance of intake (especially with respect to ability groupings) has significant associations with pupil outcomes (especially with respect to attendance and delinquency). The association is *not* due to any link with the children's observed behaviour in school *nor* is it due to any effect on the school processes as we have measured them.

Parental choice

	Mean Ranks Parental Subscription Rates			Kruskal-Wallis One-way Analysis of Variance	
	Low	Medium	High	H	p
Pupil Behaviour	6·3	6·0	4·5	0·74	NS
Attendance	8·7	5·0	3·5	5·11	NS
Academic Attainment	8·7	4·0	4·3	4·70	NS
Delinquency	6·5	3·5	2·7	3·93	NS
School Process Score	7·3	5·0	4·0	1·62	NS

Table 8.10 *Parental choice, pupil outcome and school process*

Another 'intake' variable concerns the proportion of children in each school who are there as a result of that particular school being their first choice. We did not have a direct measure of the *child's* choice, but for ten of the twelve schools we were able to use data on *parental* choice, recorded at the time of the selection process when the children were in primary school. In some schools *all* the children had had that school put down as first choice. In others the proportion was only just over half, with large numbers of children who had originally opted to go elsewhere.

As might be expected, the parental subscription rates to the schools were related to both the proportion of higher ability children in the intake ($x^2 = 5·98$; 2 df; $p < 0·05$) and the proportion of children with parents holding non-manual jobs ($x^2 = 7·32$; 2 df; $p < 0·02$). After all, these are two of the more obvious characteristics of a school and among the few which are likely to be known to parents.

On the other hand, the parental subscription rate was not significantly associated with any of the four outcome measures, nor was it significantly associated with the overall school process measure. It appears that, with respect to the longer term pupil outcomes we have been considering, parental choice at intake is of relatively little importance by comparison with other aspects of the balance of intake or with school processes. Of course, this rather negative conclusion applies strictly to the twelve schools we studied within the context of the ILEA system of secondary school selection. It may be that in other circumstances parental choice might have a much greater impact on school functioning, but in the existing situation in the inner London area with which we are concerned, it was not a crucial determinant.

Physical features and administrative organisation

The final set of variables to be considered under the heading of ecological influences consists of the physical and administrative features already considered in Chapter 6. The findings considered then showed that these variables were of negligible importance in relation to the four outcome measures. We now need to find out whether any of them were associated with the overall school process measure. Each was examined separately in this connection and none showed a significant association with school process. We may conclude that the buildings provided, the administrative organisation and the staffing resources made surprisingly little difference to school functioning. Of course, this conclusion applies only to the range of differences on these variables within our sample and to the school process measures we utilised. It is *not* suggested that the resources available to a school are of no importance, nor that the ways of running a school are uninfluenced by its size, buildings or space. Rather, the results suggest that equally *effective* schooling is possible in schools which vary substantially in physical provision and administrative organisation.

Conclusion

It has been necessary in this chapter to consider many rather complex intercorrelations and associations. However, the overall picture they provide is reasonably straightforward. The main finding is that various aspects of the balance of intake to schools are significantly associated with pupil outcome, and particularly with children's attendance and delinquency. On the other hand, the effects of intake balance appear surprisingly separate from children's observed behaviour in school, and from our many measures of different features of school process or functioning. The results of the last few chapters may be summarised by stating that children's individual characteristics, the balance of a school's intake and school processes all have significant associations with outcome. Before turning to a more speculative discussion of the possible mechanisms involved, it is necessary to put these variables all together in one statistical analysis in order to assess their relative importance when considered together. The findings on this overall statistical analysis are described in the next chapter.

9

Composite analyses of all main variables

Our research findings, as discussed in earlier chapters, have shown large differences between secondary schools in children's school attendance, behaviour, attainments and rates of delinquency. Because we had information on what the children were like before they entered secondary school, we knew that the differences had arisen as a result of changes in children's performance after secondary transfer. Their behaviour and attainments while at secondary school were *not* just a continuation of patterns already established at an earlier age. Instead, it seemed that the children's experiences during their years at secondary school had played a part in shaping their development. Of course, the finding that important changes had taken place during those years did not necessarily mean that the changes were due to experiences at school rather than elsewhere. However, the further finding that children's behaviour and attainments were systematically related to measured characteristics of the schools they attended, strongly increased the likelihood that the links with schooling were indeed a result of causal processes. This evidence carried the argument one stage further. Not only were there sizeable school differences in pupil progress but also these differences were accounted for in large part by our measures of school process. The inference* that school life had truly influenced children's attendance, behaviour and attainments was strong.

The same set of findings, however, had also shown that schooling was just one of several factors having important associations with pupil outcome. The child's own characteristics, his family circumstances and home background, and his peer group also constituted substantial influences. In a variety of different statistical analyses we

* Nevertheless, it should be emphasised that it is indeed an inference and *not* a direct demonstration of an influence (which could come only from an experimental investigation in which the effects of a planned *change* in school practice are systematically assessed).

had taken account of or controlled for these other factors in examining the possible effect of school influences. The analyses showed that school variables were still important even after these statistical controls had been introduced. On the other hand, it had usually been possible to control for only one or two other factors at a time. In order to be confident that schooling really had had an important impact on children's behaviour and attainments, it was necessary to put *all* the main variables together into one large composite statistical analysis. In this chapter we describe what this set of composite analyses showed.

The main question we needed to consider at this stage was how far school process factors were still associated with outcome differences, once full account had been taken of variations in the balance of intake to the schools (i.e. the proportion of children in the school in different ability, occupational, ethnic or behavioural groups). The earlier analyses had shown that school processes had a strong relationship with most of the outcomes, whereas the balance factors followed a more variable pattern. We had found only a *very weak* association between balance and process; in other words there was only a very slight and statistically non significant tendency for schools with the most disadvantaged intakes to have the 'worst' process scores. This suggested that although both factors were related to outcome, their effects were relatively independent of one another. On the other hand, we had not as yet examined the effects of balance and process simultaneously in the same analysis. That constituted the main purpose of these final analyses.

Log-linear modelling

In order to put all the variables together we returned to the log linear modelling procedure used previously with the delinquency data. The technique provides a systematic approach to the analysis of data which are classified in many different ways at the same time (see Everitt, 1977; also Appendix H). For example, in our own data any particular child could be categorised simultaneously according to his exam score, his verbal reasoning score, his family's occupational group, his school, his school's intake balance and his school's process score. It is readily apparent that a table showing all these various classifications, each according to a different dimension, would be exceedingly complex.

Tables of this kind are generally described as 'multidimensional', and the power of the log linear approach lies in its ability to consider *all* the variables involved at the same time, whereas the more usual simpler methods of statistical analysis demand that some categories have to be ignored while others are being analysed.

The factors in which we were interested were of two different kinds. First of all, there were variables which applied individually to all children within all schools. The child's verbal reasoning score and his family's occupational group were of this kind. Secondly, there were variables which applied only to schools as a whole; the process and balance variables (called 'parameters' in log linear analyses) were of this type. With this second type there could be only twelve scores (one for each school) so that all children in the school necessarily got the same 'score'. Moreover, it was not possible to look at balance and process factors independently of the effects of particular schools. In fact, any grouping of processes or balances was merely the rearrangement of the twelve schools into groups – either according to the balance of intake or according to process scores.

Log linear modelling is based on the proportion of children who fall into particular categories – the proportion from a particular occupational group or the proportion with a particular level of attendance or exam success. It is a more appropriate procedure for use with proportional data than the analysis of variance, although its aims are essentially similar. Both statistical techniques aim to determine which of the parameters or variables account for the greatest and which the least amount of variation in the data.*

As each school has just one process score and one balance score, it is only possible to compare process and balance by grouping schools into larger blocks – firstly according to balance and secondly according to process. Thus, schools were initially divided into two equal

---

* As described in Appendix H, the log linear procedure actually involves the creation of a 'model' to 'explain' or account for outcome, the model being based on parameters which consist of the variables or combinations of variables statistically associated with that outcome. The object of the exercise is to provide the simplest model which accounts for the outcome being investigated. Different parameters are fed into or subtracted from the model one at a time in an hierarchical fashion. Each time this is done, tests are performed to determine whether the addition or subtraction of that parameter significantly improves the explanatory model. The procedure is described more fully in Appendix H, but for present purposes it is simpler and more straightforward to consider the findings in terms of the more familiar question of which variables have the greatest 'effects' on outcome when considered both independently and in combination.

sized groups according to their balance score — creating 'high' and 'low' balance blocks. Then each block was subdivided on the basis of process scores into two subgroups. This 'nesting' procedure produced four groups: high balance and high process, high balance and low process, low balance and high process, low balance and low process. This design made it possible to examine the effects of process groupings once balance groups had been taken into account, so combining these two sets of factors in the same analysis. It was also possible to see how far school differences (within these groups) still remained after process and balance had been taken into account.

Pupil behaviour

Pupil behaviour was the single outcome variable we did not need to examine by this composite method of analysis. It was the one outcome which was *not* significantly related to the children's characteristics in primary school, and which was *not* associated with any of the ecological variables considered in the last chapter. Moreover, it was also the outcome with the strongest association with the overall measure of school process. All the analyses were in agreement in showing that the characteristics of the school itself were by far the most important of all the variables considered. We may conclude that school processes constituted the *predominant* influence on children's behaviour in the classroom and the playground (with respect to those aspects of behaviour included in our measure).

Academic outcome

Log linear analysis

In order to use a log linear analysis it was necessary first to group exam scores in some way. Three categories were used: 'O' (no result better than CSE 4); '1' (CSE 2 or 3, or 'O' level D or E only); and '2' (at least one 'O' level equivalent).

The findings can be considered in three parts. The first section is concerned with the same question as that discussed in Chapter 5,

Parameters	G^2 attributable to parameter	df	p	G^2/df^*
Exam result by:				
Occupation	21·41	4	< 0·001	5·35
VR band	220·37	4	< 0·001	55·09
School	251·63	22	< 0·001	11·44

Table 9.1 *Log linear analysis of exam results*

In this and all subsequent analyses, the numbers of children in each band by occupation and by school category were fixed by including the appropiate interaction term in the model. If not reported, all higher order interaction terms involving the response variables (i.e. exam results, attendance and delinquency) were non-significant.

namely whether there were significant differences between schools in exam success, once account has been taken of the children's verbal reasoning ability and their families' occupational background. Table 9.1 shows that, as before, the answer is 'yes'. Verbal reasoning, occupation and school all showed significant associations with exam scores (and there were no significant higher order interactions between these parameters).

The second part of the analysis is completely focused on the 'result by school' term (i.e. the contribution made by variations between schools, once the effects of VR band and occupation had been allowed for). The fact that this term was significant indicates that schools did differ in their exam results even after taking into account the differences between children in verbal ability and parental occupation. The question we move on to now is whether this 'result by school' term can be 'explained' by including balance and process in the model. In other words, is a child's exam success affected by the characteristics of the school he attends, either in terms of process (as considered in Chapter 7) or balance of intake (as considered in Chapter 8). Once again, the answers obtained by log linear modelling (see Table 9.2) are broadly in agreement with those which stemmed from our earlier analyses using rank correlation techniques. Grouping schools accor-

*The figure for G^2, considered in relation to its degrees of freedom, provides an estimate of the relative importance of any parameter. In a rough and ready kind of way, G^2/df may be used to compare the relative effects of parameters with differing degrees of freedom. Thus in the above table, the child's ability band has much the stronger effect in relation to exam success.

Parameters	G^2 attributable to parameter	df	p	G^2/df
1. Balance Groups				
(a) Academic balance				
Exam result by school (see Table 9.1)	251·63	22		
Attributable to balance groups	123·46	4	<0·001	30·87
Attributable to schools within balance groups	128·17	18	<0·001	7·12
(b) Occupational balance				
Exam result by school (see Table 9.1)	251·63	22		
Attributable to balance groups	32·88	4	<0·001	8·22
Attributable to schools within balance groups	218·75	18	<0·001	12·15
(c) Behavioural balance				
Exam result by school (see Table 9.1)	251·63	22		
Attributable to balance groups	79·97	4	<0·001	19·99
Attributable to schools within balance groups	171·66	18	<0·001	9·54
(d) Ethnic Mix				
Exam result by school (see Table 9.1)	251·63	22		
Attributable to balance groups	129·81	4	<0·001	32·45
Attributable to schools within balance groups	121·82	18	<0·001	6·77
2. Process Groups				
Exam result by school (see Table 9.1)	251·63	22		
Attributable to process groups	124·81	4	<0·001	31·20
Attributable to schools within process groups	126·82	18	<0·001	7·04

Table 9.2 *Separate effects of balance and process on exam results (Log linear analysis)*

ding to their intake balance, or their process scores, both led to significant effects. Of the various balance factors, academic and ethnic balance proved to be the most important.

The third part of the analysis deals with the issue which could not be considered before – namely how far both process and balance were important for exam success if they were considered together in *combination*. For this purpose, balance of intake was categorised in two ways – first according to the balance factors most strongly associated with exam success (namely academic balance and ethnic mix), and secondly according to a composite balance variable which combined all the separate balance factors which had been previously found to be significantly associated with exam outcome. As it turned out, the schools fell into the same balance blocks whichever procedure was followed. The process groupings of the schools were then to be 'nested' within these balance groups, as described above.

Table 9.3 shows that having allowed for balance of intake (as well as VR band and parental occupation) school process had a highly significant association with exam success. The overall conclusion from this log linear model analysis is that a child's examination success is connected, not only with his own ability level and the occupational status of his family, but also with the process and balance groups into which his school fell. While no very exact comparisons of the relative size of effect of balance of intake and school process are possible, a crude guide to the relative importance of the effects can be obtained by dividing the G^2 value by its appropriate degrees of freedom. It may be firmly concluded that *both* process and intake have strong effects.

At first sight it may seem surprising from this analysis that the effects of school process and balance of intake on examination success are much greater than the effects of parental occupation and about half as powerful as the child's own ability level (compare the G^2/df in Table 9.3 with those in Table 9.1). However, it should be appreciated in this connection that the model was set up to look at differences in academic outcome between *groups* of children and not between individuals. This was appropriate in that the object of the study was to investigate the reasons why average levels of examination success differed so markedly between schools. The answer to this question lay both in the characteristics of the schools (as reflected in balance of intake and school process) and in those of the children. However, *within* any one school there were also huge variations between children in levels of

Parameters	G^2 attributable to parameter	df	p	G^2/df
Exam results by school (see Table 9.1)	251·63	22		
Attributable to academic balance group	37·20	2	< 0·001	18·60
Attributable to process within balance group	102·86	4	< 0·001	25·72
Attributable to schools within groups	111·57	16	< 0·001	6·97

Table 9.3 *Combined effects of balance and process on exam results (Log linear analysis)*

examination success. These individual differences were, of course, largely due to variations in children's personal characteristics (including verbal ability), and their home background and experiences.

This alteration of emphasis according to whether differences between schools or differences between individual children within a school are being considered is brought out by an alternative method of multi-variate analysis. The strength and robustness of the log linear model method of analysis lies in its ability to model the associations between many variables, making only very general assumptions about their distribution. On the other hand, it suffers from the limitations imposed by having to group the data in ways which fail to take the full range of the measures into account.

Multiple linear regression

Multiple linear regression has the opposite set of strengths and weaknesses (see Maxwell, 1977). In essence, this analysis uses the pattern of correlations between variables to determine the relative effect of each variable, once its associations with other variables have been taken into account. It makes full use of the total range of all measures, but it does require the variables to have certain statistical properties which are rarely fully met in the social sciences.

Table 9.4 gives the results of an hierarchical linear regression in which the effects of the child's verbal reasoning score, parental occupa-

Order of Entry into equation		% of variance explained	Sig.
1	VR group	14·45	< 0·001
2	Parental Occupation	0·10	NS
3	% Occup. 1 Ethnic mix % Occup. 3 % Band 1 Behavioural Balance % Band 3	10·31	< 0·001
4	Process	1·06	< 0·001

Total variance explained = 25·92%
(Multiple r = 0·51)

Table 9.4 *Linear regression – exam results*

tion, and the various balance of intake scores were always examined *before* introducing school process into the equations. This was done in order to examine process effects only after taking into account the full effect of all other prior variables.

In earlier analyses, the child's VR score had proved to be much the most powerful predictor of exam success. Once VR was entered into the equation in this hierarchical approach, parental occupation showed only a non-significant contribution, but the 'process' score of the school attended was correlated significantly with exam success even after taking all other variables into account. The precise figures, of course, should not be taken too seriously because of the many hazards in employing this form of analysis with data of the type we collected.* The regression procedure is concerned with *individual* differences rather than with *school* differences and, as one would expect, the predictive power of balance of intake and of school process was much less marked in this context. However, both factors were still significant predictors, and the findings serve to support the statistically more appropriate log linear models approach. The conclusion is clear: children's levels of examination success are affected by the school they attend, and the crucial features of schooling with respect to academic outcome include both school process and balance of intake.

Attendance

Log linear analysis

The same three stage log linear analysis as that described for exam success was used to examine school attendance. For this purpose attendance was grouped into three categories: 'O' (0–10 attendance out of 20), '1' (11–19/20) and '2' (20/20). The first stage (see Table 9.5 in Appendix G) confirmed that verbal reasoning, occupation and school showed significant relationships with attendance.

---

* One of the weaknesses of this approach arises from the fact that school process and balance variables have to be used as a score for each child, so that all children at the same school necessarily receive the same score. This has two main consequences. First, because it involves the misleading assumption that all children at any one school receive the same school experiences, the result tends to *under*estimate the size of school effects. Secondly, because the *child* is taken as the unit of analysis, even small effects will be significant because of the large number of degrees of freedom involved.

The second stage, in which schools were grouped according to different intake balance factors and according to process scores, showed that occupational balance had no significant effect and could, therefore, be disregarded (see Table 9.6 in Appendix G). School process had much the strongest effect, but academic balance and behavioural mix (to a lesser extent also ethnic mix) had quite substantial and statistically significant associations with attendance.

The third stage in the analysis, introducing process groupings within the most powerful balance groups (of behavioural mix in this case), suggest that the findings on school process may need to be regarded with some caution (see Table 9.7 in Appendix G). When process was nested within balance groupings, it appeared to have rather limited effects, and differences between individual schools appeared to be of greater importance. The crudity of the groupings in this final stage in the analysis prevent us from relying too heavily on this conclusion, but it does appear that, once individual characteristics and balance factors have been taken into account, the very considerable differences which still remain between schools in attendance rates may be associated with factors other than the ones we have studied.

Multiple linear regression

Table 9.8 in Appendix G shows the results of an hierarchical linear regression in which the child's attendance, VR score, parental occupation and school balance scores are examined before introducing the school process score. Even after taking into account all the prior variables, process made a small but significant contribution to the final equation. For the reasons discussed earlier in relation to the similar analyses of the exam results, it is not possible to place much reliance on this technique. But it does seem that children's attendance is affected not only by personal variables, but also by the balance of intake to the school, the process characteristics of the school, and by other features of school life.

Delinquency

Delinquency was categorised simply on a 0–1 (none-some) basis for the log linear analysis. The first stage (Table 9.9 in Appendix G) showed that parental occupation, child's verbal reasoning score, and school were all significantly associated with delinquency, as we have seen in the earlier analyses in Chapter 5.

The second stage of the modelling in which the balance and process parameters were introduced (see Table 9.10 in Appendix G) showed that academic balance made much the strongest contribution. Neither occupational balance nor behavioural mix made any significant contribution. Ethnic mix showed a significant effect, as also did school process. It is notable that there was no significant variation left to be explained once academic balance had been introduced into the model. The strong implication was that, *un*like the case with the other outcome variables, once academic balance had been taken into account, school process made only a marginal contribution.

This was checked by proceeding to the third stage involving the nested log linear model. As there were nine boys' schools it was necessary to drop one school for this purpose. The school with the highest delinquency rate, which appeared rather separate from the others, was selected for omission. Because the nesting had to be carried out with a reduced number of schools (making only one degree of freedom for balance and two for process) the findings must be viewed with very considerable caution. However, it may be seen from Table 9.11 (see Appendix G) that they broadly confirm the conclusion that balance factors predominate over school processes in their effects on delinquency. There was, however, a significant school process effect ($G^2 = 15 \cdot 4$; 1 df; $p < 0 \cdot 001$) when the nesting was done the other way round; that is balance within process groups. Perhaps in view of the limitations of the log linear modelling procedure with just eight schools it is going too far to say that school process factors were of no importance. Nevertheless, these findings certainly demonstrate that the pattern of influences was rather different in the case of delinquency. The child's family background (with respect to occupational status) and the balance of academic intake to the school he attends were more important than in the case of the other outcome variables.

Multiple linear regression analysis

An hierarchical multiple linear regression analysis was undertaken in the same manner as that followed for exam success (see Table 9.12 in

Appendix G). The regression equation produced only a poor prediction of delinquency and little reliance can be placed on the results. School process, however, did show a significant association with outcome.

Conclusions

There are difficulties with all types of multidimensional statistical analysis, and no one procedure is obviously superior in all respects. However, with respect to our findings from this study of twelve London secondary schools, the important feature is that all analyses (both the variable by variable analyses reported in earlier chapters, and the more complex combined analyses reported in this chapter) all pointed rather consistently in the same direction. It appears that children's observed behaviour in the school was strongly associated with school process variables. Of all the outcomes considered, this is the one for which the child's personal characteristics, his home background and the balance of intake to the school were least important. Of course, there are *other* aspects of children's behaviour which may well be strongly influenced by these personal, family and social variables. But for the behaviours we considered, it seemed that to a very large extent they had developed as the child's response to the school environment he encountered.

Children's academic attainment was also strongly and consistently associated with school process influences, even after other variables had been taken statistically into account. On the other hand, in addition, a child's examination success was strongly linked with his own ability level as measured prior to secondary school transfer, and to the academic balance of the secondary school he attended.

The findings with respect to school attendance were a bit more complicated in terms of the interactions between variables. However, as with examination success, school process, the child's ability level and the intake balance of the school all stood out as important factors. In combination, their relationships seemed more complex, and it seemed that variations between individual schools, unrelated to the measures of process, were also playing an important part.

Delinquency was the one odd man out in the four outcome measures. As with the other outcomes, the child's ability level was important but, unlike the others, parental occupation was about equally important. But the biggest difference lay in the very large effect of academic balance and the much smaller effect of school process. The implication was that peer group influences of some kind were serving to shape children's behaviour. It is interesting in this context to note that it was *academic* balance which was crucial rather than any mix in terms of the socio-cultural backgrounds from which the children came.

The meaning of these associations and the practical implications which follow from them are considered in the final chapter.

10

Conclusions: speculations and implications

In previous chapters our discussion has kept rather close to the research data, dealing with a variety of methodological issues and presenting the substantive findings as objectively as possible, with only minor digressions on theoretical notions concerning school functioning or school influence. In this final chapter we will approach the findings in a more speculative fashion. The statistical results will serve as a base from which to consider the possible mechanisms and meanings which might underlie the numerical correlations, associations and differences. Of necessity, this process of interpretation is a more subjective one, so that opinions may reasonably differ on the best conceptual explanations of the results. Nevertheless, if the study findings are to be of use in educational practice, it is essential to ask *why* schools function in the ways that they do, and to consider *how* and by *which* means they have an impact on the behaviour and attainments of the children they serve.

Before discussing the educational meaning of the findings, however, it may be helpful to recapitulate the ten main conclusions which have emerged from the study.

Summary of conclusions

First, secondary schools in inner London differed markedly in the behaviour and attainments shown by their pupils. This was evident in the children's behaviour whilst at school (as observed by us as well as reported by teachers and by the pupils themselves), the regularity of their attendance, the proportions staying on at school beyond the legally enforced period, their success in public examinations, and their delinquency rates.

Second, although schools differed in the proportion of behaviourally difficult or low achieving children they admitted, these differences did *not* wholly account for the variations between schools in their pupils' later behaviour and attainment. Even when comparisons between schools were restricted to children who were quite similar in family background and personal characteristics prior to secondary transfer, marked school variations remained. This meant that children were more likely to show good behaviour and good scholastic attainments if they attended some schools than if they attended others. The implication is that experiences during the secondary school years may influence children's progress.

Third, the variations between schools in different forms of 'outcome' for their pupils were reasonably stable over periods of at least four or five years.

Fourth, in general, schools performed fairly similarly on all the various measures of outcome. That is, schools which did better than average in terms of the children's behaviour in school tended also to do better than average in terms of examination success and delinquency. There were some exceptions to this pattern, but it appeared that in most schools the different forms of success were closely connected.

Fifth, these differences in outcome between schools were *not* due to such physical factors as the size of the school, the age of the buildings or the space available; nor were they due to broad differences in administrative status or organisation. It was entirely possible for schools to obtain good outcomes in spite of initially rather unpromising and unprepossessing school premises, and within the context of somewhat differing administrative arrangements.

Sixth, the differences between schools in outcome *were* systematically related to their characteristics as social institutions. Factors as varied as the degree of academic emphasis, teacher actions in lessons, the availability of incentives and rewards, good conditions for pupils, and the extent to which children were able to take responsibility were all significantly associated with outcome differences between schools. All of these factors were open to modification by the staff, rather than fixed by external constraints.

Seventh, outcomes were also influenced by factors *outside* teachers' immediate control. The academic balance in the intakes to the schools was particularly important in this connection. Examination success tended to be better in schools with a substantial nucleus of children of at least average intellectual ability, and delinquency rates were higher in those with a heavy preponderance of the least able. Interestingly, however, while the balance of intake was significantly associated with pupil outcome, it did *not* appear to have any comparable influence on school functioning, as reflected in our school process measures.

Eighth, this effect of balance in the intake was most marked with respect to delinquency, and least important in the case of the children's observed behaviour in the classroom and elsewhere about the school.

Ninth, the association between the *combined* measure of overall school process and each of the measures of outcome was much stronger than any of the associations with individual process variables. This suggests that the *cumulative* effect of these various social factors was considerably greater than the effect of any of the individual factors on their own. The implication is that the individual actions or measures may combine to create a particular *ethos*, or set of values, attitudes and behaviours which will become characteristic of the school as a whole.

Tenth, the total pattern of findings indicates the strong probability that the associations between school process and outcome reflect in part a *causal* process. In other words, to an appreciable extent children's behaviour and attitudes are shaped and influenced by their experiences at school and, in particular, by the qualities of the school as a social institution.

Comparison with other studies

The first crucial test with any piece of research is whether comparable studies show similar results. Accordingly, before considering the implications of our findings, it is necessary to see how far the broad pattern of the results is in agreement with the previous research reviewed in the first chapter.

Our finding that secondary schools varied greatly with respect to rates of examination success, attendance, misbehaviour and delinquency is entirely in keeping with the evidence from other research. However, our investigation has taken matters a stage further by showing that these differences were not explicable in terms of the children's characteristics prior to secondary transfer. Rather, they stemmed from experiences during the secondary school years.

Earlier work has been consistent in showing that the main source of variations between schools in their effects on children did not lie in factors such as buildings or resources. We found the same. Previous investigations had pointed to the possibility that the essential difference would be found in the school's functioning as a social organisation, and as a setting for teaching and learning. Our data strongly substantiate that suggestion. Because we were able to use measures of what was *actually* done in schools (including observations in the classroom) we were able to translate the previously noted variations in school climate and morale into the specifics of school practice.

Our observations on the importance of the academic balance in a school's intake of pupils are new. Previous research has largely focused on *social* mix, and has shown, as we did, that this had only a marginal effect on scholastic attainment. The association we found between a high proportion of less able children in a school's intake and a high propensity to delinquency is in keeping with many prevailing theoretical ideas (see Hirschi and Hindelang, 1977) but earlier investigations have not obtained empirical data on this link.

In short, it is clear that at this general level, other studies (insofar as they have used comparable methods) have produced broadly similar findings. But, in several respects, our findings considerably extend knowledge on the links between school processes and school outcomes.

School process: a causal influence?

We have suggested that there is a causal relationship between school process and children's progress. Firm conclusions about causation can only come from controlled experimental studies. The only way to be sure that school practices actually influence children's behaviour and attainments is to alter those practices and then determine if this results in changes in the children's progress. In a non-experimental study, the *pattern* of statistical associations can nevertheless provide quite good guidance as to whether a relationship is likely to reflect a casual effect.

In the present study, the existence of longitudinal data was particularly helpful in showing that the pupil outcomes were associated with experiences which occurred during the years of secondary schooling. Not only did the schools differ in outcome after controlling for the children's measured characteristics at intake, but also these differences in outcome were systematically associated with measured features of the schools.

But perhaps the most crucial point concerns the pattern of correlations with school process. The question here is whether schools were as they were because of the children they admitted, or rather whether children behaved in the way they did because of school influences. Of course, interactions will take place in both directions, but the much greater correlation between school process and children's behaviour/attainments at the *end* of secondary schooling strongly implies a greater effect of schools on children than of children on schools. We may infer that it is very likely that school processes *do* influence pupil outcome.

Of course it is not suggested that the links work only in one direction. As we have already discussed, schools constitute just one element in a complex set of ecological interactions, and are shaped and constrained by a variety of societal forces outside their immediate control. They are likely to be influenced by the types of neighbourhood they serve; running a school in a remote country village is not the same as running one in inner London. Factors such as the extent of parental support and community involvement are also liable to influence how a school functions as a social unit. The teaching task in an academically selective school serving a prosperous middle-class district will be very different from that in a school with a heavy preponderance of less able pupils from socially disadvantaged homes.

Our study was not able to look at variations of this kind, but they are clearly important issues. Even within a similar geographical area, external influences, and perhaps most importantly the pupils themselves, will play a part in shaping school life. The initial teaching task is shaped by the attitudes, behaviour, interests and capabilities of the children in the class. Teacher actions then influence children's behaviour, which in turn modifies teacher behaviour, which then further impinges on the children. In this way, spirals of either improving or deteriorating behaviour (and attainments) seem likely to be built up.

The pattern of connections is complex. It is nevertheless clear that within this network, schools have a considerable degree of choice in how they are organised, and that teachers have a similar choice in their decisions on how to respond to the children they teach. Our results suggest that these decisions on how to respond are likely to affect the chances of the children improving in their behaviour and attainments.

It is not argued that schools are the *most* important influence on children's progress, and we agree with Bernstein (1970) that education cannot compensate for the inequities of society. Nevertheless, we do suggest that schools constitute one major area of influence, and one which is susceptible to change. However, for this conclusion to be of much use to practitioners, it is necessary to go on to consider some of the possible mechanisms which may be involved. The statistical associations which we have discussed in earlier chapters need to be restated in terms of the processes and meanings which they may reflect. Such a translation necessarily draws on other research as well as our own investigations, and will involve moving on from the details of our findings to some more general discussion of their possible meanings.

Schools as social organisations

Evidence for an institutional effect

The school process measures which correlated with the four types of pupil outcome included a wide variety of factors. Doubtless, as we will come to consider later, they operated by a variety of different mechanisms. It was striking, however, that their *combined* effect was much more powerful than that of any individual factor considered on its own. For this and other reasons, we have suggested that some kind of overall school 'ethos' might be involved.

Before considering how the individual process variables might operate in the context of such an institutional effect we need to ask why it is necessary to talk in terms of an ethos at all. Could it not be that school process variables act by directly shaping the behaviour of individual children? Obviously, this does occur (as we will indicate) but there are three main reasons for arguing that there is likely to be a broader institutional effect as well.

Firstly, most of the individual process variables had only a most indirect connection with the outcome with which they were statistically associated. We found a host of school factors which correlated significantly with attendance, but many of these did not involve any kind of teacher or school response to absconding or truanting as such. Moreover, some school process and balance of intake variables were significantly associated with child behaviours completely outside the school itself – as, for example, with delinquency. The implication is that the style and quality of life at school was having a relatively pervasive effect on children's behaviour – an effect which went beyond any kind of immediate shaping by direct rewards and punishments.

Secondly, we observed (although we have few quantitative measures to document this) that the *same* teacher actions sometimes led to quite *different* results in different schools. For example, if children were left alone in lessons to get on with their own work, in some schools they did just that. In others, any relaxation of direct control led to an increase in disruptive behaviour. It appeared that there was something about the way children were dealt with in general which influenced their behaviour even when there was no direct supervision by staff.

Third, many of the variables did not refer to actions which bore directly on individual children. Thus, some were concerned with conditions in the school generally (e.g. care of the buildings). Others were involved with the management of groups (for example the *dis*advantage of frequent individual interactions in class-oriented teaching) or concerned teacher behaviours which were not focused on any individual (e.g. the effect of frequently ending lessons early or beginning them late). We need to recognise that the way of responding to an individual child will have an effect on the *rest* of the class. This may be relevant, for example, in the case of unofficial sanctions. Experimental studies provide ample demonstrations of the fact that punishment can be a most effective way of controlling behaviour (see Walters and Grusec, 1977). But in a school context the ways in which punishment is used and the frequency with which it is given will carry messages to *other* children, and create an atmosphere which can run counter to the intended effect on the offending individual.

Taken together, these three aspects of our findings suggest that the importance of the separate school process measures may lie in their contribution to the ethos or climate of the school as a whole.

Concept of ethos

By introducing the concept of an ethos, we mean that it is valuable to think of schools in terms of their characteristics as social organisations (see Getzels, 1969; also Shipman, 1975). Numerous studies have documented the well-nigh universal tendency for individuals in common circumstances to form social groups with their own rules, values and standards of behaviour (see Newcomb *et al.*, 1969; Sherif and Sherif, 1969). Group influences tend to be quite powerful, and there is a general tendency for people to 'go along' with the majority (see Kelvin, 1969). Indeed, people going against the norm are likely to experience considerable anxiety (Hoffman, 1957). In approaching our findings on school processes we have drawn parallels with a variety of other somewhat similar studies of different institutions such as hospitals, hostels, children's homes and the like. All these studies have shown that any relatively self-contained organisation tends to develop its own culture or pattern; this also applies to secondary schools. We need to consider now how the individual process measures might operate in such a context.

Group management in the classroom

Both individual classes and the total school constitute different forms of social group and, as with any social groups, skills are involved in their management. The general sensitivity and efficiency with which this is done is likely to produce strong effects on the pupils' group behaviour. At least two separate issues, teaching approach and disciplinary style, arise from our research findings.

With respect to the overall organisation of class teaching, we found that children's classroom behaviour was much better when the teacher had prepared the lesson in advance, so that little time was wasted at the beginning in setting up apparatus or handing out books and papers; when the teacher arrived on time at the start of the lesson; and when, if the lesson was planned as class-oriented, the teacher mainly directed attention to the class as a whole. These results are in good agreement with previous research (see Bennett, 1978). Gump (1974) noted the marked differences between schools in the proportion of time spent moving, waiting, getting organised or clearing up. It seems as if one of the hallmarks of successful class management is keeping pupils actively engaged in productive activities rather than waiting for something to happen. Smooth transitions from one activity to the next are also characteristic of successful teaching (Brophy and Evertson, 1976). The findings suggest that when, in a class-based lesson, a teacher spends too much time dealing with the problems and activities of individual children, the attention of the rest of the class may be lost. When dealing with a group as a whole, it seems essential to keep all the children involved and interested, and to be aware of what is going on in all parts of the room (Kounin, 1970).

Good pupil behaviour was also strongly associated with the teachers' style of discipline. The amount of formal punishment made little difference, but frequent disciplinary interventions were linked with more disruptive behaviour in the classroom. Conversely, pupil behaviour was much better when teachers used an ample amount of praise in their teaching. These results are in keeping with many experimental studies of teacher-child interaction which have shown the advantages of focusing on good behaviour rather than on disruptive acts (see e.g. Becker *et al.*, 1967). It has also been found that relatively quiet reprimands are often more effective than loud ones (O'Leary *et al.*, 1970). The point is *not* that misbehaving pupils should be allowed to 'get away with it'. Indeed, simply ignoring inappropriate behaviour may lead to chaos if nothing else is done (Madsen *et al.*, 1968). Rather, the implications lie in the effects on the class as a whole. Brophy and Evertson (1976) reported that the teachers who were most successful in classroom management tended to spot disruptive behaviour early and to deal with it appropriately and firmly with the minimum of interference with the lesson.

Three different mechanisms seem to underlie the unhelpful aspects of very frequent disciplinary interventions. First, the teacher's disciplinary action towards one child may elicit rewarding responses from the others. Loud reprimands serve to draw the attention of the whole class to the disruptive pupil, and if the child's aim is to gain the interest and approval of his peers, this may be just what he wants. Secondly, there are the effects on the work of the rest of the class. Even if reprimands or punishment stop the misbehaviour of the *one* child, they will almost certainly interrupt the activities of the *others*. Thirdly, the tensions and resentment which stem from the negative atmosphere created by constant nagging and reprimands may actually provoke and perpetuate disruptive behaviour. In a very detailed study of family interactions in the home, Patterson (1977) showed that disapproval tended to increase the likelihood that the child would show hostile behaviour, and physical punishment increased the likelihood of social aggression.

Of course, the teachers' disciplinary interventions do not occur without good reason – the reprimands and punishment are used to deal with disruptive classes. The point is that this particular style of teacher response may well tend to aggravate rather than ameliorate the situation. It is also interesting in this context that the schools which used high rates of disciplinary intervention in the classroom were not necessarily those with a high proportion of problem children in their intakes.

Obviously a certain amount of firm disapproval, and also punishment, is necessary in the control of disruptive behaviour. On the other hand, our results and those of other investigations suggest that a disciplinary style which involves very frequent interventions is likely to be counterproductive. Rather, overall class management seems more likely to be successful when praise is freely given and when disciplinary actions are few but firm.

The measures we used touched on only a few aspects of classroom management and there are innumerable ways in which good management may be achieved. What is important is that teachers learn the skills involved. Probationary teachers were notably less successful in coping with their classes than their more experienced colleagues and it is important that schools provide the means for helping new recruits to learn some of the best ways of managing their classes. Experience is crucial, but the nature of the experience and the extent to which it is guided and supervised by more senior teachers is also important.

School values and norms of behaviour

The class constitutes one sort of social group; the school as a whole constitutes another. The issues with regard to the school are somewhat different from those which apply to the classroom in that (apart from school assemblies and the like) it is not usually a question of 'managing' a group of children all assembled together for a particular purpose. Instead, the questions here concern the nature of school values and norms, the degree to which these are consistent throughout the school, and the extent to which the children accept them. It is useful to consider these three issues separately, as rather different factors operate.

Strictly speaking, in discussing the meaning of our findings on the effects of school values and norms of behaviour, we are restricted to the norms which were characteristic of the particular twelve schools we studied and to the four specific outcomes we measured. However, as we emphasised at the start, these measures should be seen only as *indicators* of school success and not as the sole, or even the most important, aims of schooling. Our fifth measure, of patterns of employment, adds an essential additional dimension to outcome, but even so work is just one aspect of life. Schools may see their educational objectives as applying equally to the fostering of an enthusiasm and interest in learning, of confidence and the ability to take responsibility, of adaptability to cope with life changes, of the development of personal relationships, or of individuality. Schools have a choice in the norms they select. Our discussion of the ways in which norms may be established and accepted by pupils is concerned with social mechanisms in schools generally and *not* with the particular norms we assessed.

Norms and values can be established in a variety of different ways. So far as secondary schools are concerned, the chief mechanisms are likely to be: (i) teachers' expectations about the children's work and behaviour, (ii) the models provided by the teachers' own conduct in school, and by the behaviour of the other pupils, and (iii) the feedback that the children receive on what is acceptable performance at the school.

Expectations and standards

Children are very quick to pick up other people's expectations about both their academic competence and their behaviour. Other research has shown that, to an important extent, people tend to live up (or down) to what is expected of them. This occurs at both an individual and a group level. For example, David Farrington (1977) and Farrington *et al.* (1978) showed that youths who were publicly labelled as delinquent (through Court conviction) tended to become more delinquent as a result. This conclusion was based on the boys' own reports of their (mostly undetected) delinquency, so that the finding was not just a matter of their becoming more likely to get caught once they had become involved with the police on an earlier occasion.

Similarly, both laboratory experiments and studies of working groups show that people tend to be more or less productive according to the prevailing group norms for productivity (Vroom, 1969); working to the level of group norms in this way is most likely to occur in socially cohesive groups. Provided people see their supervisors as supportive, and provided they accept the work situation, the setting of specific, difficult but attainable goals tends to lead to better work performance (see Korman *et al.*, 1977).

Our results suggest that the same principles apply within secondary schools. Children had better academic success in schools where homework was regularly set and marked, and where the teachers expressed expectations that a high proportion of the children would do well in national examinations. It appears that both general attitudes and specific actions to emphasise academic expectations can play a part here. Children are liable to work better if taught in an atmosphere of confidence that they can and will succeed in the tasks they are set. Of course, in turn, the children's good work will tend to reinforce and support the teachers' high expectations of them. Other research, reviewed by Pilling and Pringle (1978), also indicates that teachers' expectations influence pupils' academic progress.

The same mechanisms apply as much to behaviour as to scholastic success. Thus, giving children responsibility for looking after school books and papers conveys the teacher's expectations that they will behave responsibly, and will take good care of the school property. The findings showed that schools which expected children to care for their own resources had better behaviour, better attendance and less delinquency. In a similar way, giving children posts or tasks of responsibility (such as the post of form captain or participation in school assemblies) was associated with better pupil behaviour. The message of confidence that the pupils can be trusted to act with maturity and responsibility is likely to encourage pupils to fulfil those expectations.

Models provided by teachers

Standards of behaviour in school are also set by the behaviour of the staff. There is an extensive research literature (see Bandura, 1969) which shows that children have a strong tendency to copy the behaviour of other people – especially people in positions of authority whom they like and respect. Moreover, not only do they copy specific behaviours, but they also tend to identify in a more general way with the people whom they follow, and come to adopt what they perceive to be their values and attitudes. This means that pupils are likely to be influenced – either for good or ill – by the models of behaviour provided by teachers both in the classroom and elsewhere. These will not be restricted to the ways in which teachers treat the children, but may also include the ways staff interact with one another, and how they view the school. Our observations of good care of the buildings, and the willingness of teachers to see pupils about problems at any time, provide some examples of *positive* models. These actions convey the message that the school is valued and thought to be worth keeping clean and in good decorative condition; and that staff appreciate the needs of children sufficiently to give their own time to help them when they experience difficulties. *Negative* models would be provided by teachers starting lessons late and ending them early, and by their use of unofficial physical sanctions. If teachers react with violence to provocation and disruptiveness this may well encourage pupils to do the same. Similarly, if the teachers' own behaviour suggests that they disregard timekeeping, they can scarcely expect good timekeeping and attendance from the pupils. Other research has also noted the importance of staff models of behaviour. Thus, Clegg and Megson (1968) found that attention to staff punctuality was an important element in raising the standards in one secondary school they observed.

Of course, teachers are by no means the only available models of behaviour. Secondary school pupils are likely to be influenced by their peers and, when younger, by the behaviour of pupils higher up the school. We will come to discuss peer group influences, and their very important effects, in more detail later in this chapter.

Feedback

The feedback that a child receives about what is and what is not acceptable at school will also constitute a powerful influence on his behaviour. The feedback may be direct and immediate, in terms of praise or reprimand in the classroom; it may be less direct and more delayed, in terms of annual prizes for work or sport; or it may be quite indirect, as with putting children's work up on the walls. Our findings showed that the most immediate and direct feedback in terms of praise or approval had the strongest association with pupil behaviour. Prizes for sport were associated with good attendance but not with any of the other outcomes, and prizes for work were quite unrelated to any of the outcome measures. The amount of punishment showed only weak, and generally non-significant, associations with outcome, and when the associations did reach significance, the trend was for higher levels of punishment to be associated with *worse* outcomes.

If it is assumed that effective feedback is generally helpful (and there is good evidence that it is − see, for example, Brophy and Evertson, 1976), two apparently puzzling features of these results stand out and require some discussion: (i) the relative ineffectiveness of formal prizes and (ii) the relative ineffectiveness (and sometimes adverse effects) of punishment.

There are probably three characteristics of formal prizes which tend to reduce their benefits. First, they are usually given only to a few pupils. In terms of overall school effects, the important factor is likely to be the *proportion* of pupils who receive prizes, rather than the number of rewards which are available. It may be that the discouragement felt by the majority as a result of not receiving a prize is as important as the benefits which accrue to the minority who do receive them. Second, rewards which are long delayed tend to be rather inefficient − presumably because there are such loose and indefinite links with the behaviour which the prize aims to reward. A prize may be given for generally high standards of work over a whole year, but the immediate connection in the child's mind may be with his easing off in the last few weeks as he rested on the laurels of past achievements. Thirdly, when *material* rewards are given for intrinsically interesting activities, in some circumstances the result may be a *fall-off* in motivation (Lepper, Greene and Nisbet, 1973; Smith and Pittman, 1978) − probably because the rewards have the effect of replacing intrinsic motivation with extrinsic interest which depends on the receipt of prizes. Praise and appreciation from teachers are less likely to have this inhibiting effect, and indeed may even increase the intrinsic rewards from activities which are seen to be appreciated by the teacher. For all these reasons, it is not surprising that daily appreciation in the classroom is likely to have a greater effect than occasional prizes. However, it should *not* be assumed that formal prize-givings are without merit. On the contrary, they probably help in providing a public demonstration of the value placed by the school on good achievements (in work, sport, music or other activities). Our results showed some association between prizes and good outcomes – it was just that the effects of classroom praise seemed to be much greater.

Formal punishments (such as canings or being told off by the Head) also suffer from the drawbacks associated with delay, although the delays are usually less than is the case with prizes. In addition, there are the possibly adverse secondary effects which may accompany physical or very frequent punishments – the negative atmosphere, the resentment of humiliation, and the model of violence (which may be provided). The findings from other studies are similar to our own in this area. Thus, Clegg and Megson (1968) and Reynolds and Murgatroyd (1977) found, respectively, that high rates of corporal punishment were associated with more delinquency and poorer attendance. Heal (1978) found misbehaviour worse in schools with formal punishment systems. It should not be concluded that good outcomes are most likely when there is no punishment. All of the schools in our study used punishments and reprimands fairly frequently, and it is obvious that any school must have effective means of indicating firm disapproval of misbehaviour. However, it does seem to be important that there should be the right balance between reward and punishment. Both have a place, but an excessive use of punishments is likely to be discouraging and to lead to low morale. Praise, rewards and encouragements need to outweigh negative sanctions. When giving praise it is important, however, that the currency should be *real*. Children usually know when they have done well or badly and rewards for poor quality work rapidly become devalued and ineffective.

In this connection it is relevant to note that rewards come not only from praise or prizes which are given by staff, but also are implicit in the successful accomplishment of a job well done. It seems important to organise things so that most children are able to succeed most of the time, but, of course, providing a gradient of difficulty so that there is steady progress.

Consistency of school values

Expectations, models and feedback are all likely to affect the ways in which pupils' behaviour and attitudes develop within a school.

Processes of this kind operate in all social settings – on an individual basis, in individual interactions between a teacher and pupil, in lessons, or about the school generally. As we have seen, they can lead to both good and bad results and to both intended and unintended consequences. These processes can do a great deal to establish positive values in a school but the factors are not in any way dependent on the existence of a cohesive social group for their influence. On the other hand, many studies have shown that the effects of norms are more powerful when they are clearly established as applying to a whole social group, and when the group itself is cohesive and supportive of its members (see Vroom, 1969). The 'atmosphere' of any particular school will be greatly influenced by the degree to which it functions as a coherent whole, with agreed ways of doing things which are consistent throughout the school and which have the general support of all staff.

We had several findings which suggested that this applied in the schools we studied. Outcomes tended to be better when both the curriculum and approaches to discipline were agreed and supported by the staff acting together. Thus, attendance was better and delinquency less frequent in schools where courses were planned jointly. It was not just that this facilitated continuities in teaching (although it did) but also that group planning provided opportunities for teachers to encourage and support one another.

Much the same applied with standards of discipline. Exam successes were more frequent and delinquency less common in schools where discipline was based on general expectations set by the school (or house or department), rather than left to individual teachers to work out for themselves. For obvious reasons, school values and norms are likely to be more effective if it is clear to all that they have widespread support. Discipline will be easier to maintain if the pupils appreciate that it relates to generally accepted approaches and does not simply represent the whims of the individual teacher. The particular rules which are set and the specific disciplinary techniques which are used are probably much less important than the establishment of some principles and guidelines which are both clearly recognisable and accepted by the school as a whole.

The importance of some kind of school-wide set of values and norms of behaviour was also reflected in our findings that in the more successful schools teachers reported that their senior colleagues were aware of matters such as staff punctuality and that they checked that policies were being maintained, as in the setting of homework. This was not a matter of intrusive control or supervision but rather a reflection that staff cared about the way the school functioned. It appeared that an efficient system within which teachers worked harmoniously towards agreed goals was conducive to both good morale and effective teaching.

This was also implicit in our findings on the pattern of decision making in the schools with better pupil outcomes. The importance of a sense of direction was suggested by the observation that in schools with good outcomes decisions tended to be made at a senior level rather than in the staffroom. On the other hand, in these same schools teachers stated that their views were represented and considered. It seemed necessary that teachers should feel that they had some part in the decision-making process but also that they had sufficient confidence in the staff group as a whole that they were content for their opinions and suggestions to be expressed by someone else.

For there to be this kind of staff consensus on the values and aims of the school as a whole, it is clear that it must meet the needs of teachers as well as of pupils. That was not something on which it was possible for us to focus in our study. Nevertheless, it follows from our arguments on the value of cohesive social groups that most of the issues which apply to pupils apply similarly to teachers. They, too, will be influenced by the models, expectations and feedback from senior staff (and also of course from pupils) and they, too, need to take responsibility in, to feel rewarded by and to identify with the school. The findings showed that, in themselves, physical conditions (in terms of equipment, storage space etc.) and time available (such as guaranteed free periods) were not vital – a conclusion which closely parallels that for children. The one feature which was significant was adequate clerical help, which seemed to reflect the extent to which schools took teachers' needs seriously, and attempted to meet them.

We did not study the personal relationships between staff or their own satisfactions in their teaching role or their contentment with conditions in the particular school at which they taught. However, studies of hospitals (both general and psychiatric) suggest that patients may suffer when staff morale is low (Stanton and Schwartz, 1954; Revans, 1964; see also Freeman and Giovannoni, 1969). Doubtless, too, pupils are likely to make less satisfactory progress when teaching staff are discontented or in conflict.

In short, it appears helpful for there to be some kind of consensus on how school life should be organised. For there to be an accepted set of norms which applies consistently throughout the school, it is necessary not only to have ways of ensuring that there is joint staff action but also that staff feel part of a group whose values they share. Of course, as other studies have shown (see Vroom, 1969; Sherif and Sherif, 1969; Newcomb *et al.*, 1969), uniformity of behaviour is unnecessary. Indeed the greater the group agreement on crucial issues the greater the tolerance which is possible for individuality and idiosyncracy on other matters.

Pupil acceptance of school norms

As we have seen, pupils are likely to be influenced both by the norms and values they are exposed to at school and also by the degree to which these appear to be consistent throughout the school. A third issue concerns the extent to which children accept them.

It is one thing to agree school aims and objectives, but it is quite another that these be accepted by the general body of pupils. Throughout the earlier discussion it was implicit that the effectiveness of group norms would depend on the pupils being part of a group which holds these norms. In this connection, it is important to appreciate that the relevant social group is the one to which the person *feels* he belongs (Merton and Kitt, 1950). People tend to act on the basis of their *psychological identification* with particular groups rather than in keeping with any formal membership of organisations or attendance at institutions. For this purpose, the social group is the real or imaginary collective, whose perspective is assumed by the individual (Shibutani, 1955). Pupils will form their own groups with their own distinctive values and standards. The norms of these pupil groups may be in keeping with the values of the school or they may be in opposition to them. The question, then, is what are the features of schools which make it more likely that pupils will share the educational perspective? Our own evidence suggests that the crucial influences will include (i) general conditions for, and staff attitudes to, the pupils, (ii) shared activities between staff and pupils, (iii) pupil positions of responsibility within the school system, and (iv) success and achievement.

General conditions and staff attitudes to pupils

The findings showed that pupil outcomes (especially with respect to behaviour and academic attainment) tended to be better when the schools provided pleasant working conditions for their pupils. This was evident in the significant association between good pupil behaviour and good maintenance of decorations and care of the building generally. Keeping the school clean, tidy, and well painted with attractive pictures and plants, together with furniture in a good state of repair, seemed to encourage the children to respect their surroundings and behave more appropriately. Similarly, academic attainments were better in schools which provided good pupil conditions in terms of features such as access to a telephone, availability of refreshments, and being allowed in the buildings during breaks.

Staff concern for pupil needs seemed equally important. Thus, children's behaviour was better in schools where teachers were readily available to be consulted by the children about problems, and where many children were in fact seen by teachers. The same issue was evident in the positive association between good pupil outcomes and reports by a high proportion of children that they would consult teachers about a personal problem.

These variables have not received much attention in previous studies of schools, but investigations of other institutions have suggested that people work and behave better when they are well looked after and feel that those in charge understand and respond to their personal needs. For example, Kahn and Katz (1960) found that supervisors in highly productive working groups were generally felt by employees to be supportive, understanding of their difficulties, concerned about their problems and needs, and interested in them as individuals. Holahan and Saegert (1973) observed improved social participation among psychiatric patients after the dayroom of a hospital ward had been repainted and provided with new furniture. Sinclair (1971) found that delinquents absconded less frequently from those hostels where the hostel wardens were both strict and warm.

Another aspect of the prevailing atmosphere in a school concerns the staff's response to the children's behaviour and their general evaluation of the pupils' capabilities. We have already noted that outcomes were better in schools where the teachers expected the children to achieve well and where there was substantial use of praise and approval in classroom teaching. These variables were considered earlier in relation to different mechanisms — those associated with expectations and feedback. However, they are also likely to be important in setting the emotional tone of the school and hence in influencing pupil morale. Many studies have shown that people with a positive view of their own worth tend to be more successful and achieving; and furthermore that people's self-esteem is much influenced by the manner in which they are treated by others (see Helmreich, 1972). For example, Aronson and Mettee (1962), in an experimental study, showed that people cheated more when their self-esteem was lowered by adverse comments on their personality. Our findings, similarly, suggested that pupils behaved better and achieved more when teachers treated them in ways which emphasised their successes and good potential rather than those which focused on their failings and shortcomings.

Shared activities between staff and pupils

We obtained very few measures on the extent of shared activity between staff and pupils, but it was found that schools in which a high proportion of children had been on out-of-school outings had better academic outcomes. In view of the paucity of our measures on this aspect of school life (and the fact that, through lack of resources, we were unable to study contacts between staff and parents or between the school and the community) it would be unjustified to make much of the finding. However, one of the consistent findings from other research is that shared activities towards a common goal which requires people to work together are a most effective means of reducing inter-group conflict. Mere contact in pleasant surroundings does little to reduce conflict; single episodes of co-operation have little effect; and verbal agreements on goals are not much help. Rather, it is *joint* working together over time for the same purpose which helps to break down barriers. In view of the conflict between staff and pupils which, to some extent, is an inevitable part of schooling (see discussion below), it may be that joint activities between teachers and children outside the classroom may help each to appreciate the other better and come to share some of the same goals.

Pupil positions of responsibility

The study findings showed that schools in which a high proportion of children held some kind of position of responsibility in the school system had better outcomes with respect to both pupil behaviour and examination success. This was evident in terms of the proportion of children who had been form captain or its equivalent and also in terms of the proportion who had taken some kind of active role in a school assembly or other meeting. As already mentioned, giving children these responsibilities is likely to have benefits because it conveys trust in pupils' abilities and because it sets standards of mature behaviour.

However, it probably also operates through other mechanisms. Other research has shown that people tend not only to play the social roles assigned to them (Kuhn, 1964), but also to acquire the attitudes associated with the positions they have been allocated in the social system. For example, Lieberman (1956), in a prospective study of workers in a factory, showed that those men who subsequently became foremen came to develop attitudes more favourable to the management (in spite of the fact that originally their attitudes were no different from those of their colleagues). As their position altered, so their perspectives changed. The same may apply within secondary schools. As children are able to take responsible roles, and achieve satisfaction from them, so they may become more likely to identify with educational objectives. Thus, Reynolds and Murgatroyd (1977) found that attendance was better in schools with a prefect system, and Ainsworth and Batten (1974) found that opportunities for formal status were correlated with positive social behaviour (although, unlike our own study, not with academic attainment).

Of course, much is likely to depend on how responsibilities are given and on how far the opportunities are taken to link these with particular goals. The early experimental studies of Lewin, Lippitt and White (1939; White and Lippitt, 1960) of classroom climates led to the conclusion that productivity was highest under *authoritarian* conditions when the teacher was present, but highest under *democratic* conditions when the teacher was absent. Under both conditions, productivity was least in laissez-faire groups. Aggression was either very high or very low in authoritarian groups, very high in laissez-faire groups and intermediate under democratic conditions. It was clear that leadership was an essential quality for good work, but that some democratic involvement reduced aggression and increased responsible behaviour when supervision was relaxed. A limitation of the study, and of many others that followed, was that the authoritarian leader was not only directive but unfriendly. As a consequence, the findings on the relative merits and demerits of authoritarian and democratic regimes have been rather contradictory (see Anderson, 1959; Stern, 1963). The findings with respect to worker participation in industrial decision-making are similarly inconclusive (Vroom, 1969). The notion that children can be (or indeed should be) totally identified with and committed to schools is probably as naive as similar notions about factory workers (see Dubin, 1962). Some conflict is intrinsic in the situation itself. However, other things being equal, it does appear that the combination of firm leadership and good working conditions is most likely to foster both good morale and good work. Holding positions of responsibility at school may help students' commitment to education but it is but one element in a more complex pattern of relationships.

Success and achievement

Especially during the later years at school, it is probably also crucial that the pupils are experiencing some success which is both holding them at school and providing them with satisfaction. We have few data which are relevant to this point, but it may be noted that school outcomes on exam success, pupil behaviour and attendance were fairly closely connected. Schools with good academic achievement tended to be more successful in maintaining good attendance and behaviour. It is also pertinent that school attendance rates fell off most sharply in the last school year when national examinations became a major focus for many children. The results described in the last chapter indicated that attendance rates in particular were associated with school factors not incorporated in either our process or balance of intake measures. A consideration of the schools with particularly poor attendance suggests that the relative lack of exam success may be one additional important factor.

Passing exams and being prepared for work may be the most obvious indicators of success at school, but preparation for other aspects of adult life is likely to be equally important. Achievements in activities as varied as sports, music and drama all play a part in this. But, success should not be measured merely in terms of specific task skills or paper accomplishments – even across a wide range of activities. The taking of responsibility in the school is also a most important area for success and a valuable training for the taking of responsibilities later.

Contra-school peer groups

The factors we have discussed up to this point have all related to ways in which schools may be able to increase pupil involvement in school-defined aims. Many other writers, however, have seen schools as in-evitably, and perhaps even primarily, centres of conflict. Schooling is compulsory and the very fact that children *have* to attend is likely to make for tensions and antagonism. Thus, many years ago Waller (1932) wrote, 'Teacher and pupil confront each other with attitudes from which the underlying hostility can never be altogether removed'. Gordon (1957) in his study of one American high school noted the force of the informal student subculture which stood in opposition to the official educational ideology. Coleman (1961) similarly argued that the peer group values were often non-academic. In Britain, Sugarman (1967) suggested that youth culture was linked with a thoroughgoing alienation from school; Webb (1962) saw the issue as one of a contest over control; and Delamont (1976) has described the various strategies followed by the teacher and pupil protagonists. Other writers have seen the struggle more as an extension of the social conflicts inherent in Western societies (see review by Karabel and Halsey, 1977). Un-doubtedly, there is a good deal in these views of schooling, although sometimes the evidence has been stretched rather thin in reaching dramatic conclusions (see Davies, 1976 for a critique of some of the views on social control and education). But it would be wrong to see the tensions and conflicts as similarly intense in all schools. They are not. Our observations showed marked variations between the twelve schools in the ways they functioned and, as we have discussed, the results pointed to a variety of means by which schools could increase harmony, good behaviour, and academic success.

On the other hand, it would be misleading to see matters as entirely in the hands of the teaching staff. They, like the school as a whole, are subject to many pressures and constraints outside their control. The most important feature of this kind which emerged from our study was the balance or mix in the pupil intakes. We found that outcomes tended to be worse (and especially that delinquency tended to be more frequent) in schools with a particularly high proportion of intellectually less able children. This was not just another way of saying that outcomes were usually less good for less able children (although they were) but rather that, for children of *any* level of ability, outcomes tended to be less good if the bulk of the school populations consisted of children in the lowest ability band (as determined *prior* to secondary school transfer). In other words, it was a group, rather than an individual effect, and one which seemed to operate on a school-wide basis.

Before considering the possible mechanisms underlying these results, it is necessary to mention two other features of the balance of intake findings. First, the balance or mix factor of greatest effect concerned intellectual ability and *not* either socio-cultural background of the children or their behaviour (although the latter was of some importance). Second, although the intake mix measures showed substantial correlations with pupil outcome, they showed only weak associations with our school process measures.

The implication of this last finding is that the influence of intellectual mix did *not* operate primarily through its effects on teacher attitudes or behaviour, nor through its effects on overall school functioning. The twelve schools included some which functioned very well and yet had intakes which were relatively disadvantaged. Of course, teachers' responses to their classes *are* determined in part by the characteristics of the children they teach. It would be simplistic to see the process as a one-way interaction. On the other hand, the measures of intake balance were much more strongly correlated with pupil outcome than they were with school process. The inference to be drawn is that the main mechanism was likely to be of some other kind – probably related to some aspects of the peer group itself.

One model of delinquency which might be thought to fit our observations is that of *differential association* (Sutherland, 1939; Cressey, 1964) – the notion that mixing with delinquents makes it more likely that you yourself will also become delinquent. There is indeed some evidence that this process operates (see Rutter and Madge, 1976), perhaps through the group learning of delinquent forms of behaviour, or through the lessening of individual guilt or anxiety about becoming involved in delinquent activities. In our school population, as in others which have been studied, there was a strong tendency for first offences to be committed in groups. It may be that, in this way, delinquency 'spreads' as children come into contact with others who are already delinquent, and who constitute a peer group in which delinquent activities are an accepted form of behaviour. The same process could operate with respect to patterns of poor attendance and lack of commitment to school work.

On the other hand, there are reasons for supposing that this does not constitute the whole explanation. It is pertinent in this connection that a socially disadvantaged intake to schools was *not* significantly associated with a high rate of delinquency in spite of the fact that, at an *individual* level, occupational level of the family was a good predictor of delinquency. In other words, the mix which most strongly predisposed to delinquency was *not* a mix of boys with the highest individual predisposition to delinquency. This suggests the operation of some other mechanism.

Perhaps part of the explanation lies in the effects of scholastic failure on feelings of personal worth. Schonell (1961) commented how children who fail educationally lose confidence in themselves and fail to maintain normal self-esteem; some become bored and apathetic while others develop a fierce antagonism to the educational system which so condemns their lack of academic success. Cohen (1956) pointed to the importance of 'status', the need to achieve respect in the eyes of one's peers. Children who cannot achieve scholastically may react against the school system as a whole, and seek their satisfactions elsewhere. Cohen saw the process as an active one involving the formation of delinquent groups opposed to all that schools stand for. Hargreaves (1967) described much the same thing with respect to the development of delinquent subcultures in the bottom stream of a secondary school. However, the process need not necessarily involve a subculture which is actively anti-school or pro-delinquency but rather there may be the formation of peer groups within the school which are indifferent to academic success – indifferent because they see no chance of their achieving success and hence they need to set their goals in other directions.

For children who are unlikely to gain any examination passes there may be few advantages in being part of an institution in which one of the explicit objectives is academic success and in which the norm is scholastic commitment. If the intake to any school consists of a very high proportion of less able children there will be an increased tendency for the formation of non-academic social groups indifferent or opposed to academic success.* Not only will this increase the likelihood of conflict between teachers and pupils but also new pupils to the school will be faced with the powerful social pressures which run counter to the stated objectives of the school. These alternative social groups may offer greater opportunities of satisfaction for many children.

Insofar as mechanisms of this kind do operate (and it will be appreciated that we do not have findings which allow any direct testing of the hypothesised mechanism) several implications for educational practice follow. First, it is evident that there are considerable disadvantages in an educational system which allows such an uneven distribution of children that some schools have intakes with a heavy preponderance of the intellectually less able.† (Efforts to equalise social mix seem less important.) Second, there are likely to be problems in a system which is geared to success in exams which are set at such a level that two-fifths of the child population are expected to fail.

Both these implications concern broad political issues outside the scope of our study. There are also implications for school practice even given the existing educational system. If the gathering together of a large number of academically less able children has potentially adverse effects through group influences, it might be expected that mixed ability groupings would be preferable to streaming. Our results showed no clear-cut advantage either way but the twelve schools included far too little variation to draw any useful conclusions.

Other studies have also produced rather inconclusive findings, although it does appear that there may be benefits from mixed ability groupings, at least in the early years of secondary schooling (Postlethwaite and Denton, 1978). This is an area which it would be valuable to pursue further in other investigations.

We found that delinquency rates were lower in schools where the majority of children remained in the same form or set throughout their schooling. Possibly, by ensuring the relative stability of pupil groups, these schools had increased the likelihood that the pupils would

---

* Also, of course, the same factors may lead schools to redefine their objectives in terms other than academic success.

† It has been ILEA policy for a number of years now to obtain a more even distribution of children of different measured ability in the schools.

become involved with the school and its aims, in a way which other schools which lacked this kind of secure point for identification within the school had failed to do. It also seems possible that schools can do something to counter the effects of any contra-school peer group influence by increasing the rewards and satisfactions open to the less able children in the school, and by taking steps to ensure that their particular needs are met. Although some conflict is probably inevitable (and may be useful) in all schools, it does seem that there may be a variety of ways in which it can be prevented from becoming counter-productive.

Questions arising from the research

At the time we started the study it was known that schools often varied in their rates of exam success and in their levels of good attendance and behaviour, but it was uncertain how far these differences simply reflected the characteristics of intake to the schools. Moreover, insofar as the differences were due to school influences it was not known which features of school made good outcomes more likely. Our study was designed to tackle both issues. The findings showed that school differences were *not* just a reflection of intake patterns and that much of the effects of secondary schools were linked with their features as social organisations.

However, in answering these crucial questions inevitably the study has raised others. Having found evidence of considerable differences in both the overall climates and the particular practices of schools, it is now important to go on to enquire how such climates become established and then maintained or changed. How was it that twelve schools set up to undertake the same task with children from much the same geographical area came to develop such different styles? Doubtless, part of the answer lies in the history of the schools and in a variety of external factors outside their control. In addition, however, the schools' expressed philosophies and chosen ways of working were important. Obviously, the influence of the head teacher is very considerable. We did not look in any detail at the particular styles of management and leadership which worked best; this is an issue which it is now important to investigate. Our informal observations indicated that no one style was associated with better outcomes. Indeed it was noticeable that the heads of the more successful schools took widely differing approaches. Nevertheless, it was likely that these had essential elements in common and it is important to determine what these might be.

We also did not look at the curriculum or at details of subject teaching. Teaching is the central feature which most clearly defines the purpose of schools and which differentiates them from other social institutions. An analysis of how classroom teaching is linked with school process factors as studied here would be rewarding.

Finally, our study necessarily was concerned with correlations and associations. These suggest mechanisms and causal influences, but only studies of planned change in schools can identify these with any certainty. Such investigations are needed.

Overview

One of the common responses of practitioners to any piece of research is that it seems to be a tremendous amount of hard work just to demonstrate what we knew already on the basis of experience or common sense. Was the effort really worthwhile? It might be felt that the same applies to this study. After all, it is scarcely surprising that children benefit from attending schools which set good standards, where the teachers provide good models of behaviour, where they are praised and given responsibility, where the general conditions are good and where the lessons are well conducted.

Indeed this is obvious but, of course, it might have been equally obvious if we had found that the most important factors were attending a small school in modern purpose-built premises on one site, with a particularly favourable teacher-child ratio, a year-based system of pastoral care, continuity of individual teachers, and firm discipline in which unacceptable behaviours were severely punished. In fact *none* of these items was significantly associated with good outcomes, however measured.

Research into practical issues, such as schooling, rarely comes up with findings which are totally unexpected. On the other hand, it is helpful in showing which of the abundance of good ideas available are related to successful outcome. The present study of secondary schools has just such a contribution to make. In this final chapter, we have tried to go further in considering what mechanisms might be behind the statistical findings. Our discussion of school processes has been guided by knowledge stemming from previous research, informal observations of twelve schools over three years, and numerous helpful suggestions from the teaching staff in those twelve schools with whom we have discussed our findings. However, necessarily a certain amount of imagination has been involved in making the difficult step from tables, figures and graphs to suggestions of a kind likely to be appropriate and helpful in the everyday life of a school. Nevertheless, this more speculative account of possible practical implications is based on some rather firm research findings. It is appropriate to end by summarising some of the most important of these.

First, our investigation clearly showed that secondary schools varied markedly with respect to their pupils' behaviour, attendance, exam success and delinquency. This had been observed before, but the demonstration that these differences remained *even after taking into account differences in their intake* was new. This suggested that, contrary to many views, secondary schools *do* have an important influence on their pupils' behaviour and attainments.

Secondly, we found that these variations in outcome were systematically and strongly associated with the characteristics of schools as social institutions. The pattern of findings suggested that the associations reflected a causal relationship. There were indications from previous studies that this might well be the case but it had not previously been systematically demonstrated by comparing different secondary schools.

Thirdly, the research showed *which* school variables were associated with good behaviour and attainments and which were not.

Fourth, the pattern of findings suggested that not only were pupils influenced by the way they were dealt with as individuals, but also there was a group influence resulting from the ethos of the school as a social institution.

We may conclude that the results carry the strong implication that schools can do much to foster good behaviour and attainments, and that even in a disadvantaged area, schools can be a force for the good.

Appendix A

Pupil behaviour scale

1. *Missing lessons*
From the pupil questionnaire: 'Since last September, how many times have you been in school and deliberately missed a lesson?'. Replies were coded $0 = 0$; $1 = 1$ or 2; $2 = 3–5$; $3 = 6–10$; $4 = 11–15$; $5 = 16–20$; $6 = 20+$. School scores ranged from $0·09$ to $1·61$, mean $0·87$; reliability of school means $r_s = 0·97$, $p < 0·01$.

2. *Absconding*
From the pupil questionnaire: 'Since last September, how many times have you been registered and then left school?'. Coded as item 1. School scores ranged from $0·05$ to $1·07$, mean $= 0·58$; reliability of school means $r_s = 0·90$, $p < 0·01$.

3. *Truanting*
From the pupil questionnaire: 'Since last September, how many times have you not come to school at all when you were supposed to?'. Coded as item 1. School scores ranged from $0·30$ to $1·39$, mean $= 0·87$; reliability of school means $r_s = 0·60$, $p < 0·05$.

4. *Uniform*
From the pupil questionnaire: 'How many times have you not worn school uniform in the last week?'. The actual number of times recorded by the pupils was used as the score. School scores ranged from $0·64$ to $3·14$, mean $= 1·56$; reliability of school means $r_s = 0·87$, $p < 0·01$.

5. *Uniform*
As observed during the administration of the pupil questionnaires. School score was the percentage of children not wearing the required uniform. School scores ranged from $0·30$ per cent to $47·0$ per cent, with a mean score of $12·53$ per cent. Agreement between observers obtained on 91 per cent of observations.

6. *Damage*

As observed during the administration of the pupil questionnaires. The school score was the average number of broken or cracked windows and broken chairs per room and ranged from 0 to 1·6, mean = 0·29. Agreement obtained between observers on 92 per cent of observations.

7. *Graffiti*

As observed during the administration of the pupil questionnaires. Coded, 0 = none, 1 = on a quarter of the wall area, 2 = on half of the wall area, 3 = on three-quarters of the wall area, 4 = on all wall area. School scores ranged from 0·6 to 2·3 per room, mean = 1·28; reliability between observers on 90 per cent of observations.

8. *Graffiti*

From the pupil questionnaire: 'During this term, how many times have you drawn or written anything on any part of the school building? (Do not include desks.)'. Coded 0 = never, 1 = 1 or 2, 2 = up to 10 times, 3 = 10+. School scores ranged from 0·61 to 1·22, mean = 0·95; reliability of school means $r_s = 0·92$, $p < 0·01$.

9. *Pupil violence*

As observed in school playgrounds during the third-year observation weeks. The school score was the number of fights observed during one week and ranged from 0 to 12, mean score = 2·58.

10. *Fights*

As observed during the third-year observation weeks. The score was the number of times that there was fighting between members of the third-year class during room changes. School scores ranged from 0 to 7 with a mean score of 1·67.

11. *Late*

As observed during the three-year observation weeks. The school score was the average number of children late for each lesson and ranged from 0·29 to 3·36, with a mean score of 1·44.

12. *Pencils*

As observed during the administration of the pupil questionnaires. The school score was the percentage of pupils who had to borrow a pen or pencil to complete the questionnaire. The school score ranged from 0 per cent to 30 per cent with a mean of 23·10 per cent. Agreement was obtained between observers on 82 per cent of observations.

13. *Anoraks*

As observed during the administration of the pupil questionnaires. The school score was the percentage of children wearing overcoats or anoraks in the classroom and ranged from 0 per cent to 14·5 per cent with a mean of 5·10 per cent. Agreement between observers was obtained in 100 per cent of observations.

All the remaining items are taken from the classroom observations. The definitions of each category are those which were used in training the observers. Inter-observer agreement is expressed in terms of the significance level of the correlations of scores between observers.

14. and 15. *On task*

As observed during the third year (item 14) and first year (item 15) lessons. The school score was the percentage of the observation periods in which the five selected individual pupils in each lesson were rated on task. Definition: 'Score when there is clear evidence that the child is on task, or, if only listening is required, that he is not doing anything which could preclude this. Score also if no task is prescribed.' School scores ranged from 64·54 per cent to 92·96 per cent, mean 81·49. Inter-observer agreement significant at the 0·01 level.

16. and 17. *Off task*

As observed during the third year (item 16) and first year (item 17) lessons. The school score is the percentage of the observation periods in which the five selected individual pupils in each lesson were rated off-task. Definition: 'Score when there is evidence that the child is engaged in an alternative activity which would preclude his completing the task prescribed.' [NB. A third category labelled '?', was also included in the schedule, so that ratings of on and off task were not mutually exclusive. This '?' category was scored wherever there was ambiguity about the child's activity.] School scores ranged from 1·28 per cent to 21·17 per cent, mean = 8·78. Inter-observer agreement significant at the 0·01 level.

The remaining items (with the exception of 21) are based on computed scores derived from ratings of the whole class. In each ten-second observation period, a rating was made indicating (i) whether or not the selected behaviours had occurred at all during the period, and (ii) what proportion of the class was involved. The scores thus included: 0 = no examples; $1 = 1$ or 2 children only; $2 =$ up to and including a quarter of the class; $3 =$ between a quarter and half the class; $4 =$ over half the class. The mean scores for each lesson based on these ratings thus reflect both the proportions of time during which any of the selected behaviours had occurred, and the proportion of the class involved. The scores thus give some basis on which the 'intensity' of the behaviours could be contrasted, with a score of 0·1 indicating very infrequent behaviours by a few individuals in the class, and one of 2 or more indicating fairly persistent activity by over half the class.

18. and 19. *Chat*
As observed during the third year (item 18) and first year (item 19) lessons. Definition: 'Exclude brief whispering, but include any extended or easily audible chat.' School scores ranged from 0·95 to 2·29, mean = 1·55. Inter-observer agreement significant at the 0·01 level.

20. and 22. *Class informal (mild) score*
As observed during third year (item 20) and first year (item 22) lessons. Definition: 'As a general guide, the behaviours should be such as to be noticeable in a fairly ordered classroom, but not apparently disrupting others. Exclude fidgeting, but include e.g. rhythmic tapping on desks, chewing gum, sitting on desk/feet on desk, quiet singing/humming, combing hair, and the use of swearing in general conversation or as mild expletives.' School scores ranged from 0·02 to 1·13, mean = 0·26. Inter-observer agreement significant at the 0·01 level.

21. *Individual informal (mild)*
As observed during third year lessons. School score was the percentage of the time the five selected individual pupils were rated as engaged in any of these behaviours. Definition: as above. School scores ranged from 0·8 per cent to 10·3 per cent, mean score = 3·2 per cent. Inter-observer agreement significant at the 0·01 level.

23. and 24. *Class calling out score*
As observed during third year (item 23) and first year (item 24) lessons. Definition: 'Shouting out across the room, including in answer to a question.' School scores ranged from 0·02 to 0·22, mean = 0·09. Inter-observer agreement significant at the 0·05 level.

25. *Informal severe*

As observed during third year lessons. Definition: more serious examples of 'informal mild' which are potentially or actually disruptive, e.g. loud singing, abusive swearing, throwing pencils, paper etc., and public disagreements between pupils. School scores ranged from 0 to 0·13, with a mean score of 0·02.

	1	2	3	4	5	6	7	8	9	10	11	12	13	14	15	16	17	18	19	20	21	22	23	24	25
1. Missing lessons	—	0.64	0.50	0.19	0.55	0.34	0.74	0.53	0.69	0.77	0.53	0.18	0.55	0.44	0.81	0.55	0.74	0.41	0.41	0.64	0.49	0.80	0.64	0.58	0.66
2. Absconding		—	0.50	0.29	0.62	0.42	0.63	0.46	0.88	0.59	0.47	0.34	0.61	0.55	0.56	0.62	0.70	0.32	0.40	0.54	0.35	0.74	0.59	0.70	0.53
3. Truanting			—	0.10	0.21	0.09	0.54	0.76	0.37	0.38	0.39	0.34	0.38	0.23	0.84	0.23	0.68	0.42	0.41	0.71	0.56	0.72	0.68	0.41	0.56
4. Uniform				—	0.59	0.77	0.41	0.41	0.24	0.26	0.36	-0.08	0.55	0.72	0.21	0.51	0.41	0.58	0.12	0.50	0.55	0.44	0.32	0.15	0.52
5. Uniform					—	0.62	0.74	0.64	0.60	0.26	0.59	0.42	0.81	0.64	0.49	0.39	0.73	0.27	0.51	0.52	0.50	0.74	0.64	0.64	0.64
6. Damage						—	0.64	0.23	0.51	0.52	0.53	0.81	0.66	0.83	0.36	0.53	0.51	0.58	0.72	0.54	0.56	0.61	0.57	0.51	0.22
7. Graffiti							—	0.47	0.60	0.51	0.53	0.01	0.82	0.55	0.69	0.85	0.36	0.80	0.52	0.56	0.73	0.70	0.67	0.73	0.55
8. Graffiti								—	0.30	0.65	0.85	0.37	0.53	0.37	0.71	0.26	0.11	0.61	0.31	0.23	0.47	0.38	0.74	0.58	0.26
9. Pupil violence									—	0.19	0.26	0.12	0.53	0.37	0.37	0.42	0.64	0.44	0.41	0.43	0.21	0.55	0.45	0.53	0.46
10. Fights										—	0.66	0.31	0.29	0.47	0.32	0.47	0.59	0.66	0.36	0.54	0.70	0.53	0.32	0.29	0.56
11. Late											—	0.61	0.85	0.74	0.31	0.59	0.66	0.48	0.29	0.72	0.70	0.49	0.77	0.45	0.85
12. Pencils												—	0.54	0.11	0.10	0.02	0.27	0.08	-0.05	0.41	0.34	0.19	0.56	0.30	0.45
13. Anoraks													—	0.60	0.52	0.31	0.70	0.47	0.36	0.70	0.67	0.64	0.85	0.37	0.56
14. On task														—	0.41	0.52	0.31	0.50	0.35	0.70	0.50	0.70	0.50	0.39	0.54
15. On task															—	0.41	0.41	0.50	0.56	0.73	0.68	0.70	0.50	0.39	0.68
16. Off task																—	0.31	0.42	0.31	0.51	0.50	0.59	0.38	0.61	0.38
17. Off task																	—	0.50	0.60	0.80	0.72	0.76	0.76	0.45	0.81
18. Chat																		—	0.15	0.73	0.68	0.55	0.44	-0.07	0.70
19. Chat																			—	0.31	0.35	0.56	0.44	0.59	0.33
20. Informal mild																				—	0.94	0.84	0.84	0.33	0.92
21. Informal mild																					—	0.64	0.80	0.26	0.90
22. Informal mild																						—	0.77	0.53	0.67
23. Call																							—	0.36	0.85
24. Call																								—	0.29
25. Informal severe																									—

(Most of the items relate to misbehaviour, and have been ranked from least (1) to most (12). For items which refer to good behaviour (e.g. On task) this convention has been reversed, with high levels of On task behaviour ranked 1, and low 12.)

Table A.1 Intercorrelations of pupil response items

Appendix B

School goals
(from pupil questionnaire)

Aims of this school

From this list, circle the four which you think the *teachers* in this school are most interested in:

Helping you to develop your personality and character	0
Helping you to do as well as possible in exams like CSE or GCE	1
Teaching you about right and wrong	2
Showing you how to get on with other people	3
Teaching you about what is going on in the world today	4
Keeping you occupied	5
Teaching you how to read and write well	6
Helping you to get as good a job as possible	7
Helping with things you will need to know when you leave school (for example about running a home and managing money)	8
Making school a pleasant place to be in	9

From this list circle the four which *you* think are the most important:

Helping you to develop your personality and character	0
Helping you to do as well as possible in exams like CSE or GCE	1
Teaching you about right and wrong	2
Showing you how to get on with other people	3
Teaching you about what is going on in the world today	4
Keeping you occupied	5
Teaching you how to read and write well	6
Helping you to get as good a job as possible	7
Helping with things you will need to know when you leave school (for example about running a home and managing money)	8
Making school a pleasant place to be in	9

Appendix C

Ten naughty children: examples

1. A fourth year pupil who is rather moody but never been in trouble before who gets involved in an argument with a teacher. Both teacher and pupil get angry and pupil swears at teacher. Subsequently refuses to speak to teacher.
2. A very quiet first year child is stealing small items from other pupils and keeping them in his/her locker.
3. A fifth year pupil is caught shoplifting in Woolworths. Not a difficult pupil to manage but totally uninterested in school.
4. A third year pupil who persistently larks about in lessons. Not an unpleasant child but getting more and more disruptive.
5. A second year pupil who never wears complete school uniform. Pupil owns uniform but chooses not to wear it.
6. A very withdrawn second year pupil who is no trouble in class, not very bright but works quite hard, who always looks sad. Has no friends and may be being bullied by older children.
7. A fourth year pupil who never attends more than four days/week. Not actually a problem in lessons but getting very behind in school work.
8. A fifth year pupil who is constantly aggressive. Is frequently involved in fights with other pupils and these are getting more serious. Very disruptive in lessons.
9. A third year pupil who has written names of pop stars/football teams all over playground wall.
10. Fourth year pupil caught smoking in playground. Not a troublesome child previously, in fact quite bright and hardworking.

Appendix D

Format of pupil questionnaire

1. Heading of questionnaire

SCHOOL: ☐   TEACHING SET: ☐

YEAR: ☐

HOUSE: ☐

REGISTRATION GROUP: ☐

SEX	F	0
	M	1

YEAR STARTED AT SCHOOL:

1	2	3	4	5

TODAY'S DATE ☐☐☐

PLEASE CIRCLE THE NUMBER NEXT TO YOUR CHOICE OF ANSWER

2. Sample questions

1. Have you been in the same form group (tutor group or registration group) since you started at this school?

   No 0

   Yes 1

2. Have you been in the same class for English since you started at this school?

   No 0

   Yes 1

3. How many form tutors have you had at this school?

No. of form tutors [ ]

4. How many English teachers have you had?

No. of English teachers [ ]

15. Since last September, how many times have you been in school and deliberately missed a lesson?
(If never, please put *0*)   Number of times: [ ]

16. Since last September, how many times have you been registered and then left school?

(If never, please put *0*)   Number of times: [ ]

17. Since September, how many times have you not come to school at all when you were supposed to?
(If never, please put *0*)   Number of times: [ ]

26. Since September, have you had your name read out at assembly or at any other school meeting, for doing well in:

(a) Work   No   0
             Yes   1

(b) Sport or other things   No   0
                              Yes   1

27. During this term, have you drawn or written anything on any part of the school building?   Never   0
(Do not include desks)   Once or twice   1
                           Up to 10 times 2
                           More than that 3

28. Since last September, how many times have you been kept in detention?

    (If never, please put *0*)

    No. of times ⬜

29. Have you been told off by the Head since September?

    No   0
    Yes   1

Appendix E

Details of process items

I Process items

1. *Homework in the first year*

From lesson observations. One point given for homework either set or returned in each of the four lessons observed. Each school given a score which constituted an average for all lessons (0 = no homework, 1 = set or returned in that lesson, 2 = set and returned in that lesson). Range: 0·3 to 1·3 with a mean of 0·70.

2. *Homework in the third year* – Teachers' questionnaire
Maths and English teachers of the classes we observed were asked how many minutes of homework they gave the class each week. Range of school scores 0–3 hrs. Mean 1 hr 10 mins.

3. *Homework*
Teachers' questionnaire: 'Is there any check on whether staff set homework?' Coded 0 = No, 1 = Yes. School score is the percentage of teachers saying 'Yes'. School scores varied from 10 per cent to 100 per cent with a mean of 52·3 per cent.

4. *Expected 'O' levels*
The same teachers as Item 2 were asked what percentage of the third year class they expected to pass either 'O' level or CSE grade 1. The average of these two teachers' estimates was used as the 'school score' and these range from 2·5 per cent to 45 per cent. Mean = 17·3 per cent.

5. *Work on walls*
As observed during the administration of the pupil questionnaire and the third year lesson observations (N = 239). Each room was assessed on a five point scale: 0 = nothing on walls, to 4 = all possible areas covered. The average score for each school was calculated and used as

the 'school score'. This measure was highly reliable between observers, agreement being obtained on 92 per cent of observations. School scores range from 0·25 to 1·75. Mean = 1·00.

6. *Total teaching time*
Calculated from the timetable of the third year class we observed. School scores range from 21·9 to 24·2 hours/week. Mean = 22·9 hrs.

7. *Head's reported pastoral emphasis*
From interview with head of school. A scale constructed from the replies of the head teacher to ten questions on the pastoral emphasis of the school. The items included are:
1. Use of special units. 0 = none, 1 = one, 2 = more than one.
2. Regular meetings with pupils. 0 = none, 1 = informal (e.g. lunch hour), 2 = school council.
3. Arrangement of free dinner confidentiality. 0 = none, 1 = some, 2 = positive attempt.
4. Topics discussed at last cabinet meeting. 0 = not pastoral, 1 = pastoral.
5. Allocation of form teachers. 0 = reasons other than to maintain continuity, 1 = continuity.
6. Reasons for class changes. 0 = reasons other than social or at pupils' request, 1 = social or pupils' request.
7. Topics discussed at last staff meeting. 0 = not pastoral, 1 = pastoral.
8. Stability of teachers from year to year. 0 = not school policy, 1 = class teachers only, 2 = class teachers and tutors.
9. Scale points allocated to pastoral heads. 0 = none on scale 4, 0·5 = some on scale 4, 1 = all on scale 4.
10. Role of pastoral care in school. 0 = minor emphasis, 1 = to support curriculum, 2 = a high priority in school.

School scores ranged from 2·5 to 11·0, with a mean score of 6·5.

8. *Library use*
From Pupil questionnaire: 'In the last week, have you taken any books out of the school library for enjoyment rather than work?' Coded no = 0, yes = 1. School score is the percentage of children saying 'Yes' and this ranged from 17 per cent to 56 per cent with a mean score of 33·3 per cent. Reliability of school means, $r_s = 0.73$, $p < 0.01$.

9. *Course planning*

From the teacher's interview: 'How much freedom did you have in planning the first, second and third year courses you are teaching this year?' Coded 0 = complete freedom, 1 = planned with others. The school score was the percentage of teachers who said that they planned their courses with others. The school scores ranged from 33·3 per cent to 100 per cent with a mean of 73·4 per cent.

10. *Subjects taught*

From teachers' interview: 'Which subjects are you teaching?' Coded 0 = specialist subject only, 1 = general subjects. (A teacher who helped with sports as well as his own subject would *not* be considered a 'general' teacher.) The school score was the percentage of general teachers and this ranged from 0 per cent to 50 per cent with a mean of 22·4 per cent.

11. *Per cent teachers' time on 'topic'*

Calculated from our third year lesson observations. Defined as: uninterrupted interactions focused on the subject matter in hand, or earlier or related work, and the children's acquisitions of the skills necessary in executing the work, including methods of using equipment, laying out work etc. NB. Topic can also be scored alone, without any of the interaction categories, if the teacher is clearly engaged in work related to the instructional context of the lesson, but is not interacting with the children, e.g. marking their books, watching films, listening to tapes etc. Positive comments on a child's work should be scored as 'Topic' and 'Praise'. Negative comments on a child's work should be scored as 'Topic' and 'Punishment'. Scores on this measure ranged from 64·9 per cent to 86·0 per cent, mean = 74·8 per cent, and inter-observer reliability was significant at the 0·01 level.

12. *Per cent teachers' time on 'equipment'*

Calculated from the third year lessons. Defined as: setting up of equipment, writing on board, distributing and collecting materials etc. or instructions to children on distribution of resources − but not imparting of skills and use of equipment which would be coded 'Topic'. This category can be used without interaction categories if appropriate. Scores on this measure ranged from 3·2 per cent to 13·6 per cent, mean = 9·1 per cent, and inter-observer reliability was significant at the 0·01 level.

13. *Per cent of lessons ending early*
From our observations of third year lessons. Range of school scores 0 per cent to 44 per cent. Mean = 15·3 per cent.

14. and 15. *Teachers' interventions in the classroom*
(First and third year academic lessons, 3rd yr, N = 312, 1st yr, N = 96). Percentage of teacher observation periods when teacher dealt with pupils' behaviour. This excluded 'management' of behaviour (i.e. instructions as to how the class was to behave, such as 'Everyone be quiet now', but did include subsequent actions such as 'John Smith, do stop talking'). The definition used by the observers was: directions initiated to ensure compliance with previous management instructions which have failed to produce the desired result, or to curb unacceptable behaviour − i.e. score only when the directions given are contingent upon the children's behaviour. This measure was reliable between observers at the 0·01 level.

16. *Silence*
The percentage of observation blocks when the teacher expected complete silence. A block was a five minute observation period and 'silence' would be coded if that was the predominant expectation for the whole period. Relates to third year academic lessons only (N = 312). Scores ranged from 12·9 per cent to 63·5 per cent, mean = 37·2 per cent.

17. *Teacher interaction style*
The percentage of the observation periods where teacher was interacting with the whole class (as opposed to interacting with individuals). The definitions used by the observers were: '*Individual*': score when the teacher interacts specifically with one individual, either by e.g. calling the child out to his desk, or by positioning himself next to the child, or speaking in a way which is clearly primarily directed to one individual. '*Class*': for use in all other instances of interaction with the children, i.e. for all chalk and talk sessions directed to the whole class, for question and answer sessions only involving individuals as representatives of the class, and when the teacher is going round the class, or looking at the class, whilst they are working. Scores on this measure ranged from 22·4 per cent to 60·2 per cent with a mean of 48·8 per cent, and inter-observer reliability was significant at the 0·01 level.

18. *Told off by the head teacher*
From pupil questionnaire. 'Have you been told off by the head since September?'. Coded No = 0, Yes = 1. School scores are percentage of pupils saying 'Yes' and this ranged from 12·0 per cent to 51·3 per cent with a mean of 32·5 per cent. Reliability of school means, $r_s = 0.90$, $p < 0.01$.

19. *Discipline*
From teachers' interview: 'Are there any general standards of classroom discipline which are expected at this school?'. This was coded 0 = No/Personal to teacher, 1 = Dept., Year/House or school based. The school scores ranged from 30·0 per cent to 100 per cent, with a mean score of 66·7 per cent.

20. *Detentions*
From pupil questionnaire: 'Since last September, how many times have you been kept in detention?'. Coded 0 = none, 1 = once or twice, 2 = 3–5 times, 3 = 6–10 times, 4 = 11–15 times, 5 = 16–20 times, 6 = 20+. Range of school scores 1·02 to 2·81, mean score = 1·75. Reliability of school means, $r_s = 0.94$, $p < 0.01$.

21. *Punishment – lines*
From pupil questionnaire: 'Since September, how many times have you been given lines or extra work to do?'. This was coded: 0 = never, 1 = 1, 2; 2 = 3–5; 3 = 6–10; 4 = 11–15; 5 = 16–20; 6 = 20+ and the school score was the average score for the pupils. This ranged from 0·26 to 2·83 with a mean score of 1·04. Reliability of school means, $r_s = 0.93$, $p < 0.01$.

22. *Corporal punishment*
From pupil questionnaire: 'Since September, how many times have you received corporal punishment, either in or out of class?'. Coded 0 = none, 1 = once or twice, 2 = 3–5 times, 3 = 6–10 times, 4 = 11–15 times, 5 = 16–20 times, 6 = 20+. Range of school scores 0·13 to 2·26. Mean score = 0·64. Reliability of school means, $r_s = 0.99$, $p < 0.01$.

23. *Punitive action – Ten Naughty Children scale*
A sample of teachers in each school (N = 55) was asked how they would deal with ten different problems with the children's behaviour at school. These replies were then coded on a five point scale ranging 0 = positive 'welfare' approach, 1 = no action, 2 = minor disciplinary ac-

tion, 3 = major disciplinary action, 4 = suspended or expelled. The school scores ranged from 0·59 to 1·88 with a mean score of 1·13.

24. *Named for work*

From pupil questionnaire: 'Since September, have you had your name read out at assembly or at any other school meeting for doing well in work?'. School score is the percentage of children saying 'Yes'. Range 3·7 per cent to 36·2 per cent. Mean = 17·4 per cent. Reliability of school means, $r_s = 0·88$, $p < 0·01$.

25. *Topic praise*

From third year lesson observations. Recordings of teacher praise to either individuals or groups for good work, defined as: all positive remarks including e.g. 'That's good' and 'That's right', which do not simply seem to be confirming the correctness of a statement. Score also for the distribution of any formal or tangible rewards, and enter details of these in the checklist on the initial sheet. This occurred very rarely, the range being 0·2 per cent to 2·9 per cent of observation periods, mean = 1·28 per cent, and inter-observer reliability was significant at the 0·05 level.

26. *Prizes for sport*

From pupil questionnaire: 'Since September, have you been presented with anything (for example a prize, badge, or certificate) for doing well in sport?' School score is the percentage of children saying 'Yes'. Range from 10·1 per cent to 46·9 per cent. Mean = 29·4 per cent. Reliability of school means, $r_s = 0·93$, $p < 0·01$.

27. *Prizes for work*

From pupil questionnaire: 'Since September, have you been presented with anything (for example, a prize, badge or certificate) for doing well in work?' Coded 0 = No, 1 = Yes. Range of school scores 1·3 per cent to 63·7 per cent. Mean score = 30·3 per cent. Reliability of school means, $r_s = 0·93$, $p < 0·01$.

28. *Potential consultation*

From pupil questionnaire: 'If you had a serious personal problem, which of these people would you discuss it with at school?' Choices were: form teacher or subject teacher, head of year or house, counsellor, priest or other adult at school. Each child was given a score from 0 to 3 and then the average school score was calculated. Range of school scores 0·67 to 0·34. Mean = 0·51. Reliability of school means, r_s = 0·66, p < 0·05.

29. *Outings*
From pupil questionnaire: 'Please write the names of any places you have been to with the school on outings or journeys (and put the number of outings in the total box)'. School score was coded: 0 = 0, 1 = 1, 2; 2 = 3–5; 3 = 6–10; 4 = 11–15; 5 = 16–20; 6 = 20+. Range of school scores from 0·6 to 2·9. Mean = 1·6. Reliability of school means, r_s = 0·97, p < 0·01.

30. *Pupil conditions*
A checklist of fourteen items which describe ways in which schools might be considerate of their pupils' needs – e.g. tuckshop, clean and well kept WCs, open building at break and dinner hour, good meals, school has a counsellor, no hair regulations, no sixth form uniform, school pets, etc. Each school given a score from 0 to 14. Range of school scores 1–13. Mean = 6·0.

31. *Decorations of classroom*
A score of 0 to 5 given to each classroom visited during administration of pupil questionnaire and during third year lesson observations – one point being given for each item: clean room, tidy room, plants, posters and pictures. Range of school means from 2·0 to 4·4. Mean = 2·8. Agreement obtained between observers in 96 per cent of observations.

32. *Pupils' problems*
From teacher interviews: 'If an individual child in your form/set was worried about a school/personal problem, when could he/she come to talk to you about it?' Coded 0 = any time, 1 = fixed time. Schools' scores were the percentage of teachers saying they would see a child at any time; this ranged from 0 per cent to 100 per cent with a mean of 64·47 per cent.

33. *No. of children with problems seen*
Teachers' questionnaire: 'How many children (with personal or school problems) did you see in the last two weeks?' The school score was the average number of children seen, and ranged from 0·50 to 5·63 with a mean score of 2·49.

34. *Form captain*
From pupil questionnaire: 'Have you ever been a form captain or

monitor?' School score was percentage of children answering 'Yes'. This item has high split half reliability. Range 7·3 per cent to 50·4 per cent. Mean = 32·1 per cent. Reliability of school means, $r_s = 0.90$, $p < 0.01$.

35. Pupils caring for resources
From third year lesson observations of whether pupils brought and took away their own resources (i.e. books, folders, exercise books, etc.). School score is the percentage of academic lessons where this was observed. Range 2·5 per cent to 78·5 per cent, mean 42·6 per cent.

36. Assembly participation
From pupil questionnaire: 'Have you ever taken a special part in an assembly or school/house/year meeting?' Coded $0 =$ never, $1 = 1$ or 2, $2 = 3–5$, $3 = 6–10$, $4 = 11–15$, $5 = 16–20$, $6 = 20+$. School score – the average for children at each school. Range 0·11 to 1·43, mean = 0·57. Reliability of school means, $r_s = 0.99$, $p < 0.01$.

37. Charity contributions
From pupil questionnaire: 'This term, have you contributed to any collection for charity which has been organised by the school?' School score is the percentage of children saying 'Yes'. Range from 41·8 per cent to 94·7 per cent, mean = 74·4 per cent. Reliability of school means, $r_s = 0.93$, $p < 0.01$.

38. Stability of maths and English teachers of third year pupils
The school score was the average number of terms the observed third year class had been taught by their present Maths and English teachers. School scores varied from 2 to 6 with a mean of 3·5 terms.

39. Continuity of teachers of fifth year pupils only
From pupil questionnaire: 'How many form tutors/set tutors have you had at this school?', and 'How many English teachers have you had?'. School score was the average number of each reported by the fifth year pupils. Range 5·45 to 9·16, mean 6·85. Reliability of school means, $r_s = 0.92$, $p < 0.01$.

40. Same English class
From the pupil questionnaire. The children were asked 'Have you been in the same class for English since you started at this school?'. The school score was the number of children saying 'Yes', and ranged from

40 per cent to 89 per cent with a mean of 68 per cent. Reliability of school means, $r_s = 0.98$, $p < 0.01$.

41. *Same form*
From pupil questionnaire: 'Have you been in the same form/set/tutor group/class since you started at this school?'. Score is percentage of children checking 'Yes'. Range 52 per cent to 98 per cent, mean 77·3 per cent. Reliability of school means, $r_s = 0.92$, $p < 0.01$.

42. *Friends in the same year*
From pupil questionnaire. The children were asked 'How many people in your year, but not in your class/English set have you visited at their homes, or arranged to meet out of school, since last September?'. The number of friends was coded $0 = 0$, $1 = 1$, 2; $2 = 3$–5; $3 = 6$–10; $4 = 11$–15; $5 = 16$–20; $6 = 20+$. School scores ranged from 0·99 to 3·74 with a mean of 2·21. Reliability of school means, $r_s = 0.96$, $p < 0.01$.

43. *Decision making*
From teachers' questionnaire: 'Where do you see the most important school decisions being made?' Coded: $0 =$ at senior staff level, $1 =$ at ordinary staff level. The school score is the percentage of teachers saying that decisions are taken at the senior staff level. School scores varied from 33·3 to 100 with a mean of 81·7.

44. *Representation of views at decision making*
From teachers' questionnaire: 'How are your views represented?' Coded $0 =$ through representative, $1 =$ personally. The school score is the percentage of teachers saying that they are represented by another teacher. School scores varied from 0 per cent to 100 per cent with a mean of 41·6 per cent.

45. *Late arrival at school*
From teachers' questionnaire: 'Is anyone aware if staff arrive late for school?' Coded $0 =$ No, $1 =$ Yes. School score is percentage of teachers saying 'Yes'. School scores varied from 55·6 per cent to 100 per cent with a mean of 87·9 per cent.

46. *Clerical help*
From teachers' questionnaire: 'Do you have adequate clerical help?' Coded $0 =$ definitely not, $1 =$ doubtful, $2 =$ yes. School mean scores were calculated which ranged from 0·45 to 2·00 with a mean of 1·04.

II Items in teachers' conditions scale

1. No timetable problems reported
2. Eight or more free periods/week (i.e. above mean for whole sample, mean = 7·84)
3. Guaranteed free periods
4. Three or less free periods lost in previous two weeks (mean = 3·26)
5. Has own teaching room
6. Has own storage space
7. Has adequate equipment
8. Has adequate technical help
9. Has clerical help
10. Clerical help adequate
11. Has departmental office/room
12. Has space for marking books

III Intercorrelations between process items

	1	2	3	4	5	6	7	8	9	10
1.	—	0·66	0·32	0·35	0·18	-0·21	0·49	0·21	-0·01	0·29
2.		—	*0·57*	0·15	0·18	0·12	*0·57*	0·05	-0·01	-0·11
3.			—	0·38	0·46	0·33	0·19	*0·50*	0·40	-0·24
4.				—	0·16	0·03	0·22	0·59	0·34	0·08
5.					—	0·25	-0·02	0·25	0·29	0·04
6.						—	0·33	0·47	*0·72*	0·26
7.							—	0·17	0·06	0·31
8.								—	*0·54*	0·36
9.									—	*0·51*
10.										—

All correlations significant at the 5% level are in italics

Table E.1 *Intercorrelations between academic emphasis items*

	11	12	13	14	15	16	17
11.	–	0·55	0·48	0·73	0·22	0·51	0·50
12.		–	0·30	0·26	0·17	0·61	0·15
13.			–	0·56	−0·16	0·33	0·16
14.				–	0·17	0·55	0·22
15.					–	0·17	0·62
16.						–	0·42
17.							–

Table E.2 *Intercorrelations between teacher action in lesson items*

	18	19	20	21	22	23
18.	–	0·16	0·17	−0·15	−0·10	0·23
19.		–	0·08	0·01	−0·54	−0·14
20.			–	0·64	0·56	0·66
21.				–	0·54	0·27
22.					–	0·13
23.						–

Table E.3 *Intercorrelations of punishment items*

	24	25	5	26	27
24.	–	0·52	0·32	0·29	0·73
25.		–	0·05	−0·03	0·13
5.			–	0·52	0·06
26.				–	0·41
27.					–

Table E.4 *Intercorrelations between reward items*

	28	29	30	31	32	33
28.	–	0·41	0·29	0·01	0·40	0·10
29.		–	0·66	0·54	0·15	0·35
30.			–	0·37	0·06	0·39
31.				–	0·59	0·50
32.					–	0·40
33.						–

Table E.5 *Intercorrelations between pupil conditions items*

	34	35	36	37
34.	–	0·19	0·90	0·20
35.		–	0·24	0·55
36.			–	0·20
37.				–

Table E.6 *Intercorrelations between responsibility and participation measures*

38 × 39		= −0·31	

Table E.7 *Correlation between item 38 and item 39*

	40	41	42
40.	–	0·75	0·37
41.		–	0·62
42.			–

Table E.8 *Intercorrelations between peer group stability items*

	9	43	44	45	46	3
9.	–	0·23	0·34	0·73	0·20	0·40
43.		–	0·12	0·23	0·26	0·58
44.			–	0·14	0·05	0·34
45.				–	0·01	0·30
46.					–	0·07
3.						–

Table E.9 *Intercorrelations between staff organisation measures*

Appendix F

Observations

I. Lesson observations: sample category definitions

1. Teacher section

The principle throughout this section is that the predominant activity in which the teacher has been engaged during the observation period should be selected and recorded, and that all likely sorts of behaviour should be covered by one or other of the categories.

The focus in this section should be the person principally in charge of instructing the class, i.e. if someone other than the class teacher takes the children for a time, the focus would be on this person.

(A) *Interaction categories*

If interaction of any kind constitutes the major activity during the observation period, one of the 'interact' categories, together with one of the 'type' categories, must always be scored.

(i) *Individual*: Score when the teacher interacts specifically with one individual, either by e.g. calling the child out to his desk, or by positioning himself next to the child, or speaking in a way which is clearly primarily directed to one individual. In mixed schools, enter M or F according to the sex of the child. If the teacher continues to interact with the same child during a second or subsequent observation period, mark these later entries ✓ (or M+).

(ii) *Class*: For use in all other instances of interaction with the children, i.e. for all chalk and talk sessions directed to the whole class, for question and answer sessions only involving individuals as representatives of the class (N.B. taking registers would also be marked 'Class' on these grounds) and when the teacher is going round the class, or looking at the class, whilst they are working.

(B) *Type of interaction*

In all cases where interaction is scored, one and only one of the following categories must also be scored:

(i) *Topic categories*

(a) *Equipment*: Score for setting up of equipment, writing on board, distributing and collecting materials etc., or for instructions to children on distribution of resources – but not NB imparting of skills re use of equipment, which would be coded 'Topic'.
This category can also be used alone (i.e. with no interaction category) if appropriate.

(b) *Topic*: Uninterrupted interactions focused on the subject matter in hand, on earlier or related work, and the children's acquisition of the skills necessary in executing the work, including methods of using equipment, laying out work and so on.
Positive comments on a child's work should be scored as 'Topic' and 'Praise'.
Negative comments on a child's work should be scored as 'Topic' and 'Punishment'.
NB Topic can also be scored alone, without any of the interaction categories, if the teacher is clearly engaged in work related to the instructional context of the lesson, but is not interacting with the children, e.g. marking their books, consulting registers or records, listening to tapes, or generally surveying the children while they are working.

(ii) *Behaviour categories*: In all cases, score only for non-task related references to behaviour or dress (i.e. references to appropriate behaviour in laboratories would be coded as topic).
(a) *Management*: Score when the teacher gives initial instructions, or directions to prevent trouble occurring.
(b) *Control*: Directions initiated to ensure compliance with previous management instructions which have failed to produce the desired result, or to curb unacceptable behaviour – i.e. score only when the directions given are contingent upon the children's behaviour. If any verbal rebuke is included, score also 'Punishment'.
If comments are made about the children's *good* behaviour, these

should also be scored as control (i.e. as contingent on behaviour), but qualified by 'Praise'.

(iii) *Other*

(a) *Personal*: Score for specifically personal comments, which would usually indicate some background knowledge of, or interest in, the child, home or activities. On these grounds include also references to other non-school activities which seem to have no relationship to the task, e.g. discussion of football teams would probably be rated as 'Personal' in a maths lesson (but could be topic in a games lesson!).

(b) *Admin*: Score for points of school administration, outside the immediate requirements of the particular classroom – e.g. collection of school fund money, announcing general notices etc. and for taking of attendance registers.

2. Individual children

In this section, certain behaviours only have been selected as of interest, and thus the principles to be applied in scoring entries are in some cases different from those in the 'Teacher' section, as any instances of the selected behaviours, however brief, may be coded.

(i) *Task categories*

Always score one, and only one, of these, relating to the predominant activity during the period:

(a) *On*: Score when there is clear evidence that the child is on task, or, if only listening is required, that he is not doing anything which could preclude this. Score also if no task is prescribed.

(b) *?*: Score when it is not clear whether the child is on task, e.g. if he is engaged in an activity which does not absolutely preclude being on task, but may make it unlikely.

(c) *Off*: Score when there is evidence that the child is engaged in an alternative activity which would preclude his completing the task prescribed.

(ii) *Chat etc.*

The remaining categories are not mutually exclusive, and any instances, however brief, should be scored (but NB definition of chat).

(a) *Chat*: Exclude brief whispering, but include extended or easily audible chat.

(b) *Informal — mild*: Exclude fidgeting, but include e.g. rhythmic tapping on desk, chewing gum, sitting on desk/feet on desk, quiet singing/humming, and the use of swearing in general conversation or as mild expletives. As a general guide, the behaviours should be such as to be noticeable in a fairly ordered classroom, but not apparently disrupting others.

3. Class

Once again, any instances of the selected behaviours should be scored here or a score of *0* if none has occurred. Otherwise, ratings should be made in all cases on the following basis:

0 (i.e. blank) = no examples
1   = 1 or 2 children
2   = up to and including quarter of class
3   = between quarter and half class
4   = over half class

Definitions as for individual children above.

Procedures for checking inter-observer agreement

Twenty-two lessons were observed by pairs of observers to check levels of agreement. Some of these checks were made before the main series of observations, and others in the weeks intervening between the main data collection weeks. Total scores per lesson for each category (i.e. the units used in the analysis) for each observer were correlated to provide a measure of agreement. As three observers were involved, three series of correlations were made — A with B and C, B with A and C, and C with A and B. The probabilities given for the individual items included in Appendices A and E relate to these product-moment correlations. The mean scores of each observer on each category were also examined for possible variations. Certain behaviours occurred too infrequently during the check lessons to allow for adequate assessments of inter-observer agreement.

II. Checklist for beginning and ending of lessons

TO LESSON

33	Start/after break/N.K.		0
	Same room/Double		1
	V. slow		2

34	Lost	0	1
35	Fight	0	1
36	750 yards	0	1

START

37	Outside:	Mill	0
		Enter room	1
		Line up	2
	Inside:	Muddle	0
		Sit	1
		Stand	2

39	Off-task chat to T	0	1
40	Silence	0	1
41	Greeting	0	1
42	Register	0	1
43	Ritual	0	1

44	Seating:	Chosen by children	0
		T directs some	1
		T directs all	2
		N/K	9
45	Resources:	Brought by children	0
		On desk	1
		Distrib. by T	2
		Distrib. by monitors	3
		Collected by children	4

46–7 Time to start of work:

48   No. Late:

END

49	Timing:	Long	0
		Good	1
		Short	2
		Dismiss before bell	3

50	Stand behind chairs	0	1
51	Silence	0	1
52	Farewell	0	1
53	Line-up	0	1
54	Off-task chat to T	0	1
55	Tidy room	0	1
56	Dismiss by row/group/sex	0	1
57	Reports:	Individual	0	1
58		Class	0	1

59	Resources:	
	Collected by T	0
	Collected by monitor	1
	Replaced by children	2
	Kept by children	3

CHECKLIST

60	Homework set	0	1
61	Homework returned	0	1

Outings/trips

Formal punishments:

Formal rewards:

Jobs of e.g. monitors

Definitions for beginnings and endings of lessons

Initial sheet

Entries in each of the main sections have been coded in one of two ways:
(a) Items with mutually exclusive alternatives: 0–9. Circle the appropriate coding.
(b) Single items which may be present or absent: Circle 0 for absent, 1 for present.

(i) *To lesson*

Lost = fewer children in the current lesson than the previous one, where the number should be the same.

Fight = involving members of the class being observed.

(ii) *Start*

Resources = select the coding which seems to be the norm for the majority of resources.

Time to start of lesson: enter the time after the pips at which the majority of the class has settled to work, or the teacher has control of the class to start the lesson.

Late: enter the number of children arriving after the time entered above.

(iii) *End*

Timing: Short = Teacher finishes early, and there is time to fill before the pips, but the children are kept until then.

Long = Teacher does not finish in time, and the lesson overruns the pips.

Dismiss before bell = Teacher finishes early, and allows children to go.

Resources: As above

(iv) *Checklist*

Complete entries for any of the listed items which occur (and add notes on any other points of interest not otherwise recorded).

 (a) Outings/trips: note details, and whether subject or school-based.
 (b) Formal punishments: note types of punishment given, numbers of children involved, and, if possible, relevant 'offences'.

(c) Formal rewards: again, note types of reward, number involved, and relevant standards of work or behaviour.
(d) Jobs: note details of any jobs referred to during the lesson.

III Classroom observation schedule

1. Number   Late
2. Pencils
3. Uniform
4. Overcoats

5. Chairs
6. Windows

7. Condition   Clean
                    Tidy
                    Plants
                    Posters
                    Pictures

   Total

8. Work on walls   0   1   2   3   4
9. Graffiti   0   1   2   3   4

Classroom observation schedule – definitions

This observation schedule was used during the series of classroom observations of the third year and during the administration of the pupil questionnaire.

1. The number of pupils in the class and the number who arrived after the start of the lesson.
2. The number of pencils borrowed from the researchers during the administration of the questionnaire.
3. The number of children not in correct school uniform (as defined by the school).
4. The number of children in outdoor coats or anoraks.

5. The number of broken chairs in the classroom.
6. The number of broken or cracked windows.
7. The decorative condition of the room. One point was given for each of the five items and a total score assigned to each room.
8. The amount of children's work on the walls, coded from 0 to 4. 0 = none, 1 = one quarter of available wall space, 2 = one half of available wall space, 3 = three quarters of available wall space, 4 = all available wall space.
9. The amount of graffiti, coded as item 8.

Classroom observation schedule – procedures for checking inter-observer agreement

The reliability of the items in this schedule was assessed by comparing the ratings given by the three observers in 33 lessons when all three were present. The 'percentage agreement' figures given in Appendices A and E are the proportion of these 33 lessons in which all three observers gave the same coding.

Appendix G

Additional tables

Source	SS	df	MS	F	p
Band	1384·00	2	692·00	21·24	
Occupation	222·40	2	111·20	3·41	
School	2768·73	11	251·70	7·73	
Band x Occup.	36·87	4	9·21	0·28	NS
Band x School	1167·26	21	55·58	1·71	0·025
Occup. x School	1123·78	22	51·08	1·57	0·046
Band x Occup. x School	1322·89	39	33·92	1·04	NS
Residual	57442·80	1763	32·58		
Total	65527·66	1864	33·15		

(Hierarchical ANOVA with variables entered in the order shown above)

Table 5.1 *Analysis of variance (ANOVA) of 5th Year attendance by band, occupation and school*

Source	SS	df	MS	F	p
Occupation	240·83	2	120·42	3·92	0·020
School	1412·80	11	128·44	4·18	0·001
Residual	32817·93	1069	30·70		
Total	34471·56	1082	31·86		

(Hierarchical ANOVA with variables entered in the order shown above)

N.B. In this and all subsequent tables, non-significant higher order interactions have been pooled with the residual term.

Table 5.2 *Analysis of variance of 5th year attendance (band 2 pupils only) by school*

Designation	Girls % delinquent	(total no.)	Boys % delinquent	(total no.)
Low score	4·10	(439)	23·99	(296)
High score-total	16·00	(75)	33·33	(90)
Emotional	9·68	(31)	28·57	(28)
Conduct	21·05	(38)	38·89	(54)
Mixed	16·67	(6)	12·50	(8)

'*Chi-squared*' tests

Girls
Delinquency by high/low score $x^2 = 16·49$ p $< 0·001$
Delinquency by conduct/all other groups $x^2 = 17·25$ p $< 0·001$

Boys
Delinquency by high/low score $x^2 = 3·13$ NS
Delinquency by conduct/all other groups $x^2 = 5·25$ p $< 0·05$

Table 5.4 *Teacher questionnaire designation and delinquency*

Source	SS	df	MS	F	p
Verbal reasoning	1907·56	6	317·93	146·25	0·001
School	465·79	11	42·34	19·48	0·001
Residual	4743·22	2182	2·17		
Total	7116·54	2199	3·24		

(Hierarchical ANOVA with variables entered in the order shown above)

Table 5.9 *Analysis of variance of examination scores by verbal reasoning group and school*

Source	SS	df	MS	F	p
Occupation	85·05	2	42·52	15·78	0·001
School	356·74	11	32·43	12·03	0·001
Residual	2937·38	1090	2·69		
Total	3379·17	1103	3·06		

(Hierarchical ANOVA with variables entered in the order shown above)

Table 5.10 *Analysis of variance of examination scores, parental occupation and school (Middle VR band pupils only)*

Source	SS	df	MS	F	p
Verbal reasoning	39·04	1	39·04	16·88	0·001
School	170·00	11	15·46	6·68	0·001
Residual	1549·15	670	2·31		
Total	1758·19	682	2·58		

(Hierarchical ANOVA with variables entered in the order shown above)

Table 5.11 *Analysis of variance of CSE grades 4 and 5 for pupils in verbal reasoning groups 6 and 7 only – by school*

Source	SS	df	MS	F	p
Verbal reasoning	182·25	2	91·12	25·92	0·001
School	153·60	11	13·96	3·97	0·001
Residual	2067·44	588	3·52		
Total	2403·28	601	3·99		

(Hierarchical ANOVA with variables entered in the order shown above)

Table 5.12 *Analysis of variance of 'O' Level equivalents for pupils in VR groups 1 to 3 only – by school*

Source	SS	df	MS	F	p
Verbal reasoning	1181·34	6	196·89	80·35	0·001
School	300·55	11	27·32	11·15	0·001
Residual	2619·52	1069	2·45		
Total	4101·41	1086	3·78		

(Hierarchical ANOVA with variables entered in the order shown above)

Table 5.13 *Analysis of variance of examination scores by school, after excluding poor attendance, early leavers and delinquents*

Source	SS	df	MS	F	p
Band	679·83	2	339·92	148·03	
Occupation	29·40	2	14·70	6·40	
Area	39·77	2	19·88	8·66	
Band × Occupation	7·39	4	1·85	0·81	
Band × Area	25·63	4	6·41	2·79	
Occupation × Area	3·58	4	0·90	0·39	
Band × Occupation × Area	56·18	7	8·03	3·49	0·001
Residual	2417·91	1053	2·29		
Total	3261·44	1078	3·02		

(Hierarchical ANOVA with variables entered in the order shown)

Table 8.1 *Analysis of variance of examination scores (boys only) by VR band, parental occupation and home area*

Source	SS	df	MS	F	p
Area	13·08	2	6·54	2·59	0·076
School	125·12	8	15·64	6·19	0·001
Residual	1658·62	657	2·52		
Total	1796·81	667	2·69		

(Hierarchical ANOVA with variables entered in the order shown)

Table 8.2 *Analysis of variance of examination scores (for VR band 2 boys only), by home area and school*

Source	SS	df	MS	F	p
Band	1564·43	2	782·22	20·08	0·001
Occupation	25·04	2	12·52	0·321	0·725
Area	130·54	2	65·27	1·67	0·188
Residual	40948·86	1051	38·96		
Total	43190·60	1076	40·14		

(Hierarchical ANOVA, with variables entered in the order shown)

Table 8.3 *Analysis of variance of 5th year attendance (boys only) by VR band, parental occupation and home area*

Source	SS	df	MS	F	p
Area	22·20	2	11·10	0·31	0·732
School	696·21	8	87·03	2·45	0·013
Residual	23275·31	655	35·53		
Total	23993·72	665	36·08		

(Hierarchical ANOVA with variables entered in the order shown)

Table 8.4 *Analysis of variance of 5th year attendance (for VR band 2 boys only), by home area and school*

Parameters	G^2 attributable to parameter	df	p	G^2/df
Attendance by:				
Occupation	10·80	4	< 0·05	2·70
VR band	21·24	4	< 0·001	5·31
School	106·19	22	< 0·001	4·83

Table 9.5 *Log linear analysis of 5th year attendance*

Parameters	G^2 attributable to parameter	df	p	G^2/df
1. *Balance groups*				
(a) *Academic balance*				
Attendance by school (see Table 9·5)	106·19	22		
Attributable to balance groups	31·90	4	< 0·001	7·98
Attributable to schools within balance groups	74·29	18	< 0·001	4·13
(b) *Occupational balance*				
Attendance by school (see Table 9·5)	106·19	22		
Attributable to balance groups	6·04	4	NS	1·51
Attributable to schools within balance groups	100·15	18	< 0·001	5·56
(c) *Behavioural balance*				
Attendance by school (see Table 9·5)	106·19	22		
Attributable to balance groups	48·41	4	< 0·001	12·10
Attributable to schools within balance groups	57·78	18	< 0·001	3·21
(d) *Ethnic mix*				
Attendance by school (see Table 9·5)	106·19	22		
Attributable to balance groups	23·63	4	< 0·001	5·91
Attributable to schools within balance groups	82·56	18	< 0·001	4·59

Parameters	G^2 attributable to parameter	df	p	G^2/df
2. *Process groups*				
Attendance by school (see Table 9·5)	106·19	22		
Attributable to process groups	66·06	4	< 0·001	16·51
Attributable to schools within process groups	40·13	18	< 0·01	2·23

Table 9.6 *Separate effects of balance and process on attendance (log linear analysis)*

Parameters	G^2 attributable to parameter	df	p	G^2/df
Attendance by school (see Table 9·5)	106·19	22		
Attributable to behavioural balance groups	64·61	2	< 0·001	32·31
Attributable to process within balance groups	7·48	4	NS	1·87
Attributable to schools within groups	34·10	16	<0·01	2·13

Table 9.7 *Combined effects of balance and process on attendance (log linear analysis)*

Order of entry into equation		% of variance explained	p
1	VR group	2·80	< 0·001
2	Parental occupation	0·07	NS
3	% Occup. 1 Ethnic mix % Occup. 3 % Band 1 Behavioural balance % Band 3	14·28	< 0·001
4	Process	0·75	< 0·001

Total variance explained = 17·90% (Multiple r = 0·42)

Table 9.8 *Linear regression – attendance*

Parameters	G^2 attributable to parameter	df	p	G^2/df
Delinquency by:				
Occupation	12·05	2	< 0·01	6·03
VR Band	13·93	2	< 0·001	6·97
School	32·50	8	< 0·001	4·06

Table 9.9 *Log linear analysis of delinquency (Boys only)*

Parameters	G^2 attributable to parameter	df	p	G^2/df
1. Balance groups				
(a) Academic balance				
Delinquency by school (see Table 9.9)	32·50	8		
Attributable to balance groups	24·90	2	< 0·001	12·45
Attributable to schools within balance groups	7·60	6	NS	1·27
(b) Occupational balance				
Delinquency by school (see Table 9.9)	32·50	8		
Attributable to balance groups	0·37	2	NS	0·18
Attributable to schools within balance groups	32·13	6	< 0·001	5·36
(c) Behavioural mix				
Delinquency by school (see Table 9.9)	32·50	8		
Attributable to balance groups	5·74	2	NS	2·87
Attributable to schools within balance groups	26·76	6	< 0·001	4·46
(d) Ethnic mix				
Delinquency by school (see Table 9.9)	32·50	8		
Attributable to balance groups	19·54	2	< 0·001	9·77
Attributable to schools within balance groups	12·96	6	< 0·05	2·16
2. Process				
Delinquency by school (see Table 9.9)	32·50	8		
Attributable to process groups	13·01	2	< 0·01	6·51
Attributable to schools within process groups	19·49	6	< 0·01	3·25

Table 9.10 *Separate effects of balance and process on delinquency (log linear analysis)*

Parameters	G^2 attributable to parameter	df	p	G^2/df
Delinquency by school	24·19	7	< 0·001	3·46
Attributable to academic balance group	11·53	1	< 0·001	11·53
Attributable to process within balance group	1·12	2	NS	0·56
Attributable to schools within groups	11·54	4	< 0·05	2·89

Table 9.11 *Combined effects of balance and process on delinquency log linear analysis: 8 schools only*

Order of entry into equation	Boys	p	Girls	p
1 VR group	3·49	< 0·001	2·00	< 0·001
2 Parental occupation	0·09	NS	1·76	< 0·001
3 % Occup. 1 Ethnic mix % Occup. 3 % Band 1 Behavioural balance % Band 3	1·53	NS	1·09	NS
4 Process	1·29	< 0·001	< 0·05	NS
Total variance explained	6·40%		4·90%	
(Multiple r =	0·25		0·22)	

Table 9.12 *Linear regression – delinquency*

Appendix H

Analysis of multiway contingency tables by log linear models

When data are categorised into cells on two or more discrete variables the resulting contingency table can be analysed using a variety of methods. One method which enables the possible interactions between variables to be assessed is the log linear model. This approach, with various extensions, has been applied to such tables as they arose in the analysis of the present data set. Before the model itself is described, the general multiway contingency table and its sub-tables will be briefly discussed as an introduction to the problems of such data.

Multiway contingency tables

In such a table each unit or individual is independently characterised by a number of variables which are measured on a discrete scale, e.g. nominal variables with two categories such as male and female, or ordered scales such as number of children which could be scored in a variety of ways and could be created as an ordinal scale.

The table thus consists of counts of the number of units with the same characteristics. Table H.1 is such a table defined by the following variables: (1) Verbal reasoning band at ten years, (2) Occupation of parent at fourteen years, and, (3) The exam results based on 'O' level passes. Thus the table gives the numbers of children falling in each of eighteen categories defined by the combination of levels of the above variables.

A question we may wish to answer is 'Does result depend on occupation?'. Clearly it can be seen that different bands have somewhat differing proportions of occupations, and band is also related to result. Thus we may need to take these interactions into account. We could ignore the band variable altogether and produce Table H.2 below.

Band	1			2			3		
Occupation of Parent	1	2	3	1	2	3	1	2	3
Exam Result 1. No 'O' level passes	6	5	2	17	29	35	4	16	21
2. At least 1 'O' level pass	5	6	3	21	22	10	2	2	2

Table H.1 *Distribution of 'O' level passes by band and parental occupation*

Exam Results	Parental Occupation		
	1	2	3
No 'O' levels	27	50	58
At least 1 'O' level	28	30	15

Table H.2 *'O' level results by occupation of parent*

This table is called a margin to the larger three-way table. The question originally asked could to some extent be answered by this table, but it would still be left uncertain since this table may be no more than a reflection of the relation between parental occupation and band. Also, it can be seen from Table H.1 that the association between parental occupation and result is not so clear-cut in verbal reasoning bands 1 and 3. Thus, we need a method to overcome these difficulties and to utilise all the information from the main table, rather than combining results from sub-tables or taking at face value results from two-variable marginal tables. Notice also that there are two further two-variable marginal tables – band by result and band by parent's occupation in addition to the three single variable margins. In two-way tables hypotheses are tested using the single variable margins to provide expected values.

For multiway tables hypotheses can be tested using information not only from the single variable but from combinations of other marginal tables to provide expected values. The log linear model approach enables a model of the data to be built from sets of interaction terms, as in the analysis of variance and its linear model. On the basis of the most parsimonious model, if one is available, answers can be provided to such questions as the significance of interactions and information can be given as to which variables, if any, should be omitted in collapsing the table to simplify the representation of those interactions correctly.

Variable 1	Variable 2						Totals
	1	2	.	.	.	c	(row)
1	n_{11} . n_{12}		.	.	.	n_{1c}	n_1
2	n_{21}	n_{22}	.	.	.	n_{2c}	n_2
.							
.							
r	n_{r1}	n_{r2}				n_{rc}	n_r
Totals (column)	$n_{.1}$	$n_{.2}$				$n_{.c}$	$n_{..}$

Table H.3

Log linear models in a two-dimensional table

This section briefly describes the log linear model and its parameters for the simple two-way table with variables 1 and 2 having r and c levels respectively, n_{ij} represents the numbers of individuals at level i of variable 1 and level j of variable 2. The marginal totals $n_{i.}$ and $n_{.j}$ (for rows and columns) represent the number of individuals at level i of variable 1, disregarding levels of variable 2, and the number of individuals at level j of variable 2 disregarding variable 1 respectively.

The usual chi-square test of significance is based on a model of independence between the two variables. That is F_{ij}, the number of individuals expected at level i of 1 and j of 2, is equal to the product of the probabilities of level i on variable 1 and level j on variable 2 separately, multiplied by the sample size.

$$F_{ij} = p_i * p_j * n_{..}$$

Taking logarithms

$$\log_e F_{ij} = \log_e p_i + \log_e p_j + \log_e n_{..}$$

This provides a basis for the log linear model which is of the following form:

$$\log_e p_{ij} = u + u_1(i) + u_2(j) + u_{12}(ij)$$

That is, the logarithm of the cell probability is the sum of four sets of terms

(1) u — a grand mean term

(2) $u_1(i)$ — a term to represent the 'main effect' of variable 1 at level i (r parameters)

(3) $u_2(j)$ — a similar term for variable 2
(c parameters)
(4) $u_{12}(ij)$ — a term to represent the effects of an interaction between the variables 1 and 2 in cell ij ($r \times c$ parameters)

Under the hypothesis of no interaction, or independence, this model for the population probabilities reduces to

$$\log_e P_{ij} = u + u_1(i) + u_2(j)$$

and for a sample of size $N(= n..)$ the number F in cell ij would be given by

$$\log_e F_{ij} = \log_e(Np_{ij}) = \log_e P_{ij} + \log_e N = u' + u_1(i) + u_2(j)$$

where $u' = u + \log_e N$. Thus, if a text of the fit of this model were to be constructed we would be able to assess our hypothesis of independence. From the logarithms of the theoretical frequencies we can obtain expressions for the 'u' terms as follows:

$$u' = \frac{1}{rc} \sum_i \sum_j \log_e F_{ij}$$

$$u_1(i) = \frac{1}{c} \sum_j \log_e F_{ij} - u'$$

$$u_2(j) = \frac{1}{r} \sum_i \log_e F_{ij} - u'$$

And since $u_1(i)$ and $u_2(j)$ represent deviations from the 'grand mean' term $u,'$ the set of constraints familiar to users of analysis of variance applies as below

$$\sum_i u_1(i) = \sum_j u_2(j) = 0.$$

Thus to implement the model we need a method of estimation and a goodness of fit test, both of which are provided by using maximum likelihood methods.

Although this does seem a long-winded process for a simple two-way table where the Pearson Chi-square statistic has been shown to adequately test the hypothesis of independence, the ideas of log linear models generalise readily to multiway tables. In such cases the choice of hypotheses regarding independence is much more complex.

Three-way tables

In this section we consider the hypotheses that can arise in such a table as presented in the first section. These hypotheses are directly related to log linear models by the inclusion of specific terms. This is easily seen to be generalisable to tables of four or more variables. The question of choice of particular models for a table is left for discussion in a subsequent section.

Hypotheses of independence in three-way tables

If we adopt a similar notation to the previous section, p_{ijk} represents the probability of an observation falling in the i-th level of variable 1, the j-th level of variable 2 and the k-th level of variable 3. Then we can describe all the marginal tables of probabilities using the dot notation as before.

(a) $p_{i..}$ represents the probability of the i-th level of the first variable disregarding the second and third variables

$$p_{i..} = \sum_{jk} p_{ijk}$$

similarly we have $p_{.j.}$ and $p_{..k}$.

(b) $p_{ij.}$ is the probability of an observation falling in the ij-th cell of the table formed from the first two variables alone. That is $p_{ij.} = \sum_{k} p_{ijk}$ is the probability of an observation being at level i on variable 1 and level j on variable 2. Similarly the other two tables are represented by $p_{i.k}$ and $p_{.jk}$.

Complete independence

This hypothesis is directly related to two variable independence and states that $p_{ijk} = p_{i..} \times p_{.j.} \times p_{..k}$
That is, the probability of an observation falling in cell ijk is the product of the univariate marginal probabilities for the i, j and k levels on each of the variables 1, 2 and 3. Or we can express expected frequencies

$$F_{ijk} = p_{i..} \times p_{.j.} \times p_{..k} \times N \ (N = n_{...} \text{ the sample size})$$

We can then estimate $p_{i..}$ by $\dfrac{n_{i..}}{n_{...}}$,

$$p_{.j.} \text{ by} \dfrac{n_{.j.}}{n_{...}} \text{ and } p_{..k} \text{ by} \dfrac{n_{..k}}{n_{...}}$$

to obtain expected values

$$E_{ijk} = \dfrac{n_{i..} \times n_{.j.} \times n_{..k}}{N \times N}$$

i.e. $\quad E_{111} = \dfrac{27 \times 55 \times 135}{210 \times 210} = 4.55$

Then we could use the chi-square test statistic

$$x^2 = \sum_{ijk} \dfrac{(n_{ijk} - E_{ijk})^2}{E_{ijk}}$$

with the appropriate degrees of freedom.

However we can express this hypothesis in terms of the log linear model in the following form

$$\log_e F_{ijk} = u + u_1(i) + u_2(j) + u_3(k)$$

where $u_1(i)$ is a term to represent an effect for the i-th level of variable 1 similarly $u_2(j)$ and $u_3(k)$ for variables 2 and 3. The usual constraints hold, that is

$$\sum_i u_1(i) = \sum_j u_2(j) = \sum_k u_3(k) = 0$$

For variable 1 of Table H.1 the $u_1(i)$ term represents three parameters, one for each level of the variable, but only two are independent because of the constraints imposed. For variables 2 and 3 there are two and one independent parameters in the terms $u_2(j)$ and $u_3(k)$ respectively for exactly the same reasons. Thus we have a model with $2 + 2 + 1 = 5$ independent parameters to represent main effects, and 1 grand mean parameter, and hence in total 6 independent parameters. We have 18 cells or points at which to fit the model, and hence the model has $18 - 6 = 12$ degrees of freedom. In general, the degrees of freedom are calculated from the equation below:

degrees of freedom = no. of cells – no. of independent parameters. We have a model then for complete independence – no interaction between any variables is postulated.

Partial independence

This is where two variables, say variables 1 and 2, are associated, but both are independent of variable 3. In terms of Table H.1, verbal reasoning band and parental occupation are associated, but neither is associated with result. We can then write the probabilities of cell ijk as follows:

$$p_{ijk} = p_{ij.} \times p_{..k}$$

This is called partial independence.

The reason to test such an hypothesis could be that the dependence of band on occupation is known but, although it is of little interest, it has to be taken into account. Alternatively, if the sampling had been stratified in such a way that the proportions for the band and occupation table had been fixed beforehand. Thus the interaction is now just some artefact of the sampling scheme which again needs to be taken into account in order to assess the independence of result from both band and occupation.

We can directly find the expected values from

$$E_{ijk} = \frac{n_{ij} \times n_{..k}}{N}$$

$$\text{for instance } E_{111} = \frac{11 \times 135}{210} = 7 \cdot 07$$

and we could again use chi-square tests. The log linear model in this situation is written as

$$\text{Log}_e F_{ijk} = u + u_1(i) + u_2(j) + u_3(k) + u_{12}(ij)$$

Where the same constraints apply to the $u_1(i)$, $u_2(j)$ and $u_3(k)$ $u_{12}(ij)$ represent the effect of the interaction between variables 1 and 2 in cell ij and similar constraints apply to this;

that is

$$\sum_i u_{12}(ij) = \sum_j u_{12}(ij) = 0$$

Hence for Table H.1 the $u_{12}(ij)$ represent 3×3 parameters but only $2 \times 2 = 4$ independent because of the constraints used. Hence the model contains $1 + 2 + 2 + 1 + 4 = 10$ independent parameters and has $18 - 10 = 8$ degrees of freedom. Clearly we could have chosen the dependency between pairs of variables — the first order interaction — in two other ways. The dependency could have been either between variables 1 and 3, or between 2 and 3, which would have been represented by terms $u_{13}(ik)$ or $u_{23}(jk)$. Thus there are three models of partial independence which could have been specified. Yet another type of independence – conditional independence – could arise when two of the terms $u_{12}(ij)$, $u_{23}(jk)$ and $u_{13}(ik)$ are put in the model. For instance we could specify a relation between band and occupation, and also band and result, and then wish to test the hypothesis that result is independent of occupation once the band of the observation is given. The log linear model in this instance is

$$\text{Log}_e \, F_{ijk} = u + u_1(i) + u_2(j) + u_3(k) + u_{12}(ij) + u_{13}(ik)$$

The terms, again, are subject to constraints and hence for Table H.1 the model would have $1 + 2 + 2 + 1 + 4 + 2 = 12$ independent parameters and hence 6 degrees of freedom.

Also it is clear that the choice of pairs of first order interactions could have been made in another two ways.

Finally we could include all first order interactions, and this could be best interpreted as the hypothesis of no second order interaction. This is expressible in the following probabalistic statement:

for an $r \times c \times l$ table as:

$$\frac{p_{rcl} \; p_{ij1}}{p_{icl} \; p_{rj1}} = \frac{p_{rck} \, p_{ijk}}{p_{ick} \, p_{rjk}}, \qquad \begin{aligned} i &= 1, \ldots, r-1 \\ j &= 1, \ldots, c-1 \\ k &= 1, \ldots, l-1 \end{aligned}$$

which again suggests that the relationship between *any* two variables does not change from one level to another of the third.

The second order interaction term, $u_{123}(ijk)$, if included in the model, would lead to a perfect fit, since all the degrees of freedom would have been exhausted. This model is called the saturated model, and is used in certain instances as a guide to the location of significant terms and thus model reduction. We have thus seen 8 models of interest for a three-way table, each model represented by the inclusion of a set of terms in an equation for the expected frequencies. The next section describes how the estimates of the parameters and goodness of fit are obtained.

The expected frequencies calculable from the probability statements also get complicated since in general they are not directly calculable, and some iterative process such as Deming-Stephan scaling has to be used (see Everitt, 1977). As can be imagined, the modelling of tables of four or more variables leads to an even larger number of models of interest, involving not only first order interactions but also second and higher orders. This leads to another problem – that of choice of model, which is discussed later.

Estimation

A variety of procedures have been suggested for the estimation of parameters in the log linear model, each with its own goodness of fit statistic. The analysis in previous chapters was based on maximum likelihood estimation, the exact details of which are far beyond this appendix. The associated goodness of fit statistic is the maximum likelihood chi-square known as G^2

$$G^2 = 2 \Sigma \text{ observed } \log_e \left[\frac{\text{observed}}{\text{expected}} \right], \text{ where the}$$

summation is over all the cells in the table.

The degrees of freedom for G^2 are the degrees of freedom for the model – that is the number of independent parameters subtracted from the number of cells in the table. The usual chi-square tables are applicable, since for large sample sizes G^2 is distributed as a chi-square variate as is the Pearson chi-square statistic and others.

In general the maximum likelihood procedure can use almost any distribution of scores but the programme used, called Everymans Contingency Table Analysis, developed by L. A. Goodman, is based on a multinomial distribution. That is, the counts in the cells are assumed to be from a multinomial distribution. In fact, a Poisson distribution will give the same numerical results. The likelihood of the table is then written down in terms of the parameters involved in the model. This function is then maximised with respect to these unknown parameters and, using an iterative process, the estimates of parameters found. Standard errors for these estimates can be also calculated using the maximum likelihood theory for large samples. An equivalent procedure can be used, since the inclusion of a term in effect fixes the marginal table implied by that term. The Deming-Stephan iterative scaling procedure can be used on these fixed margins to estimate expected values. Then it is a simple matter to calculate the goodness of fit and to estimate the parameters involved from combinations of the logarithms of the expected values.

Readers interested in the maximum likelihood procedure or its alternatives and the asymptotic distributional properties are referred to Bishop, Fienberg and Holland (1975) for a fuller discussion.

Model selection and hypothesis testing

The principle of first smoothing the data and then drawing inference is adopted. That is where we have no a priori hypotheses about a set of data and we wish to determine the model (or models) that fits the data, such that the model contains all the important features of the data. This is achieved by adopting a stepwise procedure. As our choice of models is restricted by the estimation procedure which requires all lower order interaction terms to be present if they are implied by a higher order term, this is called the hierarchy principle. For example, inclusion of a second order term u_{123} requires the inclusion of u_{12}, u_{13}, u_{23}, u_1, u_2, u_3 and u.

Thus this means that a backward stepwise procedure is required initially – i.e. starting at the higher order interactions and then working in some manner as suggested by Goodman (1971) or Aitkin (1978). Both methods use the fact that differences in fit as measured by differences in the G^2 statistic reflect addition or subtraction of parameters in the model. For example, we may take the data from Table H.1. Table H.4 shows the terms omitted from the saturated model, and the corresponding G^2 for each model considered. First, the second order interaction term between band, parental occupation and result is omitted. The non-significant G^2 implies that we could drop this term which leads to a non-significant decrease in fit from the saturated model. Then following Aitkin (1978) we drop all first order interactions. This model itself gives a bad fit to the data and leads to a significant decrease in fit when compared with the first model tried (using an appropriate significance level for considering the three terms together). This suggests one or more of these three terms are non-zero. Hence each, in turn, is omitted from model 1 and the changes in G^2 compared for significance. The decrease in fit for the omission of u_{23} is non-significant, and hence could be dropped from model, and hence we would adopt model 5, which includes interactions between band and result and also occupation and result. Thus our original question is answered if we consider the change in G^2 when each of these two interactions is omitted. This process for general tables need not lead to unique models.

	Model (terms omitted)	G^2	df	Change in G^2 from model 1	df
1.	u_{123}	3·84	4	–	–
2.	$u_{12}, u_{23}, u_{13}, u_{123}$	40·14	12	36·30	8
3.	u_{12}, u_{123}	12·66	6	8·82	2
4.	u_{13}, u_{123}	15·73	6	11·89	2
5.	u_{23}, u_{123}	10·37	8	6·53	4
6.	u_{23}, u_{12}, u_{123}	23·72	10	13·35 * from 5	2
7.	u_{23}, u_{13}, u_{123}	26·79	10	16·42 * from 5	2

Table H.4

Nested designs

Where in previous chapters we have a term school within groups on the basis of some balance factor we can still apply the log linear approach using a set of parameters equivalent to the usual nested analysis of variance design. The effect of groups in an interaction term containing schools can be assessed by omitting the school within group part of this interaction and then omitting the whole term from the model (provided, of course, the models chosen are admissible with respect to the hierarchy principle). From the changes in fit, as measured by G^2, we can ascertain what proportion of the chi-square the school within groups interaction accounts for, and whether this is a significant component of the model.

Appendix I

Attainment at the end of the first year in the sixth form

In the main body of analyses on academic attainment we focused largely on examination results at the end of the fifth year. We had also collected information on any further CSE or 'O' levels gained by pupils in the main sample during their first years in the sixth form. Overall some 27 per cent of pupils stayed on into the sixth form, but there was considerable variation between schools, the proportions in individual schools ranging from under 10 per cent to over 40 per cent. A few children took courses of 'A' levels only, and some stayed on simply to extend their general education, without sitting further exams. The majority, however, stayed on to re-sit CSE or 'O' levels, or to extend their qualifications at this level. Altogether, 494 pupils sat further exams of these kinds during the first year sixth, and 425 of these improved their earlier grades, or gained further passes. These 425 pupils constituted just under 20 per cent of the total fifth year group we had studied, but again the proportions in individual schools varied, from 10·4 per cent to 39·0 per cent. The remainder of this appendix summarises the findings on this group of sixth form 'improvers'.

Characteristics of sixth form improvers

By comparison with the sample as a whole, it was clear that these pupils who improved their exam scores in the first year sixth differed from their peers in terms of measured ability, parental occupation, fifth year attendance, delinquency rates and fifth year exam results.

Compared with the total sample of pupils in this age group, twice as many of these sixth formers were in the top ability band (22·6 per cent vs 11·6 per cent), and only half as many in the bottom band (15·1 per cent vs 31·1 per cent). This means that this sixth form group constituted 37·6 per cent of the top band, 21·0 per cent of the middle band, and only 9·4 per cent of the bottom band in the original sample ($x^2 = 100·67$ $df = 2$ $p < 0·001$).

VR Band	Sixth Form Improvers (N = 425)	Others (N = 1775)	Total Sample (N = 2200)
	%	%	%
1	22·6	8·9	11·6
2	63·3	56·1	58·3
3	15·1	34·9	31·1
	$x^2 = 100·67$ df = 2 $p < 0·001$		

Table I.1 *Verbal reasoning band and sixth form exam improvement*

Parental Occupation	Sixth Form Improvers (N = 395)	Others (N = 1511)	Total Sample (N = 1906)
	%	%	%
Non-Manual	18·7	12·4	13·7
Skilled Manual	48·9	45·7	46·4
Semi-skilled/unskilled	32·4	41·8	39·9
	$x^2 = 16·65$ df = 2 $p < 0·001$		

Table I.2 *Parental occupation and sixth form exam improvement*

Source	SS	df	MS	F	p
Between groups	5695·50	1	5695·50	134·93	0·001
Within groups	92776·94	2198	42·21		
Total	98472·44	2199			

Table I.3 *Fifth year attendance and sixth year exam improvement (oneway analysis of variance)*

The sixth form improvers were less likely to have parents in the lower occupational groups (see Table I.2), and there was a clear tendency for them to have been better attenders during the fifth year (a mean attendance of 17·85 out of 20, by comparison with 13·78 for other pupils – see Table I.3).

Finally, both boys and girls amongst the sixth form improvers were much less likely to have been involved in delinquent activities. Only 8·7 per cent of the sixth form boys were delinquent by comparison with 28·1 per cent in the whole sample. The comparable figures for girls were 0·9 per cent and 6 per cent (see Table I.4).

(a) *BOYS*

	Sixth Form Improvers (N = 208)	Others (N = 1042)	Total sample (N = 1250)
	%	%	%
Delinquent	8·7	32·0	28·1
Non-delinquent	91·3	68·0	71·9

$$x^2 = 45·48 \ \ df = 1 \ \ p < 0·001$$

(b) *GIRLS*

	Sixth Form Improvers (N = 217)	Others (N = 733)	Total sample (N = 950)
	%	%	%
Delinquent	0·9	7·5	6·0
Non-delinquent	99·1	92·5	94·0

$$x^2 = 11·72 \ \ df = 1 \ \ p < 0·001$$

Table I.4 *Delinquency and sixth year exam improvement*

As might be expected from all these factors, this sixth form group had achieved considerably better exam scores than their peers at the end of the fifth year. Excluding Easter leavers from the comparison (and so concentrating only on pupils who had actually stayed on to sit exams at the end of the fifth year), this sixth form group had mean exam scores which were significantly higher than the other pupils in each ability band (see Table I.5).

VR Band

	Sixth Form Improvers			Others excluding Easter Leavers				
	N	X	(SD)	N	X	(SD)	F	p
1	96	4·57	(2·01)	145	2·57	(2·19)	51·02	0·001
2	265	2·86	(1·82)	844	1·38	(1·55)	168·65	0·001
3	64	1·23	(1·22)	464	0·51	(0·84)	36·88	0·001

Table I.5 *Fifth year exam scores and sixth year exam improvements*

Exam scores of the sixth form improvers

As shown in Table I.6, the sixth form group showed very substantial improvements in their final exam scores by comparison with those they had obtained at the end of the sixth year. The improvement was greatest in absolute terms for the top VR group, but larger in propor-

	VR Group						
Exam score	*1* (N = 28)	*2* (N = 68)	*3* (N = 103)	*4* (N = 93)	*5* (N = 69)	*6* (N = 33)	*7* (N = 31)
Score at end of							
1st year sixth	7·68	5·81	5·40	4·52	3·73	2·86	1·77
Improvements	2·04	1·68	1·84	1·73	1·83	1·38	0·79

Table 1.6 *Sixth form mean exam scores, and improvement over 5th year scores by VR group*

tion for those at the lower end of the ability range. Translating these scores at the end of the sixth year into actual numbers and grades of pass, the small number (28) of pupils in VR group 1 had gained on average 6·4 'O' level equivalents, those in the middle group had 2·6 'O' level equivalents and 3·8 grade 2 or 3 CSEs or 'O' levels at grades D and E, while the 31 pupils in the lowest group had an average 2·4 of these lower graded passes.

It was clear then that these sixth form pupils, a majority of those who had stayed on into the sixth form, had benefited considerably from their extra year of schooling, and that they would be relatively well-equipped with formal qualifications if they left school at this point.

School differences

(a) *Exam scores at end of fifth year*

Source	SS	df	MS	F	p
VR	600·99	6	100·16	40·92	0·001
School	192·98	11	17·54	7·17	0·001
Residual	996·27	407	2·45		
Total	1790·25	424	4·22		

(b) *Exam scores at end of first year sixth*

Source	SS	df	MS	F	p
VR	824·73	6	137·45	38·40	0·001
School	223·51	11	20·32	5·68	0·001
Residual	1456·89	407	3·58		
Total	2505·12	424	5·91		

Table I.7 *School differences on exam scores of sixth form improvers*
(Hierarchical analysis of variance)

Marked school differences were evident in the exam scores of the group of sixth form improvers, both at the end of the fifth year and at the end of the first year sixth. The various school fifth year mean scores, adjusted for VR, ranged from 0·68 to 3·94 with an overall average of 3·00 ($F = 7·167$; 11 df, $p < 0·001$). The sixth year school averages, adjusted for VR, ranged from 2·28 to 5·62 with an overall average of 4·69 ($F = 5·68$; 11 df; $p < 0·001$). The school rankings on the final exam scores of the sixth form improvers correlated 0·87 with the academic outcome rankings for the total sample of children at the twelve schools.

The findings add considerable weight to our earlier conclusions on school differences. It appeared that some quite strong school influences were operating to produce differences which persisted into the sixth form even with this atypical group of relatively high achieving and less disadvantaged pupils.

References

ACLAND, H. (1973) Social determinants of educational achievement: an evaluation and criticism of research. Ph.D. Thesis, University of Oxford.

AINSWORTH, M. E. and BATTEN, E. J. (1974) *The Effects of Environmental Factors on Secondary Educational Attainment in Manchester: A Plowden Follow-Up.* London: Macmillan.

AITKIN, M. (1978) The analysis of unbalanced cross-classifications. *Journal of the Royal Statistical Society (Series A),* 141, 195–211.

ANDERSON, R. C. (1959) Learning in discussions: A résumé of the authoritarian-democratic studies. *Harvard Educational Review,* 29, 201–15.

ARONSON, E. and METTEE, D. R. (1962) Dishonest behavior as a function of differential levels of induced self-esteem. *Journal of Personality and Social Psychology,* 9, 121–7.

AVERCH, H. A., CARROLL, S. J., DONALDSON, T. S., KIESLING, H. J. and PINCUS, J. (1972) *How Effective is Schooling? A critical review and synthesis of research findings.* Santa Monica, California: Rand Corporation.

BANDURA, A. (1969) Social-learning theory of identificatory processes. In Goslin, D. A. (ed.) *Handbook of Socialization Theory and Research.* Chicago: Rand McNally. Pp. 325–46.

BARKER, R. G. and GUMP, P. V. (1964) *Big School, Small School.* Stanford, California: Stanford University Press.

BARNES, J. H. and LUCAS, H. (1974) Positive discrimination in education: individuals, groups and institutions. In Leggatt, T. (ed.) *Sociological Theory and Survey Research.* London: Sage.

BARTAK, L. and RUTTER, M. (1973) Special educational treatment of autistic children: A comparative study. I: Design of study and characteristics of units. *Journal of Child Psychology and Psychiatry,* 14, 161–79.

BECKER, W. C. (1973) Applications of behavior principles in typical classrooms. In Thoresen, C.E. (ed.) *Behavior Modification in Education.* The 72nd Year Book of the National Society for the Study of Education. Chicago: University of Chicago Press. Pp. 77–106.

BECKER, W. C., MADSEN, C. H., ARNOLD, C. R. and THOMAS, D. R. (1967) The contingent use of teacher attention and praise in reducing classroom behavior problems. *Journal of Special Education,* 1, 287–307.

BENNETT, S. N. (1976) *Teaching Styles and Pupil Progress.* London: Open Books.

BENNETT, S. N. (1978) Recent research on teaching: a dream, a belief and a model. *British Journal of Educational Psychology,* 48, 127–47.

BERGER, M., YULE, W. and RUTTER, M. (1975) Attainment and adjustment in two geographical areas. II: The prevalence of specific reading retardation. *British Journal of Psychiatry,* 126, 510–19.

BERNSTEIN, B. (1970) Education cannot compensate for society. *New Society,* 387, 344–7.

BISHOP, Y. M. M., FIENBERG, S. E. and HOLLAND, F. W. (1975) *Discrete Multivariate Analysis.* Massachusetts Institute of Technology Press.

BOWLES, S. (1971) Unequal education and the reproduction of the social division of labor. *Review of Radical Political Economics,* **3.** (Reprinted in Karabel, J. and Halsey, A. H., 1977.)

BOWLES, S. and GINTIS, H. (1976) *Schooling in Capitalist America: Educational Reform and the Contradictions of Economic Life.* New York: Basic Books.

BRIMER, M. A., MADAUS, G. F., CHAPMAN, B., KELLAGHAN, T. and WOOD, R. (1977) *Sources of Difference in School Achievement.* Report to the Carnegie Corporation, New York.

BROPHY, J. E. and EVERTSON, C. M. (1976) *Learning From Teaching.* Boston: Allyn & Bacon.

BROWN, G. W., BHROLCHAIN, M. N. and HARRIS, T. (1975) Social class and psychiatric disturbance among women in an urban population. *Sociology,* **9,** 225–54.

CLEGG, A. and MEGSON, B. (1968) *Children in Distress.* Harmondsworth, Middx: Penguin Books.

COHEN, A. K. (1956) *Delinquent Boys: The culture of the gang.* London: Kegan Paul.

COLEMAN, J. S. (1961) *The Adolescent Society.* New York: Free Press.

COLEMAN, J. S. (1975) Methods and results in the IEA studies of the effects of school on learning. *Review of Educational Research,* **45,** 335–86.

COLEMAN, J. S. *et al.* (1966) *Equality of Educational Opportunity.* Washington: US Government Printing Office.

CRESSEY, D. R. (1964) *Delinquency, Crime and Differential Association.* The Hague: Martinus Nijhoff.

DAVIES, B. (1976) *Social Control and Education.* London: Methuen.

DAVIS, D. (1977) Where comprehensives score. *Times Educational Supplement,* 25.3.77.

DELAMONT, S. (1976) *Interaction in the Classroom.* London: Methuen.

DOUGLAS, J. W. B. (1964) *The Home and the School.* London: MacGibbon and Kee.

DOUGLAS, J. W. B., ROSS, J. M. and SIMPSON, H. R. (1968) *All Our Future: A longitudinal study of secondary education.* London: Peter Davies.

DUBIN, R. (1962) Industrial workers' worlds: A study of the 'central life interests' of industrial workers. In Rose, A. M. (ed.) *Human Behaviour and Social Processes: An Interactionist Approach.* London: Routledge and Kegan Paul.

EGGLESTON, J. (1977) *The Ecology of the School.* London: Methuen.

EVERITT, B. S. (1977) *The Analysis of Contingency Tables.* London: Chapman & Hall.

FARRINGTON, D. P. (1972) Delinquency begins at home. *New Society,* **21,** 495–7.

FARRINGTON, D. P. (1977) The effects of public labelling. *British Journal of Criminology,* **17,** 112–25.

FARRINGTON, D. P., OSBORN, S. G. and WEST, D. J. (1978) The persistence of labelling effects. *British Journal of Criminology,* **18,** 277–84.

FINLAYSON, D. J. (1973) Measuring school climate. *Trends in Education,* April 1973.

FINLAYSON, D. J. and LOUGHRAN, J. L. (1975) Pupils' perceptions in low and high delinquency schools. *Educational Research,* **18,** 138–45.

FOGELMAN, K. (1978) School attendance, attainment and behaviour. *British Journal of Educational Psychology,* **48,** 148–58.

FREEMAN, H. E. and GIOVANNONI, J. M. (1969) Social psychology of mental health. In Lindzey, G. and Aronson, E. (eds) *The Handbook of Social Psychology* (2nd edition). Vol. 5: *Applied Social Psychology.* London: Addison-Wesley. Pp. 660–719.

GALLOWAY, D. (1976) Size of school, socio-economic hardship, suspension rates and persistent unjustified absence from school. *British Journal of Educational Psychology,* **46,** 40–47.

GARDNER, D. E. M. (1966) *Experiment and Tradition in Primary Schools*. London: Methuen.

GATH, D., COOPER, B., GATTONI, F. and ROCKETT, D. (1977) *Child Guidance and Delinquency in a London Borough*. Maudsley Monographs No. 24. London: Oxford University Press.

GETZELS, J. W. (1969) A social psychology of education. In Lindzey, G. and Aronson, E. (eds) *The Handbook of Social Psychology* (second edition). Vol. 5: *Applied Social Psychology*. London: Addison-Wesley. Pp. 459–537.

GOOCH, S. and PRINGLE, M. L. KELLMER (1966) *Four Years On: A follow-up study at school leaving age of children formerly attending a traditional and a progressive junior school*. London: Longmans.

GOODMAN, L. A. (1971) The analysis of multidimensional contingency tables: stepwise procedures and direct estimation methods for building models for multiple classifications. *Technometrics*, **13**, 33–61.

GORDON, W. (1957) *The Social System of the High School*. Glencoe, Ill: Free Press.

GUMP, P. V. (1974) Operating environments in schools of open or traditional design. *School Review*, **82**, 575–94.

HALPIN, A. (1966) *Theory and Research in Administration*. London: Macmillan.

HARGREAVES, D. N. (1967) *Social Relations in a Secondary School*. London: Routledge & Kegan Paul.

HEAL, K. H. (1978) Misbehaviour among school children: the role of the school in strategies for prevention. *Policy and Politics*, **6**, 321–32.

HELMREICH, R. (1972) Stress, self-esteem and attitudes. In King, B. T. and McGinnies, E. (eds) *Attitudes, Conflict and Social Change*. London: Academic Press.

HIRSCHI, T. and HINDELANG, M. J. (1977) Intelligence and delinquency: a revisionist review. *American Sociological Review*, **42**, 571–87.

HOFFMAN, M. L. (1957) Conformity as a dense mechanism and a formal resistance to genuine group influence. *Journal of Personality*, **25**, 412–24.

HOLAHAN, C. J. and SAEGERT, S. (1973) Behavioral and attitudinal effects of large scale variation in the physical environment of psychiatric wards. *Journal of Abnormal Psychology*, **82**, 454–62.

Inner London Educational Authority (1970) *Literacy Survey*. Mimeographed report.

JENCKS, C., SMITH, M., ACLAND, H., BANE, M. J., COHEN, D., GINTIS, H., HEYNS, B. and MICHELSON, S. (1972) *Inequality: A reassessment of the effect of family and schooling in America*. New York: Basic Books.

JENSEN, A. R. (1969) How much can we boost IQ and scholastic achievement? *Harvard Educational Review*, **39**, 1–123.

JEPHCOTT, A. P. and CARTER, M. P. (1954) *The Social Background of Delinquency*. Nottingham: University of Nottingham.

KAHN, R. L. and KATZ, D. (1960) Leadership practices in relation to productivity and morale. In Cartwright, D. and Zander, A. (eds), *Group Dynamics: Research and Theory, Vol. 2*. New York: Harper & Row.

KARABEL, J. and HALSEY, A. H. (1977) Educational research: a review and an interpretation. In Karabel, J. and Halsey, A. H. (eds) *Power and Ideology in Education*. New York: Oxford University Press. Pp. 1–85.

KELSALL, R. K. and KELSALL, H. M. (1971) *Social Disadvantage and Educational Opportunity*. New York: Holt, Rinehart & Winston.

KELVIN, P. (1969) *The Bases of Social Behavior: An approach in terms of order and value*. London: Holt, Rinehart & Winston.

KING, R. (1973) *School Organisation and Pupil Involvement: A study of secondary schools*. London: Routledge and Kegan Paul.

KING, R. D., RAYNES, N. V. and TIZARD, J. (1971) *Patterns of Residential Care:*

Sociological studies in institutions for handicapped children. London: Routledge & Kegan Paul.

KORMAN, A. K., GREENHAUS, J. H. and BADIN, I. J. (1977) Personal attitudes and motivation. *Annual Review of Psychology,* **28,** 175–96.

KOUNIN, J. S. (1970) *Discipline and Group Management in Classrooms.* New York: Holt, Rinehart & Winston.

KUHN, M. H. (1964) Major trends in symbolic interaction theory in the past twenty-five years. *Sociological Quarterly,* **5,** 61–84.

LACEY, C. (1970) *Hightown Grammar: The School as a Social System.* Manchester: Manchester University Press.

LACEY, C. (1974) Destreaming in a 'pressured' academic environment. In Eggleston, J. (ed.) *Contemporary Research in the Sociology of Education.* London: Methuen.

LEPPER, M. R., GREENE, D. and NISBET, R. E. (1973) Undermining children's intrinsic interest with extrinsic reward: A test of the over-justification hypothesis. *Journal of Personality and Social Psychology,* **28,** 129–37.

LEWIN, K., LIPPITT, R. and WHITE, R. (1939) Patterns of aggressive behavior in experimentally created social climates. *Journal of Social Psychology,* **10,** 271–99.

LIEBERMAN, S. (1956) The effects of changes in roles on the attitudes of role occupants. *Human Relations,* **9,** 385–402.

LUNN, J. C. B. (1970) *Streaming in the Primary School.* Slough: NFER.

MABEY, C. (1974) *Social and ethnic mix in schools and the relationship with attainment of children aged 8 and 11.* London: Centre for Environmental Studies, Research Paper No. 9.

McDILL, E. L. and RIGSBY, L. C. (1973) *Structure and Process in Secondary Schools.* Baltimore: Johns Hopkins University Press.

MADAUS, G. F., KELLAGHAN, T. and RAKOW, E. A. (1976) School and class differences in performance on the leaving certificate examination. *Irish Journal of Education,* **10,** 41–50.

MADSEN, C. H., BECKER, W. C. and THOMAS, D. R. (1968) Rules, praise and ignoring: elements of elementary classroom control. *Journal of Applied Behavior Analysis,* **1,** 139–50.

MARLAND, M. (1975) *The Craft of the Classroom: A Survival Guide.* London: Heinemann Educational.

MAXWELL, A. E. (1977) *Multivariate Analysis in Behavioural Research.* London: Chapman and Hall.

MERTON, R. K. and KITT, A. S. (1950) Contributions to the theory of reference group behaviour. In Merton, R. K. and Lazarsfeld, P. F. (eds) *Continuities in Social Research: Studies in the Scope and Method of 'The American Soldier'.* Glencoe, Ill.: Free Press. Pp. 40–105.

MILLER, L. B. and DYER, J. L. (1975) Four preschool programs: their dimensions and effects. *Monographs of the Society for Research in Child Development,* **40,** Serial No. 162.

MILLHAM, S., BULLOCK, R. and CHERRETT, P. (1975) *After Grace – Teeth.* London: Human Context Books.

MOSTELLER, F. and MOYNIHAN, D. P. (eds) (1972) *On Equality of Educational Opportunity.* New York: Random House.

NEWCOMB, T. M., TURNER, R. H. and CONVERSE, P. E. (1969) *Social Psychology: The Study of Human Interaction.* London: Holt, Rinehart and Winston.

NIE, N. H., HULL, C. H., JENKINS, J. G., STEINBRENNER, K. and BENT, D. H. (1975) *Statistical Package for the Social Sciences.* New York: McGraw Hill.

Office of Population Censuses and Surveys (1973) *Young People's Employment Study: Preliminary Report No. 1.* London: OPCS Social Survey Division.

Office of Population Censuses and Surveys (1974) *Young People's Employment Study: Preliminary Report No. 2.* London: OPCS Social Survey Division.

O'LEARY, K. D., KAUFMAN, K. F., KASS, R. E. and DRABMAN, R. S. (1970) The effects of loud and soft reprimands on the behavior of disruptive students. *Exceptional Children,* **37,** 145–55.

PASSOW, A. H., GOLDBERG, M. and TANNENBAUM, A. J. (eds) (1967) *Education of the Disadvantaged: A book of readings.* New York: Holt, Rinehart and Winston.

PATTERSON, G. R. (1977) Accelerating stimuli for two classes of coercive behaviors. *Journal of Abnormal Child Psychology,* **5,** 335–50.

PIDGEON, D. (1965) *Non-verbal Test 5.* Slough: NFER.

PILLING, D. and PRINGLE, M. KELLMER (1978) *Controversial Issues in Child Development.* London: Paul Elek.

PLOWDEN REPORT (1967) *Children and Their Primary Schools.* London: HMSO.

POSTLETHWAITE, K. and DENTON, C. (1978) *Streams for the Future? The long-term effects of early streaming and non-streaming – the Final Report of the Banbury Enquiry.* Banbury: Pubansco Publications.

POSTLETHWAITE, T. H. (1975) The surveys of the International Association for the Evaluation of Educational Achievement (IEA): Implications of the IEA surveys of achievement. In Purvis, A. C. and Levine, D. V. (eds) *Educational Policy and International Assessment.* Berkeley, Calif.: McCutchen.

POWER, M. J., ALDERSON, M. R., PHILLIPSON, C. M., SCHOENBERG, E. and MORRIS, J. N. (1967) Delinquent schools? *New Society,* **10,** 542–3.

POWER, M. J., BENN, R. T. and MORRIS, J. N. (1972) Neighbourhood, school and juveniles before the Courts. *British Journal of Criminology,* **12,** 111–32.

PRATT, J. (1978) Calculating your LEA's generosity. *Where,* **136,** 73–5.

QUINTON, D. (1979) The socio-cultural environment. In Rutter, M. and Quinton, D. (eds) *The Child, His Family and the Community.* London: Wiley. In preparation.

RAYNES, N. V., PRATT, M. W. and Roses, S. (1977) Aides' involvement in decision-making and the quality of care in institutional settings. *American Journal of Mental Deficiency,* **81,** 570–7.

REVANS, R. W. (1964) *Standards for Morale: Cause and Effect in Hospitals.* London: Oxford University Press.

REYNOLDS, D., JONES, D. and St LEGER, S. (1976) Schools do make a difference. *New Society,* **37,** 321.

REYNOLDS, D. and MURGATROYD, S. (1977) The sociology of schooling and the absent pupil: the school as a factor in the generation of truancy. In Carroll, H. C. M. (ed.) *Absenteeism in South Wales: Studies of Pupils, Their Homes and Their Secondary Schools.* Swansea: Faculty of Education, University of Swansea.

ROSENTHAL, R. and JACOBSON, L. (1968) *Pygmalion in the Classroom.* New York: Holt, Rinehart and Winston.

ROSS, J., BUNTON, W. J., EVISON, P. and ROBERTSON, T. S. (1972) *A Critical Appraisal of Comprehensive Schooling: A research report.* Slough: NFER.

RUTTER, M. (1967) A children's behaviour questionnaire for completion by teachers: Preliminary findings. *Journal of Child Psychology and Psychiatry,* **8,** 1–11.

RUTTER, M. (1977) Prospective studies to investigate behavioural change. In Strauss, J. S., Babigian, H. M. and Roff, M. (eds) *The Origins and Course of Psychopathology.* New York: Plenum Publishing.

RUTTER, M. and BARTAK, L. (1973) Special educational treatment of autistic children: A comparative study. II: Follow-up findings and implications for services. *Journal of Child Psychology and Psychiatry,* **14,** 241–70.

RUTTER, M. and MADGE, N. (1976) *Cycles of Disadvantage.* London: Heinemann.

RUTTER, M., TIZARD, J. and WHITMORE, K. (eds) (1970) *Education, Health and*

Behaviour. London: Longmans.

RUTTER, M., YULE, W., BERGER, M., YULE, B., MORTON, J. and BAGLEY, C. (1974) Children of West Indian immigrants. I: Rates of behavioural deviance and of psychiatric disorder. *Journal of Child Psychology and Psychiatry*, **15**, 241–62.

RUTTER, M., COX, A., TUPLING, C., BERGER, M. and YULE, W. (1975a) Attainment and adjustment in two geographical areas. I: The prevalence of psychiatric disorder. *British Journal of Psychiatry*, **126**, 493–509.

RUTTER, M., YULE, B., MORTON, J. and BAGLEY, C. (1975b) Children of West Indian immigrants. III: Home circumstances and family patterns. *Journal of Child Psychology and Psychiatry*, **16**, 105–23.

RUTTER, M., YULE, B., QUINTON, D., ROWLANDS, O., YULE, W. and BERGER, M. (1975c) Attainment and adjustment in two geographical areas. III: Some factors accounting for area differences. *British Journal of Psychiatry*, **126**, 520–33.

SCHONELL, F. J. (1961) *The Psychology and Teaching of Reading*. Edinburgh: Oliver and Boyd.

Schools Council (1968) *Enquiry 1: Young School Leavers, part 2*. London: HMSO.

SEAVER, W. J. (1973) Effects of naturally induced teacher expectancies. *Journal of Personality and Social Psychology*, **28**, 333–42.

SHAW, C. R. and MCKAY, H. D. (1942) *Juvenile Delinquency and Urban Areas*. Chicago: University of Chicago Press.

SHAYCOFT, M. (1967) *The High School Years: Growth in Cognitive Skills*. Pittsburgh: American Institutes for Research and School of Education, University of Pittsburgh.

SHERIF, M., HARVEY, O. J., WHITE, B. J., HOOD, W. R. and SHERIF, C. (1961) *Intergroup Conflict and Cooperation: The Robbers' Cave Experiment*. Norman, Oklahoma: University of Oklahoma Book Exchange.

SHERIF, M. and SHERIF, C. W. (1969) *Social Psychology*. London: Harper and Row.

SHIBUTANI, T. (1955) Reference groups as perspectives. *American Journal of Sociology*, **60**, 562–9.

SHIPMAN, M. D. (1975) *The Sociology of the School* (2nd edition). London: Longmans.

SIEGEL, S. (1956) *Nonparametric Statistics for the Behavioural Sciences*. New York: McGraw Hill.

SINCLAIR, I. A. C. (1971) *Hostels for Probationers*. London: HMSO.

SKODAK, M. and SKEELS, H. M. (1949) A final follow-up study of one hundred adopted children. *Journal of Genetic Psychology*, **75**, 85–125.

SMITH, T. W. and PITTMAN, T. S. (1978) Reward, distraction and the over-justification effect. *Journal of Personality and Social Psychology*, **36**, 565–72.

STALLINGS, J. (1975) Implementation and child effects of teaching practices in follow through classrooms. *Monographs of the Society for Research in Child Development*, **40**, Serial No. 163.

STANTON, A. H. and SCHWARTZ, M. S. (1954) *The Mental Hospital*. New York: Basic Books.

Statistics of Education 1976 (1978) Vol. 2, School Leavers, C.S.E. and G.C.E. Department of Education and Science (London: HMSO)

STERN, G. G. (1963) Measuring noncognitive variables in research on teaching. In Gage, N. L. (ed.) *Handbook of Research on Teaching*. Chicago, Ill.: Rand McNally. Pp. 398–447.

SUGARMAN, B. (1967) Involvement in youth culture, academic achievement and conformity in school: an empirical study of London school boys. *British Journal of Sociology*, **18**, 151–64.

SUMMERS, A. A. and WOLFE, B. L. (1977) Do schools make a difference? *American Economic Review*. In press.

SUTHERLAND, E. H. (1939) *Principles of Criminology*. Philadelphia: Lippincott.

268 FIFTEEN THOUSAND HOURS

TIZARD, J. (1975) Race and IQ: the limits of probability. *New Behaviour*, 1, 6–9.

VROOM, V. H. (1969) Industrial social psychology. In Lindzey, G. and Aronson E. (eds) *The Handbook of Social Psychology* (second edition). Vol. 5: *Applied Social Psychology*. London: Addison-Wesley. Pp. 196–268.

WALLER, W. (1932) *The Sociology of Teaching*. New York: Wiley.

WALLIS, C. P. and MALIPHANT, R. (1967) Delinquent areas in the County of London: ecological factors. *British Journal of Criminology*, 7, 250–84.

WALTERS, G. C. and GRUSEC, J. E. (1977) *Punishment*. San Francisco: Freeman.

WATTS, A. F. (1955) *Sentence Reading Test 1*. Slough: NFER.

WEBB, J. (1962) The sociology of a school. *British Journal of Sociology*, 13, 264–72.

WEBBER, R. J. (1977) *The national classification of residential neighbourhoods: An introduction to the classification of wards and parishes*. Technical paper no. 23. London: Planning Research Applications Group.

WEST, D. J. and FARRINGTON, D. (1973) *Who Becomes Delinquent?* London: Heinemann Educational.

WHITE, R. and LIPPITT, R. (1960) Leader behaviour and member reaction in three 'social climates'. In Cartwright, D. and Zander, A. (eds) *Group Dynamics in Research and Theory* (second edition). New York: Harper and Row.

WING, J. and BROWN, G. (1970) *Institutionalism and schizophrenia: A comparative study of three mental hospitals, 1960–1968*. Cambridge: Cambridge University Press.

YINGER, J. M., IKEDA, K., LAYCOCK, F. and CUTLER, S. J. (1977) Middle Start: An experiment in the educational enrichment of young adolescents. London: Cambridge University Press.

YULE, B. and RUTTER, M. (1979) In preparation.

YULE, W., BERGER, M., RUTTER, M. and YULE, B. A. (1975) Children of West Indian immigrants. II. Intellectual performance and reading attainment. *Journal of Child Psychology and Psychiatry*, 16, 1–17.

Name index

Subject index